Betty Crocker

money saving meals

200
DELICIOUS WAYS TO EAT ON THE CHEAP

WILEY

Wiley Publishing, Inc.

GENERAL MILLS

Editorial Director: Jeff Nowak

Publishing Manager: Christine Gray

Manager and Editor, Cookbooks:
Lois Tlusty

Recipe Development and Testing:
Betty Crocker Kitchens

Photography: General Mills
Photography Studios and Image
Library

WILEY PUBLISHING, INC.

Publisher: Natalie Chapman

Associate Publisher:
Jessica Goodman

Executive Editor: Anne Ficklen

Editor: Adam Kowit

Assistant Editor: Meaghan McDonnell

Production Manager: Michael Olivo

Cover Design: Suzanne Sunwoo

Art Director: Tai Blanche

Manufacturing Manager: Kevin Watt

The Betty Crocker Kitchens seal
guarantees success in your kitchen.
Every recipe has been tested on
America's Most Trusted Kitchens™ to
meet our high standards of reliability,
easy preparation and great taste.

Find more great ideas at
BettyCrocker.com

For general information on our other products and services or for technical support, please contact our Customer Care Department within the United States at (800) 762-2974, outside the United States at (317) 572-3993 or fax (317) 572-4002.

Wiley also publishes its books in a variety of electronic formats. Some content that appears in print may not be available in electronic books. For more information about Wiley products, visit our web site at www.wiley.com.

Library of Congress Cataloging-in-Publication Data

Crocker, Betty.
  [Money saving meals]
  Betty Crocker money saving meals.
    p. cm.
  Includes index.
  ISBN 978-0-470-53076-4
  1. Quick and easy cookery. 2. Low budget cookery. I. Title. II.
Title: Money saving meals.
  TX833.5.C694 2009
  641.5'55—dc22

                            2009029119

Manufactured in the United States of America

10 9 8 7 6 5 4 3 2 1

Cover photo: Chicken- and Spinach-Stuffed Shells (page 106)

COST PER SERVING

The cost per serving was calculated using national supermarket average price per ingredient based on Nielsen Scanner Data (January 2009). These costs are guidelines and may vary due to regional and seasonal prices. Some ingredients may be less expensive at club stores, discount supermarkets, farmers' markets and co-ops. Ingredients purchased on sale and/or using coupons will help reduce the cost per serving too.

Dear Friends,

At the end of the day, when everyone is hungry, it's so easy to splurge on expensive drive-through or convenience foods that can make a real dent in your food budget. Fortunately, cooking at home can be a lot less expensive than a meal out and doubly delicious. Here are 200 family-pleasing recipes that prove tasty dishes don't have to cost a lot. The cost per serving is included for every recipe—along with an inspiring photo—so picking what to make is easy.

Before you dive into making dinner, check out the great information up front giving strategies to make shopping and cooking easier, cheaper and more efficient. Follow this handy advice and watch your grocery bill go down!

The most crucial element to budget cooking is planning. Page 8 outlines a simple budget pantry to help you whip up a delicious dinner in a flash. In many recipes, ingredients marked with a star indicate Best Budget Picks—a set of super-versatile main ingredients and flavors that you can grab on sale, then use a new way each time you cook (see the list on pages 314–15 for recipes that use each one). To make choosing a recipe even easier, there are five icons flagging recipes throughout, from Fast recipes that are ready in a flash to Great for Kids dishes that will please the younger crowd.

It's never been a better time to be a smart shopper and cook—and luckily, it's never been easier.

Happy Cooking!

Betty Crocker

|| CONTENTS ||

Stretching the Food Dollar

Making a dollar go far these days seems like more of a challenge than ever before, and it's no different when it comes to getting affordable meals on the table.

Many of the quickest and simplest foods to cook, like steaks and chops, are often the most expensive, and convenience items like jarred sauces can quickly add up. The good news is that a few simple strategies for smart shopping, storing and cooking can translate into big savings.

It Pays to Plan

The most effective way to save money on meals is to plan ahead. This allows you to buy in economical quantities and helps ensure the food you buy will get used and not wasted. It can also save time in the kitchen. One simple idea that saves time and money is to get a head start on weekday meals by making a large entrée or doubling a recipe on a Sunday night that can be used to create another dinner during the week. Double the meat loaf recipe (page 58) or many of the poultry recipes, and—depending on how many people you're feeding—you'll have two dinners squared away and/or a lunch or two to boot! Look for recipes tagged with the GREAT LEFTOVERS icon: These would be delicious the next day, and many can be reused in new ways—like in salads or sandwiches or tossed with pasta.

Cooking with an eye on your wallet may mean limiting certain costly convenience products, but it doesn't mean you can't get dinner on the table fast. Check out recipes tagged FAST, which are all ready in 30 minutes or less. And recipes tagged ONE-DISH MEAL are an easy path to cost-saving dinners. What about dining out? Nobody wants to give up restaurants entirely, so save them for special occasions. In between, why not prepare your favorite restaurant dishes at home? Check out the recipes tagged RESTAURANT FAVE for treats like shrimp scampi and French dip sandwiches that can easily be created at home for a lot less than what they'd cost at a restaurant.

Shop Smart

Before you set out for the supermarket, take inventory of what you have on hand so you don't duplicate, especially if you're shopping for perishables. It's easy to forget that fresh parsley that's at the back of your crisper drawer, still perfectly usable. Before you make a shopping list, plan your weekly meals. Then make a detailed list that will meet the needs of your meal plans, and don't forget to account for leftovers. It may be easier to keep a running grocery list on the computer so you can use last week's list as a starting place.

Once at the store, stick to your list, avoiding impulse purchases that can really add up. If you can, shop solo during off-peak hours and allow time to browse. This will help you avoid the distractions that may prompt you to grab something off the shelf in order to get out fast, even if it wasn't on your list.

TIPS FOR SHOPPING SUCCESS

Here are a few pointers that will save you time, money and frustration when you shop for groceries:

- Before you shop, check your supermarket's website (many do have them!) to see what's on sale for the current week. Some supermarket websites also post their weekly circulars and let you sign up for weekly emails alerting you to future specials and promotions.

- Don't shop without a list! It's amazingly easy to forget a crucial ingredient in the dish or dishes you plan to make. Stores can be quite distracting, and in fact, some supermarkets are organized to make you want to buy items you don't really want or need. Simply sticking to your list can save an enormous amount of money.

- Have a backup meal in mind when you go shopping, just in case your store is out of a crucial ingredient.

- Don't food shop when you're hungry! You'll have more trouble resisting the urge to buy the "junk food" that so many of us crave.

Pantry Power

If you do find yourself in the supermarket without a plan for dinner, it's much easier to plan a meal on the spot if you have a well-stocked basic pantry back at home.

You're far less likely to splurge on foods you don't need, and you can just pick up a couple of items to round out the meal. Here's a list of pantry staples that appear in many of the recipes in this book. Get in the habit of keeping this list with you when you go shopping, and stock up on any of these ingredients whenever you see them on sale at the supermarket.

All-purpose flour

Bacon (freeze any extra after opening)

Balsamic vinegar

Bisquick or Bisquick Heart Smart®

Black pepper, preferably whole peppercorns if you have a grinder

Bottled barbecue sauce

Bread crumbs, regular or panko

Butter or margarine

Canned beans, various kinds

Canned chopped green chiles

Canned diced tomatoes

Canned low-sodium chicken broth

Canned tuna, packed in water

Cooking spray

Couscous

Dried oregano

Dried pasta, various kinds

Frozen vegetables, various kinds

Garlic (1 head; keep in a dark, dry place, not the refrigerator)

Mayonnaise

Mustard

Olive oil

Parmesan cheese, whole or grated (keep refrigerated)

Red pepper flakes (if you like spicy food)

Rice, white and/or brown

Salt

Sugar

Taco seasoning mix

If you always have these—or at least most of these—on hand, dinner can come together more easily and inexpensively because you won't have to make multiple trips to the store and buy them in small, more expensive quantities. And most of them will store well for a long time.

Best Budget Picks

When it comes to the main ingredient or flavoring in a recipe, it can help your wallet to take advantage of a few super-versatile items. These **Best Budget Picks,** flagged ★ in this book, are used in numerous recipes in each chapter. That means you can get a lot of mileage from a few foods. To get the most value out of these items, buy them in bulk or large-quantity packages—then turn to pages 314–15 for a quick-reference list giving you plenty of recipes to put that purchase to good use.

- **Ground Beef:** A mainstay in casseroles, pastas and more. Look for ground beef in bulk or in "family-size" portions. Ground beef freezes well, so when you get home, take what you need right away, then divide the remainder into smaller portions, wrap tightly in plastic and store in the freezer for 3 to 4 months.

- **Chicken Breasts:** Take advantage of the better price for a large-size package, then rewrap them individually and store in the freezer. That way you can defrost just the amount you need. For extra convenience, cook and cube the chicken before freezing (see "Pre-Cooked Chicken," right).

- **Canned Soups:** Canned soups come in handy for all sorts of uses, like making sauces in a jiffy, adding liquid and flavor to a casserole and rounding out a stew—not to mention an easy quick meal on their own! Save more by buying them in bulk-size packages.

- **Bottled Dressing:** Bottled salad dressings are more versatile than just for dressing salads. Vinaigrette-type dressings are ideal for use as a quick marinade or baste for meat, chicken and fish. And with a little imagination, many dressings can be turned into sauces, dips or flavor-boosters for all sorts of recipes.

- **Canned Beans:** These are endlessly useful in rounding out a meal—meat or meatless—quickly and inexpensively. Make sure to rinse and drain the beans before using, then stir into a stew or toss with a salad or pasta to make the dish more substantial.

- **Canned Tomatoes:** Canned tomatoes are called for in so many recipes—not just pasta—that you almost can't have too many cans on hand. Plus, they're much cheaper than many brands of jarred pasta sauce.

PRE-COOKED CHICKEN

It's not much effort to pre-cook chicken breasts to have on hand when the need arises. Cook 4 boneless skinless chicken breasts (about 5 oz each) until the juice is clear when center of thickest part is cut (170°F). You'll get approximately 2½ cups chopped, cubed or shredded chicken. Refrigerate cooked chicken up to 2 days or freeze up to 1 month.

To Microwave: Place chicken in microwavable dish large enough to hold the pieces in a single layer. Cover with plastic wrap, folding back one corner to vent, or waxed paper. Microwave on Medium for 14 to 16 minuets. Let stand 5 minutes, then chop, cube or shred.

To Poach: Place chicken in pan of simmering water or chicken broth (season with salt and pepper if you like). Cover and simmer over medium-low heat about 20 minutes. Refrigerate chicken in poaching liquid until cool enough to handle, then chop, cube or shred.

Use pre-cooked chicken in this Chicken-Veggie Casserole (page 288).

Store It Right

Proper storage will save you lots of money, ensure food safety and keep foods tasting great. Follow these tips for keeping fresh vegetables, herbs and fruits fresh longer.

IN THE REFRIGERATOR

- The coldest part of your refrigerator is the lowest—the crisper drawer. Most vegetables should be stored there, usually in plastic bags.

- Don't wash vegetables before refrigerating them. Water can remove that natural protective layer that keeps vegetables fresh.

- Don't refrigerate garlic, shallots, whole uncut winter squash or potatoes. Instead, store in a cool, dry place with minimal light.

- Leafy vegetables with stems intact, the way arugula is often sold, should be stored with wet paper towels wrapped around the stems, in plastic bags or wrap.

- Whole heads of lettuce will generally keep longer than loose leafy greens.

- Tomatoes or avocadoes should be ripened on your kitchen counter until they are very ripe, and then eaten as soon as possible.

- Peppers and mushrooms last longer in paper bags in the crisper.

- Since fruit is often sold unripe, it is often good to let the fruit ripen at room temperature. You can speed up the ripening process by placing the fruit in a brown paper bag, turning the bag every day. Adding an apple to the bag will further hasten ripening.

- Bananas can be stored at room temperature until very ripe. Then the banana should be refrigerated. The skin will turn black, but the banana itself will be fine for a few days.

- Most ripe fruits should be stored in the refrigerator in a plastic bag or a sealed container.

- Freezing works well for many foods, but the following don't freeze well: soft cheeses, cooked pasta, fried foods, hard-boiled eggs, garlic, mayonnaise and milk-based sauces.

- Foods must be stored in tightly sealed containers or wrapping.

- Be sure to write the date that you froze any food on the wrapping or on freezer tape.

- To freeze raw vegetables, plunge briefly into boiling water to set the color, then quickly plunge them into ice water to stop cooking. Dry the vegetables well, pack them in freezer bags, squeeze out as much air as you can, and seal tightly.

- Herbs (other than basil) freeze well, but they should then be used as ingredients in a recipe, not as a garnish.

- To freeze herbs, wash them, pat or spin them dry and arrange them on a cookie sheet in a single layer. Freeze them, then transfer them into labeled, sealed containers. You can use the herbs straight out of the freezer.

Get the Most from Bulk Bins

Buying food from bulk bins can mean big savings. Food sold in bulk is often cheaper than food sold in small portions, especially if you go for grains, rice, dried beans, nuts, seeds and pasta. You can also buy exactly the portion you need, which is perfect when you only want a little of something, like a few tablespoons of pine nuts to make pesto or a new whole grain you want to try. When stored in a cool, dry place, most grains can last up to a year. In the freezer, they can last up to two years. Whole grains containing oil can become rancid and must be stored in the refrigerator or freezer and will last for up to six months. These grains include barley, brown rice, bulgur, kasha, whole-grain cornmeal, wheat germ and whole-wheat flour.

COOKING GRAINS— AT A GLANCE

So you bought grains in bulk and are wondering how to cook them? Here's a cheat sheet:

Long-grain white rice: Heat 1 cup rice and 2 cups water to boiling. Reduce heat to low. Cover and simmer 15 minutes. Makes: 3 cups

Long-grain brown rice: Heat 1 cup rice and 2¾ cups water to boiling. Reduce heat to low. Cover and simmer 45 to 50 minutes. Makes: 4 cups

Wild rice: Heat 1 cup wild rice and 2½ cups water to boiling. Reduce heat to low. Cover and simmer 40 to 50 minutes. Makes: 3 cups

Barley: Heat 4 cups water to boiling. Stir in barley. Reduce heat to low. Cover and simmer 45 to 50 minutes. Makes: 4 cups

Bulgur: Pour 3 cups boiling water over bulgur. Cover and soak 30 to 60 minutes (do not cook). Drain if needed. Makes: 3 cups

Kasha: Pour 2 cups boiling water over kasha. Cover and soak 10 to 15 minutes (do not cook). Drain if needed. Makes: 4 cups

CHAPTER 1

Poultry That
Pays Off

Chicken Dishes on the Fly

Chicken breasts are one of the most versatile foods in the kitchen—and so useful in a pinch. For a smart buy, buy a large package of boneless skinless chicken breasts, then rewrap them individually and store in your freezer (see page 9). Then, if you're pressed for time, they'll be in easy reach to use in one of these three speedy recipes for a great-tasting dish done in under 20 minutes.

FRESH HERB CHICKEN

Melt 1 tablespoon butter in 12-inch nonstick skillet over medium heat. Add 4 boneless skinless chicken breasts and brown on each side. Add $\frac{1}{4}$ cup dry white wine or chicken broth, 2 tablespoons chopped fresh basil, dill or chives, and $\frac{1}{4}$ teaspoon salt. Cook about 8 minutes, turning once, or until chicken is no longer pink in center.

PESTO CHICKEN

Heat 1 tablespoon olive oil in 12-inch nonstick skillet over medium heat. Add 4 boneless skinless chicken breasts and cook about 10 minutes, turning once, until chicken is no longer pink in center. A few minutes before removing from heat, spoon 1 to 2 tablespoons purchased pesto over each piece and sprinkle with shredded mozzarella cheese; cover skillet to melt cheese.

RANCH CHICKEN

Heat 2 tablespoons oil in 12-inch nonstick skillet over medium heat. Dip 4 boneless skinless chicken breasts in $\frac{1}{4}$ cup ranch dressing, then coat with $\frac{1}{3}$ cup dry Italian-style or seasoned bread crumbs. Cook about 10 minutes, turning once, or until chicken is no longer pink in center.

Oven-Fried Chicken

Prep Time: **20 Minutes** || Start to Finish: **1 Hour 20 Minutes** || **6 Servings**

¼ cup butter or margarine

½ cup all-purpose flour

1 teaspoon paprika

½ teaspoon salt

¼ teaspoon pepper

1 cut-up whole chicken
(3 to 3½ lb)

1 Heat oven to 425°F. Melt butter in 13×9-inch pan in the oven.

2 In large food-storage plastic bag, mix flour, paprika, salt and pepper. Place a few pieces of chicken at a time in bag, seal bag and shake to coat with flour mixture. Place chicken, skin sides down, in a single layer in butter in pan.

3 Bake uncovered 30 minutes. Remove pan from oven; turn chicken pieces over, using tongs. Bake uncovered about 30 minutes longer or until juice of chicken is clear when thickest pieces are cut to bone (170°F for breasts; 180°F for thighs and legs on an instant-read thermometer). If chicken sticks to pan, loosen it gently with turner or fork.

1 Serving: Calories 330; Total Fat 21g (Saturated Fat 9g, Trans Fat 1g); Cholesterol 105mg; Sodium 330mg; Total Carbohydrate 8g (Dietary Fiber 0g) **Exchanges:** ½ Starch, 3½ Lean Meat, 2 Fat **Carbohydrate Choices:** ½

Lighten Up Oven-Fried Chicken: Remove skin from chicken before cooking. Do not melt butter in pan; instead, spray pan with cooking spray. Decrease butter to 2 tablespoons; melt butter and drizzle over chicken after turning in step 3 for 11 grams of fat and 240 calories per serving.

budget smart

"To save a little more money on this recipe, substitute 3½ lb of chicken thighs and drumsticks for the cut-up whole chicken. Just be sure to cook the pieces to 180°F."

94¢
per serving

Home-Style Chicken Dinner

Prep Time: **30 Minutes** || Start to Finish: **1 Hour 20 Minutes** || **4 Servings**

2 teaspoons dried basil leaves

1 teaspoon seasoned salt

1 teaspoon garlic pepper blend

2 tablespoons olive or
 vegetable oil

1 cut-up whole chicken (3- to
 3½-lb), skin removed if
 desired

6 small unpeeled red potatoes,
 cut into quarters (2 cups)

2 medium dark-orange sweet
 potatoes, peeled, cut into
 1-inch pieces (3 cups)

1 medium green bell pepper,
 cut into 1-inch pieces (1 cup)

3 plum (Roma) tomatoes, cut
 into quarters

1 Heat oven to 400°F. Spray 13×9-inch (3-quart) glass baking dish with cooking spray. In large bowl, mix basil, seasoned salt, garlic pepper and oil. Brush about half of the mixture on chicken. Add remaining ingredients to bowl; toss to coat.

2 Place vegetables in baking dish. Place chicken on vegetables. Brush with any remaining oil mixture.

3 Bake uncovered 45 to 50 minutes or until vegetables are tender and juice of chicken is clear when centers of thickest pieces are cut to bone (170°F for breasts; 180°F for thighs and drumsticks). Serve with pan juices.

1 Serving: Calories 610; Total Fat 27g (Saturated Fat 7g, Trans Fat 0.5g); Cholesterol 130mg; Sodium 480mg; Total Carbohydrate 51g (Dietary Fiber 7g) **Exchanges:** 2 Starch, 1 Other Carbohydrate, 1 Vegetable, 5 Medium-Fat Meat **Carbohydrate Choices:** 3

budget smart

" Sweet potatoes bring this homey classic right up to date and help make it a one-dish meal. "

$2.60
per serving

★ **Best Budget Picks** (for more uses, see pages 314–15)

Zesty Roasted Chicken and Potatoes

Prep Time: **10 Minutes** || Start to Finish: **45 Minutes** || **6 Servings**

★ **6 boneless skinless chicken breasts (about 1³/₄ lb)**

8 small (unpeeled) red potatoes, cut into quarters (about 1 lb)

¹/₃ cup mayonnaise or salad dressing

3 tablespoons Dijon mustard

¹/₂ teaspoon pepper

2 cloves garlic, finely chopped, or ¹/₄ teaspoon garlic powder

Chopped fresh chives, if desired

1 Heat oven to 350°F. Spray 15×10×1-inch pan with cooking spray.

2 Place chicken and potatoes in pan. In small bowl, mix remaining ingredients except chives; brush over chicken and potatoes.

3 Roast uncovered 30 to 35 minutes or until potatoes are tender when pierced with a fork and juice of chicken is clear when center of thickest part is cut (170°F). Sprinkle with chives.

1 Serving: Calories 310; Total Fat 14g (Saturated Fat 2.5g, Trans Fat 0g); Cholesterol 85mg; Sodium 330mg; Total Carbohydrate 15g (Dietary Fiber 2g) **Exchanges:** 1 Starch, 4 Very Lean Meat, 2 Fat **Carbohydrate Choices:** 1

Lighten Up Zesty Roasted Chicken and Potatoes: Use low-fat mayonnaise for 9 grams of fat and 270 calories per serving.

budget smart

"The Dijon mustard and garlic give the chicken a nice little kick. Leftover chopped chives freeze very well for future use: store them in a resealable freezer plastic bag with all the air squeezed out."

$1.91 per serving

Chicken Tortilla Casserole

Prep Time: **20 Minutes** || Start to Finish: **1 Hour 15 Minutes** || **8 Servings**

★ 1 can (10³⁄₄ oz) 98% fat free 45% less sodium condensed cream of chicken soup

1 can (4.5 oz) chopped green chiles

1 container (8 oz) fat-free sour cream

¹⁄₂ cup fat-free (skim) milk

★ 2¹⁄₂ cups shredded cooked chicken breast

8 yellow corn tortillas (6 or 7 inch), torn into bite-size pieces

1 medium green bell pepper, chopped (1 cup)

1 large tomato, chopped (1 cup)

1¹⁄₂ cups shredded sharp Cheddar cheese or Mexican cheese blend (6 oz)

1 Heat oven to 350°F. Spray 13×9-inch (3-quart) glass baking dish with cooking spray. In large bowl, mix soup, chiles, sour cream and milk until blended. Stir in chicken, tortillas and bell pepper. Stir in tomato and 1 cup of the cheese. Spoon and spread mixture in baking dish.

2 Cover with foil. Bake 40 minutes. Uncover; sprinkle with remaining ¹⁄₂ cup cheese. Bake uncovered 5 to 10 minutes longer or until cheese is melted and mixture is bubbly. Let stand 5 minutes.

1 Serving: Calories 270; Total Fat 11g (Saturated Fat 5g, Trans Fat 0g); Cholesterol 60mg; Sodium 610mg; Total Carbohydrate 22g (Dietary Fiber 2g) **Exchanges:** 1¹⁄₂ Starch, 2¹⁄₂ Very Lean Meat, 1¹⁄₂ Fat **Carbohydrate Choices:** 1¹⁄₂

budget smart

" To save some money, get in the habit of shredding your own cheese—it's often less expensive than buying pregrated cheese. For easy cleanup, shred over a piece of waxed paper or foil, lift sides and slide cheese right into measuring cup or into a resealable food-storage plastic bag. "

$1.67 per serving

★ **Best Budget Picks** (for more uses, see pages 314–15)

Crunchy Garlic Chicken

Prep Time: **30 Minutes** || Start to Finish: **55 Minutes** || **6 Servings**

2 tablespoons butter or margarine, melted

2 tablespoons milk

1 tablespoon chopped fresh chives or parsley

$\frac{1}{2}$ teaspoon salt

$\frac{1}{2}$ teaspoon garlic powder

2 cups corn flake cereal, crushed (1 cup)

3 tablespoons chopped fresh parsley

$\frac{1}{2}$ teaspoon paprika

★ 6 boneless skinless chicken breasts (about 1$\frac{3}{4}$ lb)

2 tablespoons butter or margarine, melted

1 Heat oven to 425°F. Spray 13×9-inch pan with cooking spray. In shallow dish, mix 2 tablespoons butter, the milk, chives, salt and garlic powder.

2 In another shallow dish, mix crushed cereal, parsley and paprika. Dip chicken into milk mixture, then coat lightly and evenly with cereal mixture. Place in pan. Drizzle with 2 tablespoons butter.

3 Bake uncovered 20 to 25 minutes or until juice of chicken is clear when centers of thickest pieces are cut.

1 Serving: Calories 245; Total Fat 11g (Saturated Fat 5g; Trans Fat 0.5); Cholesterol 90mg; Sodium 410mg; Total Carbohydrate 8g (Dietary Fiber 0g) **Exchanges:** 4 Lean Meat **Carbohydrate Choices:** $\frac{1}{2}$

budget smart

" The crunchy cereal coating for this chicken is a great way to use up the last bits of a box of cereal that are already mostly crushed. Reheated leftovers make a delicious sandwich with lettuce, tomato and mayonnaise. "

$1.60 per serving

Parmesan-Dijon Chicken

Prep Time: **15 Minutes** || Start to Finish: **45 Minutes** || **6 Servings**

¾ **cup dry bread crumbs**

¼ **cup grated Parmesan cheese**

2 **tablespoons Dijon mustard**

¼ **cup butter or margarine, melted**

★ **6 boneless skinless chicken breasts (about 1¾ lb)**

1 Heat the oven to 375°F.

2 In large food-storage plastic bag, mix bread crumbs and cheese. In shallow dish, stir mustard into melted butter until well mixed.

3 Pat chicken dry with paper towels. Dip 1 piece of chicken at a time into butter mixture, coating all sides. Then place in bag of crumbs, seal bag and shake to coat with crumb mixture. In ungreased 13×9-inch pan, place chicken in a single layer.

4 Bake uncovered 20 to 30 minutes, turning chicken over once with tongs, until juice of chicken is clear when center of thickest pieces are cut (170°F). If chicken sticks to pan during baking, loosen it gently with turner or fork.

1 Serving: Calories 330; Total Fat 17g (Saturated Fat 8g, Trans Fat 0g); Cholesterol 110mg; Sodium 540mg; Total Carbohydrate 11g (Dietary Fiber 0g) **Exchanges:** ½ Starch, 5 Very Lean Meat, 3 Fat **Carbohydrate Choices:** 1

budget smart

"The bread crumb–Parmesan-mustard crust keeps the chicken moist and juicy. Use any leftover chicken to make Parmesan-Dijon sandwiches for the next day's lunch—top with lettuce, tomato and some additional Dijon mustard."

$1.56
per serving

Lemon Chicken with Olives

Prep Time: **20 Minutes** || Start to Finish: **20 Minutes** || **4 Servings**

★ **4 boneless skinless chicken breasts (about 1¼ lb)**

2 teaspoons olive or canola oil

1 tablespoon lemon juice

1 teaspoon salt-free lemon-pepper seasoning

¼ cup sliced ripe olives

4 thin slices lemon

1 Set oven control to broil. Spray broiler pan rack with cooking spray. Starting at thickest edge of each chicken breast, cut horizontally almost to opposite side. Open cut chicken breast so it is an even thickness.

2 In small bowl, mix oil and lemon juice. Drizzle over both sides of chicken breasts. Sprinkle both sides with lemon-pepper seasoning. Place on rack in broiler pan.

3 Broil with tops 4 inches from heat about 10 minutes, turning once, until juice of chicken is clear when center of thickest part is cut (170°F). During last 2 minutes of broiling, top with olives and lemon slices.

1 Serving: Calories 170; Total Fat 7g (Saturated Fat 1.5g, Trans Fat 0g); Cholesterol 75mg; Sodium 140mg; Total Carbohydrate 0g (Dietary Fiber 0g); **Exchanges:** 4 Very Lean Meat, ½ Fat **Carbohydrate Choices:** 0

budget smart

"Lemon, olives and chicken go together so beautifully that many recipes combine them (try the Mediterranean Chicken Packets, page 32). This recipe uses both lemon juice and whole lemon slices from the same lemon: Cut off the 4 lemon slices, then squeeze the remainder for the tablespoon of juice."

$1.68 per serving

★ **Best Budget Picks** (for more uses, see pages 314-15)

Chicken Marsala

Prep Time: **45 Minutes** || Start to Finish: **45 Minutes** || **4 Servings**

¹⁄₄ **cup all-purpose flour**

¹⁄₄ **teaspoon salt**

¹⁄₄ **teaspoon pepper**

★ **4 boneless skinless chicken breasts (about 1¹⁄₄ lb)**

2 tablespoons olive or vegetable oil

2 cloves garlic, finely chopped

1 cup sliced mushrooms (3 oz)

¹⁄₄ **cup chopped fresh parsley or 1 tablespoon parsley flakes**

¹⁄₂ **cup dry Marsala wine or chicken broth**

1 In shallow dish, mix flour, salt and pepper. Coat chicken with flour mixture; shake off excess flour.

2 In 10-inch skillet, heat oil over medium-high heat. Cook garlic, mushrooms and parsley in oil 5 minutes, stirring frequently.

3 Add chicken to skillet. Cook uncovered about 8 minutes, turning once, or until chicken is brown. Add wine. Cook uncovered 8 to 10 minutes longer, turning once, or until juice of chicken is clear when center of thickest part is cut (170°F).

1 Serving: Calories 290; Total Fat 11g (Saturated Fat 2g, Trans Fat 0g); Cholesterol 85mg; Sodium 230mg; Total Carbohydrate 9g (Dietary Fiber 0g) **Exchanges:** ¹⁄₂ Starch, 4¹⁄₂ Very Lean Meat, 2 Fat **Carbohydrate Choices:** ¹⁄₂

budget smart

" This twist on veal marsala is both easy and impressive—especially the second time you make it. That's because marsala wine has a much longer shelf life than most wines and if you buy it once, you can hold on to it for the next time you make this recipe! "

$2.12
per serving

Lime- and Chili-Rubbed Chicken Breasts

Prep Time: **20 Minutes** || Start to Finish: **20 Minutes** || **4 Servings**

2 teaspoons chili powder

2 teaspoons packed brown sugar

2 teaspoons grated lime peel

½ teaspoon salt

¼ teaspoon garlic powder

⅛ teaspoon ground red pepper (cayenne)

★ 4 boneless skinless chicken breasts (about 1¼ lb)

2 teaspoons olive or canola oil

1 Heat gas or charcoal grill. In small bowl, mix chili powder, brown sugar, lime peel, salt, garlic powder and ground red pepper. Rub both sides of chicken with oil, then with spice mixture.

2 Place chicken on grill over medium heat. Cover grill; cook 10 to 15 minutes, turning once or twice, until juice of chicken is clear when center of thickest part is cut (170°F).

1 Serving: Calories 200; Total Fat 7g (Saturated Fat 1.5g, Trans Fat 0g); Cholesterol 85mg; Sodium 390mg; Total Carbohydrate 3g (Dietary Fiber 0g) **Exchanges:** 4½ Very Lean Meat, 1 Fat **Carbohydrate Choices:** 0

budget smart

" Looking for a way to use up the fruit of the lime after grating the peel? Try it in Southwestern Chicken Scaloppine on the facing page which calls for lime juice. "

$1.81
per serving

★ **Best Budget Picks** (for more uses, see pages 314-15)

Southwestern Chicken Scaloppine

Prep Time: **30 Minutes** || Start to Finish: **30 Minutes** || **4 Servings**

★ **4 boneless skinless chicken breasts (about 1¼ lb)**

¼ cup all-purpose flour

1 teaspoon ground cumin

½ teaspoon salt

2 tablespoons vegetable oil

½ cup chicken broth

¼ teaspoon red pepper sauce, if desired

2 tablespoons lime juice

2 tablespoons chopped fresh cilantro

1 Between pieces of plastic wrap or waxed paper, place chicken breast with smooth side down; gently pound with flat side of meat mallet or rolling pin until about ¼ inch thick. Repeat with remaining chicken. Cut chicken into smaller pieces if desired.

2 In shallow dish, mix flour, cumin and salt. Coat chicken with flour mixture. Reserve 1 teaspoon flour mixture.

3 In 12-inch nonstick skillet, heat oil over medium heat. Add chicken; cook 3 to 5 minutes on each side or until golden brown and no longer pink in center. Remove chicken from skillet; cover to keep warm.

4 In small bowl, stir reserved 1 teaspoon flour mixture into broth. Gradually stir broth mixture and red pepper sauce into skillet. Heat to boiling; stir in lime juice and cilantro. Serve sauce over chicken.

1 Serving: Calories 260; Total Fat 12g (Saturated Fat 2.5g, Trans Fat 0g); Cholesterol 85mg; Sodium 500mg; Total Carbohydrate 7g (Dietary Fiber 0g) **Exchanges:** ½ Other Carbohydrate, 4½ Very Lean Meat, 2 Fat **Carbohydrate Choices:** ½

$1.62 per serving

budget smart

"The cilantro helps give this dish a Southwestern accent, but you can also use fresh parsley instead. If you don't have a mallet or rolling pin, use the bottom of a small saucepan to flatten the chicken."

Chicken with Oregano-Peach Sauce

Prep Time: **15 Minutes** || Start to Finish: **35 Minutes** || **4 Servings**

½ cup peach preserves

¼ cup raspberry vinegar

2 tablespoons chopped fresh
    oregano leaves, if desired

★ 4 boneless skinless chicken
    breasts (1¼ lb)

½ teaspoon garlic-pepper blend

½ teaspoon seasoned salt

1 Heat gas or charcoal grill. In 1-quart saucepan, heat preserves and vinegar to boiling, stirring constantly, until melted. Spoon about ¼ cup mixture into small bowl or custard cup for brushing on chicken. Stir oregano into remaining mixture, and reserve to serve with chicken.

2 Sprinkle chicken with garlic-pepper blend and seasoned salt.

3 Place chicken on grill over medium heat. Cover grill; cook 15 to 20 minutes, turning once and brushing with ¼ cup preserves mixture during last 10 minutes of cook time, until juice of chicken is clear when center of thickest pieces are cut (170°F). Discard any remaining preserves mixture brushed on chicken. Serve chicken with reserved preserves mixture with oregano.

1 Serving: Calories 280; Total Fat 4.5g (Saturated Fat 1.5g, Trans Fat 0g); Cholesterol 85mg; Sodium 260mg; Total Carbohydrate 28g (Dietary Fiber 0g) **Exchanges:** 2 Other Carbohydrate, 4 Very Lean Meat, ½ Fat **Carbohydrate Choices:** 2

budget smart

" Adding oregano to the remaining preserves mixture turns it into a refreshing sauce for the cooked chicken. If you can't find fresh oregano, substitute fresh thyme leaves or minced fresh sage leaves, or 2 teaspoons of dried oregano. You can also substitute ¼ teaspoon of garlic powder and ¼ teaspoon ground black pepper for the garlic-pepper blend. "

★ **Best Budget Picks** (for more uses, see pages 314–15)

$1.91
per serving

Feta-Topped Chicken

Prep Time: **10 Minutes** || Start to Finish: **25 Minutes** || **4 Servings**

★ **4 boneless skinless chicken breasts (about 1¼ lb)**

★ **2 tablespoons balsamic vinaigrette dressing**

1 teaspoon Italian seasoning

¼ teaspoon seasoned pepper

1 large plum (Roma) tomato, cut into 8 slices

¼ cup crumbled feta cheese (1 oz)

1 Set oven control to broil. Brush both sides of chicken breasts with dressing. Sprinkle both sides with Italian seasoning and seasoned pepper. Place on rack in broiler pan.

2 Broil with tops 4 inches from heat about 10 minutes, turning once, until juice of chicken is clear when center of thickest part is cut (170°F). Top with tomato and cheese. Broil 2 to 3 minutes longer or until cheese is lightly browned.

1 Serving: Calories 230; Total Fat 9g (Saturated Fat 2.5g, Trans Fat 0g); Cholesterol 95mg; Sodium 230mg; Total Carbohydrate 3g (Dietary Fiber 0g) **Exchanges:** 4½ Very Lean Meat, 1½ Fat **Carbohydrate Choices:** 0

budget smart

"Feta is a great budget-friendly cheese to have on hand because there are so many uses for it—in salads, tossed with pasta and in main dishes like this chicken entrée. French and American feta cheeses are usually less salty than Greek; American feta tends to be the least expensive."

★ **Best Budget Picks** (for more uses, see pages 314–15)

Chicken Milano

Prep Time: **25 Minutes** || Start to Finish: **25 Minutes** || **4 Servings**

Salad

1 cup tightly packed arugula
   leaves

$\frac{1}{2}$ cup diced tomatoes

2 tablespoons diced red onion

Dressing

1 tablespoon olive or
   vegetable oil

2 teaspoons red wine vinegar

$\frac{1}{8}$ teaspoon salt

Chicken

2 tablespoons all-purpose flour

1 cup Italian-style crispy bread
   crumbs

1 egg

★ 4 boneless skinless chicken
   breasts (about 1$\frac{1}{4}$ lb)

2 tablespoons olive or
   vegetable oil

$\frac{1}{4}$ cup crumbled tomato-basil
   or regular feta cheese (1 oz)

1 In medium bowl, place salad ingredients. In small bowl, beat dressing ingredients with wire whisk. Pour over salad; toss to coat.

2 On separate plates, place flour and bread crumbs. In medium bowl, beat egg with fork. Coat both sides of chicken with flour. Dip chicken into beaten egg, then coat well with bread crumbs.

3 In 12-inch nonstick skillet, heat 2 tablespoons oil over medium heat. Add chicken; cook 8 to 10 minutes, turning once, until juice of chicken is clear when center of thickest part is cut (170°F) and coating is golden brown. Serve chicken topped with salad and sprinkled with cheese.

1 Serving: Calories 440; Total Fat 24g (Saturated Fat 4g, Trans Fat 0g); Cholesterol 145mg; Sodium 650mg; Total Carbohydrate 21g (Dietary Fiber 0g) **Exchanges:** 1 Starch, $\frac{1}{2}$ Other Carbohydrate, 4$\frac{1}{2}$ Very Lean Meat, 4 Fat **Carbohydrate Choices:** 1$\frac{1}{2}$

budget smart

" This is a poultry spin on a classic veal dish from Milan, Italy. The arugula and tomato salad is the traditional accompaniment, but baby spinach leaves would work, too. Chicken can be cut into strips and tossed with additional arugula or other green for an easy crispy chicken salad. "

★ **Best Budget Picks** (for more uses, see pages 314–15)

$2.40
per serving

Mediterranean Chicken Packets

Prep Time: **45 Minutes** || Start to Finish: **45 Minutes** || **4 Servings**

1 package (4 oz) crumbled tomato-basil feta cheese (1 cup)

2 tablespoons grated lemon peel

1 teaspoon dried oregano leaves

★ 4 boneless skinless chicken breasts (about 1¼ lb)

4 plum (Roma) tomatoes, each cut into 3 slices

1 small red onion, finely chopped (1 cup)

20 pitted kalamata olives or pitted jumbo ripe olives

1 Heat gas or charcoal grill. Cut 4 (18×12-inch) sheets of heavy-duty foil. In small bowl, mix cheese, lemon peel and oregano. On center of each foil sheet, place 1 chicken breast, 3 tomato slices, ¼ cup onion and 5 olives. Spoon ¼ of the cheese mixture over chicken and vegetables on each sheet.

2 For each packet, bring up 2 sides of foil over chicken and vegetables so edges meet. Seal edges, making a tight ½-inch fold; fold again, allowing space for heat circulation and expansion. Fold other sides to seal.

3 Place packets on grill over medium heat. Cover grill; cook 20 to 25 minutes, rotating packets ½ turn after 10 minutes, until juice of chicken is clear when center of thickest part is cut (170°F). Place packets on plates. To serve, cut large X across top of each packet; carefully fold back foil to allow steam to escape.

1 Serving: Calories 290; Total Fat 13g (Saturated Fat 6g, Trans Fat 0g); Cholesterol 110mg; Sodium 570mg; Total Carbohydrate 7g (Dietary Fiber 2g) **Exchanges:** 1 Vegetable, 5 Very Lean Meat, 2 Fat **Carbohydrate Choices:** ½

budget smart

" Grilling chicken breasts with vegetables and seasoning in foil packets is a wonderful way to lock in all those flavors, and cleanup is a breeze! The crumbled tomato-basil feta is really convenient, but you can also crumble your own plain or flavored feta—or try using goat cheese for an interesting twist. "

★ **Best Budget Picks** (for more uses, see pages 314-15)

$2.71
per serving

Grilled Sesame-Ginger Chicken

Prep Time: **25 Minutes** || Start to Finish: **25 Minutes** || **4 Servings**

2 tablespoons teriyaki sauce

1 tablespoon sesame seed, toasted*

1 teaspoon ground ginger

★ 4 boneless skinless chicken breasts (about 1¼ lb)

1 Brush grill rack with vegetable oil. Heat gas or charcoal grill. In small bowl, mix teriyaki sauce, sesame seed and ginger.

2 Place chicken on grill. Cover grill; cook over medium heat 15 to 20 minutes, brushing frequently with sauce mixture and turning after 10 minutes, until juice of chicken is clear when center of thickest part is cut (170°F). Discard any remaining sauce mixture.

*To toast sesame seed, cook in ungreased heavy skillet over medium-low heat 5 to 7 minutes, stirring frequently until browning begins, then stirring constantly until golden brown.

1 Serving: Calories 190; Total Fat 6g (Saturated Fat 1.5g, Trans Fat 0g); Cholesterol 85mg; Sodium 420mg; Total Carbohydrate 2g (Dietary Fiber 0g) **Exchanges:** 4½ Very Lean Meat, 1 Fat **Carbohydrate Choices:** 0

budget smart

“This homemade twist on teriyaki chicken has only four ingredients! The sauce mixture would also be good brushed on grilled pork chops, grilled fish like salmon or grilled vegetables. ”

★ **Best Budget Picks** (for more uses, see pages 314–15)

$1.63
per serving

Grilled Taco-Barbecue Chicken

Prep Time: **25 Minutes** || Start to Finish: **25 Minutes** || **4 Servings**

2 tablespoons taco seasoning mix (from 1-oz package)

1 teaspoon dried oregano leaves

★ 4 boneless skinless chicken breasts (about 1¼ lb)

1 tablespoon olive or vegetable oil

¼ cup barbecue sauce

2 tablespoons chili sauce

½ teaspoon ground cumin

1 Heat gas or charcoal grill. In shallow bowl, mix taco seasoning mix and oregano. Brush chicken with oil; sprinkle with taco seasoning mixture.

2 Place chicken on grill. Cover grill; cook 10 to 15 minutes or until juice of chicken is clear when center of thickest part is cut (170°F).

3 Meanwhile, in small microwavable bowl, mix barbecue sauce, chili sauce and cumin. Cover; microwave on High 30 to 60 seconds or until hot. Serve sauce over chicken.

Oven Directions: Heat oven to 375°F. Line shallow baking pan with foil, or spray with cooking spray. Place coated chicken in pan. Bake 25 to 30 minutes or until juice of chicken is clear when center of thickest part is cut (170°F).

1 Serving: Calories 240; Total Fat 8g (Saturated Fat 2g, Trans Fat 0g); Cholesterol 85mg; Sodium 780mg; Total Carbohydrate 11g (Dietary Fiber 0g) **Exchanges:** ½ Other Carbohydrate, 4½ Very Lean Meat, 1 Fat **Carbohydrate Choices:** 1

$1.83 per serving

budget smart

"Taking chicken breasts south of the border is a great way to spice up a weeknight summer dinner. This recipe puts your spice cabinet to work with taco seasoning, dried oregano and cumin."

★ **Best Budget Picks** (for more uses, see pages 314-15)

Cacciatore-Style Chicken

Prep Time: **55 Minutes** || Start to Finish: **55 Minutes** || **4 Servings**

★ 3 boneless skinless chicken breasts (³/₄ to 1 lb)

1 tablespoon olive or vegetable oil

1 medium onion, chopped (¹/₂ cup)

2 cloves garlic, finely chopped

¹/₂ cup chopped green bell pepper

³/₄ cup sliced zucchini or yellow summer squash

³/₄ cup sliced mushrooms

★ 1 can (14.5 oz) diced tomatoes, undrained

¹/₂ teaspoon Italian seasoning

¹/₈ teaspoon pepper

2 cups uncooked bow-tie (farfalle), radiatore (nuggets) or rotini pasta

1 Cut each chicken breast half crosswise into 3 pieces. In 10-inch skillet, heat oil over medium-high heat. Cook chicken in oil about 5 minutes, stirring frequently, until brown; move chicken to one side of skillet.

2 Add onion, garlic, bell pepper, zucchini and mushrooms to other side of skillet. Cook vegetables about 3 minutes, stirring occasionally, until crisp-tender.

3 Stir tomatoes, Italian seasoning and pepper into vegetables and chicken. Heat to boiling; reduce heat. Cover and simmer 25 minutes or until chicken is no longer pink in center. Meanwhile, cook and drain pasta as directed on package.

4 Uncover chicken mixture and simmer 5 minutes longer. Serve over pasta.

1 Serving: Calories 280; Total Fat 8g (Saturated Fat 1.5g, Trans Fat 0g); Cholesterol 80mg; Sodium 310mg; Total Carbohydrate 29g (Dietary Fiber 3g) **Exchanges:** 1¹/₂ Starch, 1 Vegetable, 2¹/₂ Very Lean Meat, 1 Fat **Carbohydrate Choices:** 2

budget smart

" This simple spin on the Italian classic is made easy by using boneless chicken breasts, which you can buy in bulk for extra savings. The canned diced tomatoes are another great budget staple. "

$2.47 per serving

Chicken-Rice Skillet

Prep Time: **15 Minutes** || Start to Finish: **20 Minutes** || 4 Servings

1 tablespoon vegetable oil

★ 1¼ lb boneless skinless chicken breasts, cut into 1-inch pieces

2 cups water

1 tablespoon butter or margarine

1 bag (1 lb) frozen broccoli, red peppers, onions and mushrooms (or other combination), thawed, drained

2 cups uncooked instant rice

1 teaspoon salt

¼ teaspoon pepper

1 cup shredded Cheddar cheese (4 oz)

1 In 12-inch skillet, heat oil over medium-high heat. Cook chicken in oil 3 to 4 minutes, stirring occasionally, until no longer pink in center.

2 Add water and butter; heat to boiling. Stir in vegetables, rice, salt and pepper. Sprinkle with cheese; remove from heat.

3 Cover and let stand about 5 minutes or until water is absorbed.

1 Serving: Calories 580; Total Fat 21g (Saturated Fat 9g, Trans Fat 0g); Cholesterol 125mg; Sodium 870mg; Total Carbohydrate 54g (Dietary Fiber 3g) **Exchanges:** 3 Starch, 2 Vegetable, 4½ Lean Meat, 1 Fat **Carbohydrate Choices:** 3½

budget smart

"Frozen mixed vegetables save time and money: A bag contains just the right amount of each vegetable and the prep work's already done! Store several bags in the freezer to use in quick weeknight dinners, like this 20-minute meal."

★ **Best Budget Picks** (for more uses, see pages 314-15)

$2.42
per serving

Chicken and Noodles Skillet

Prep Time: **40 Minutes** || Start to Finish: **40 Minutes** || **4 Servings (1¼ cups each)**

1 tablespoon vegetable oil

★ 1 lb boneless skinless chicken breasts, cut into bite-size pieces

1 medium onion, chopped (½ cup)

1 cup ready-to-eat baby-cut carrots, cut lengthwise in half

1 cup frozen cuts broccoli

1 cup uncooked egg noodles (2 oz)

1 can (14 oz) chicken broth

★ 1 can (10¾ oz) condensed cream of chicken soup

Chopped fresh parsley, if desired

1 In 12-inch nonstick skillet, heat oil over medium-high heat. Cook chicken and onion in oil 6 to 8 minutes, stirring frequently, until browned and onion is just tender.

2 Stir in remaining ingredients except parsley. Heat to boiling; reduce heat. Cover and simmer 10 minutes. Uncover and simmer 5 to 8 minutes longer, stirring occasionally, until chicken is no longer pink in center and noodles are tender. Sprinkle with parsley.

1 Serving: Calories 340; Total Fat 13g (Saturated Fat 3.5g, Trans Fat 0g); Cholesterol 85mg; Sodium 1080mg; Total Carbohydrate 24g (Dietary Fiber 3g) **Exchanges:** 1 Starch, 2 Vegetable, 3½ Lean Meat, ½ Fat **Carbohydrate Choices:** 1½

budget smart

❝ This lightly creamy chicken noodle skillet is a great and economical way to get kids to eat their veggies. And it's on the table in well under an hour. ❞

★ **Best Budget Picks** (for more uses, see pages 314–15)

$2.07
per serving

Chicken Sesame Stir-Fry

Prep Time: **20 Minutes** || Start to Finish: **20 Minutes** || **2 Servings**

1 cup water

Dash salt

½ cup uncooked instant brown rice

2 tablespoons reduced sodium soy sauce

1 teaspoon lemon juice

2 teaspoons cornstarch

½ teaspoon toasted sesame oil

1 teaspoon canola oil

½ lb uncooked chicken breast tenders (not breaded), pieces cut in half lengthwise

1½ cups frozen bell pepper and onion stir-fry (from 1-lb bag), thawed, drained

½ teaspoon sesame seed

1 In 1-quart saucepan, heat ⅔ cup of the water and the salt to boiling over high heat. Stir in rice. Reduce heat to low. Cover; simmer about 10 minutes or until water is absorbed. Fluff with fork.

2 Meanwhile, in small bowl, stir remaining ⅓ cup water, the soy sauce, lemon juice, cornstarch and sesame oil; set aside.

3 Heat nonstick wok or 10-inch skillet over medium-high heat. Add canola oil; rotate wok to coat side. Add chicken; cook and stir 2 to 3 minutes. Add stir-fry vegetables; cook and stir 3 to 5 minutes or until chicken is no longer pink in center and vegetables are crisp-tender.

4 Stir soy sauce mixture into chicken mixture; heat to boiling. Cook and stir until sauce is thickened. Sprinkle with sesame seed. Serve with rice.

1 Serving: Calories 300; Total Fat 5g (Saturated Fat 0g, Trans Fat 0g); Cholesterol 50mg; Sodium 750mg; Total Carbohydrate 35g (Dietary Fiber 2g) **Exchanges:** 1½ Starch, ½ Other Carbohydrate, 1 Vegetable, 3 Very Lean Meat, ½ Fat **Carbohydrate Choices:** 2

budget smart

"Want to cook with Chinese flavors but not sure which flavorings you really need? Start with soy sauce and toasted sesame oil—they're the most frequently called for ingredients in a range of Chinese-style dishes, like this simple stir-fry. Toasted sesame oil lends a delightful, unmistakable Chinese flavor but must be used sparingly. Store it in the refrigerator to preserve freshness."

$1.33
per serving

Italian Chopped Salad

Prep Time: **20 Minutes** || Start to Finish: **20 Minutes** || **4 Servings**

6 cups chopped (1 large bunch or 2 small bunches) romaine lettuce

2 large tomatoes, chopped (2 cups)

2 medium cucumbers, chopped (1½ cups)

1 cup cut-up cooked chicken or turkey

1 package (3 oz) Italian salami, chopped

★ 1 can (15 oz) cannellini beans

1 cup fresh small basil leaves

★ ²⁄₃ cup red wine vinaigrette or Italian dressing or homemade dressing

In large bowl, place lettuce, tomatoes, cucumbers, chicken, salami, beans and basil leaves. Pour vinaigrette over salad, and toss until ingredients are coated.

1 Serving: Calories 500; Total Fat 29g (Saturated Fat 6g, Trans Fat 0g); Cholesterol 55mg; Sodium 1050mg; Total Carbohydrate 33g (Dietary Fiber 9g) **Exchanges:** 1 Starch, ½ Other Carbohydrate, 2 Vegetable, 3 Medium-Fat Meat, 2½ Fat **Carbohydrate Choices:** 2

Homemade Italian Dressing: In a container with a tight-fitting lid, combine 1 cup olive or vegetable oil, ¼ cup white or cider vinegar, 2 tablespoons finely chopped onion, 1 teaspoon dried basil, 1 teaspoon sugar, 1 teaspoon ground mustard, ½ teaspoon salt, ½ teaspoon dried oregano leaves, ¼ teaspoon pepper, and 2 finely chopped cloves garlic. Cover and shake all ingredients. Shake before using. Store tightly covered in refrigerator.

budget smart

" This main-dish salad benefits from cannellini beans, which cost little and are high in fiber. Try adding canned beans to other salads to make them more substantial. "

$3.53 per serving

★ **Best Budget Picks** (for more uses, see pages 314–15)

Summer Harvest Chicken-Potato Salad

Prep Time: **15 Minutes** || Start to Finish: **30 Minutes** || **4 Servings**

4 medium red potatoes (1 lb), cut into ³/₄-inch cubes

¹/₂ lb fresh green beans, trimmed, cut into 1-inch pieces (about 2 cups)

¹/₂ cup plain fat-free yogurt

★ ¹/₃ cup fat-free ranch dressing

1 tablespoon prepared horseradish

¹/₄ teaspoon salt

Dash pepper

★ 2 cups cut-up cooked chicken breast

²/₃ cup thinly sliced celery

Torn salad greens, if desired

1 In 2-quart saucepan, heat 6 cups lightly salted water to boiling. Add potatoes; return to boiling. Reduce heat; simmer uncovered 5 minutes. Add green beans; cook uncovered 8 to 12 minutes longer or until potatoes and beans are crisp-tender.

2 Meanwhile, in small bowl, mix yogurt, dressing, horseradish, salt and pepper; set aside.

3 Drain potatoes and green beans; rinse with cold water to cool. In large serving bowl, mix potatoes, green beans, chicken and celery. Pour yogurt mixture over salad; toss gently to coat. Line plates with greens; spoon salad onto greens.

1 Serving: Calories 270; Total Fat 3.5g (Saturated Fat 1g, Trans Fat 0g); Cholesterol 60mg; Sodium 410mg; Total Carbohydrate 32g (Dietary Fiber 5g) **Exchanges:** 1¹/₂ Starch, ¹/₂ Other Carbohydrate, 1 Vegetable, 2¹/₂ Very Lean Meat **Carbohydrate Choices:** 2

$2.14 per serving

budget smart

❝ Can't decide between chicken or potato salad? Here you get the best of both! This summery salad keeps the calories down by using fat-free yogurt and ranch dressing, but you can use regular if that's what you have on hand. You could also substitute 2 cups of chopped cooked ham for the chicken. ❞

Turkey and Green Chile Stuffing Casserole

Prep Time: **25 Minutes** || Start to Finish: **1 Hour 40 Minutes** || **6 Servings**

2 tablespoons butter or
   margarine

1 medium onion, chopped
   (1/2 cup)

1 small red bell pepper, chopped
   (1/2 cup)

4 cups seasoned cornbread
   stuffing mix

1 cup frozen whole kernel corn

1 can (4.5 oz) chopped green
   chiles, undrained

1 1/2 cups water

2 turkey breast tenderloins
   (about 3/4 lb each)

1/2 teaspoon chili powder

1/2 teaspoon peppered
   seasoned salt

1 Heat oven to 350°F. Spray 11×7-inch (2-quart) glass baking dish with cooking spray. In 12-inch nonstick skillet, melt butter over medium-high heat. Cook onion and bell pepper in butter 2 to 3 minutes, stirring frequently, until tender. Stir in stuffing mix, corn, chiles and water. Spread stuffing mixture in baking dish.

2 Sprinkle both sides of turkey tenderloins with chili powder and peppered seasoned salt. Place on stuffing, pressing into stuffing mixture slightly. Spray sheet of foil with cooking spray. Cover baking dish with foil, sprayed side down.

3 Bake 1 hour. Uncover and bake 10 to 15 minutes longer or until juice of turkey is no longer pink when centers of thickest pieces are cut.

1 Serving: Calories 360; Total Fat 7g (Saturated Fat 3g, Trans Fat 0.5g); Cholesterol 85mg; Sodium 990mg; Total Carbohydrate 43g (Dietary Fiber 3g) **Exchanges:** 3 Starch, 3 1/2 Very Lean Meat, 1/2 Fat **Carbohydrate Choices:** 3

budget smart

" Turkey and chile stuffing combine to make this easy one-dish meal with a Tex-Mex twist. The chopped canned chiles are mildly spicy, but not hot. If you do want more heat, just add a little more chili powder. "

Honey-Mustard Turkey with Snap Peas

Prep Time: **10 Minutes** || Start to Finish: **25 Minutes** || **4 Servings**

1 lb uncooked turkey breast
   slices, about ¼ inch thick

½ cup Dijon and honey
   marinade

1 cup ready-to-eat baby-cut
   carrots, cut lengthwise
   in half

2 cups frozen sugar snap peas

1 In shallow glass or plastic dish, place turkey. Pour marinade over turkey; turn slices to coat evenly. Cover dish and let stand 10 minutes at room temperature.

2 Spray 10-inch skillet with cooking spray; heat over medium heat. Drain most of marinade from turkey. Cook turkey in skillet about 5 minutes, turning once, until brown.

3 Add carrots, lifting turkey to place carrots on bottom of skillet. Top turkey with peas. Cover and simmer about 7 minutes or until carrots are tender and turkey is no longer pink in center.

1 Serving: Calories 260; Total Fat 11g (Saturated Fat 2g, Trans Fat 0g); Cholesterol 75mg; Sodium 260mg; Total Carbohydrate 10g (Dietary Fiber 3g) **Exchanges:** ½ Other Carbohydrate, 1 Vegetable, 4 Very Lean Meat, 1½ Fat **Carbohydrate Choices:** ½

budget smart

"Using precut ingredients can shave precious minutes from a meal, as in this 25-minute dinner. If you'd prefer to shave pennies, use regular carrots, peeled and cut into ¼-inch slices instead of the baby-cut carrots. Slicing up your own turkey breast saves even more."

$1.34
per serving

★ **Best Budget Picks** (for more uses, see pages 314–15)

Onion-Topped Turkey Divan

Prep Time: **15 Minutes** || Start to Finish: **1 Hour 10 Minutes** || **4 Servings (1 cup each)**

1 bag (14 oz) frozen broccoli florets, thawed

2 cups diced cooked turkey

★ 1 can (10¾ oz) condensed cream of chicken soup

½ cup mayonnaise or salad dressing

½ cup milk

1 cup shredded Cheddar cheese (4 oz)

1 cup French-fried onions (from 2.8-oz can), coarsely crushed

1 Heat oven to 350°F. Spray 8-inch square (2-quart) glass baking dish with cooking spray.

2 Layer broccoli and turkey in baking dish. In medium bowl, mix soup, mayonnaise and milk; stir in cheese. Spread over turkey and broccoli. Cover baking dish with foil.

3 Bake 30 minutes. Sprinkle with onions. Bake uncovered 20 to 25 minutes longer or until bubbly and broccoli is tender.

1 Serving: Calories 560; Total Fat 37g (Saturated Fat 12g, Trans Fat 2.5g); Cholesterol 110mg; Sodium 1130mg; Total Carbohydrate 22g (Dietary Fiber 3g) **Exchanges:** 1½ Starch, 4 Lean Meat, 5 Fat **Carbohydrate Choices:** 1½

budget smart

"Everyone loves those canned French-fried onions that go on top of the famous potluck vegetable dish of green beans with cream of mushroom gravy. Try them on other casseroles to add crunch, like this easy turkey and broccoli divan."

$2.22
per serving

Curried Turkey Stir-Fry

Prep Time: **30 Minutes** || Start to Finish: **30 Minutes** || **4 Servings (1¼ cups each)**

1¼ cups uncooked instant brown or white rice

2 cups water

¼ teaspoon salt

2 teaspoons canola oil

1 lb uncooked turkey breast strips for stir-fry

1 medium red bell pepper, cut into thin strips

2 cups small fresh broccoli florets

★ 1 can (10½ oz) ready-to-serve chicken broth soup

4 teaspoons cornstarch

4 teaspoons curry powder

½ teaspoon ground ginger

¼ teaspoon salt

1 Cook brown rice as directed on package, using water and ¼ teaspoon salt.

2 Meanwhile, in 12-inch nonstick skillet, heat oil over medium-high heat. Add turkey; cook 5 to 8 minutes, stirring frequently, until browned. Stir in bell pepper and broccoli. Cook 2 minutes.

3 In small bowl, mix remaining ingredients. Stir into turkey and vegetables. Heat to boiling. Reduce heat; cover and cook 2 to 3 minutes or until vegetables are crisp-tender and turkey is no longer pink in center. Serve over brown rice.

1 Serving: Calories 320; Total Fat 5g (Saturated Fat 0.5g, Trans Fat 0g); Cholesterol 75mg; Sodium 770mg; Total Carbohydrate 35g (Dietary Fiber 4g) **Exchanges:** 2 Starch, 1 Vegetable, 3½ Very Lean Meat, ½ Fat **Carbohydrate Choices:** 2

budget smart

" If you can't find turkey breast strips or if you already have turkey breasts on hand, use a pound of whole turkey breast. Slice into finger-sized strips. You may find it easier to gently pound the meat into uniform thickness before slicing; flatten between sheets of waxed paper using the flat side of a meat mallet or rolling pin. "

★ **Best Budget Picks** (for more uses, see pages 314–15)

$1.99
per serving

Caribbean Turkey Stew

Prep Time: **15 Minutes** || Start to Finish: **30 Minutes** || **2 Servings (1³/₄ cups each)**

2 teaspoons olive oil

1 turkey breast tenderloin
(¹/₂ lb), cut into 1-inch pieces

1 small onion, coarsely chopped
(¹/₄ cup)

1 clove garlic, finely chopped

2 small red potatoes, cut into
eighths (³/₄ cup)

¹/₂ dark-orange sweet potato,
peeled, cut into 1-inch pieces
(³/₄ cup)

★ 1 can (14 oz) chicken broth

¹/₄ teaspoon ground nutmeg

¹/₈ teaspoon pepper

1 dried bay leaf

¹/₂ cup frozen sweet peas,
thawed

1 In 3-quart saucepan, heat oil over medium-high heat. Add turkey, onion and garlic; cook 4 to 5 minutes, stirring frequently, until onion is softened.

2 Stir in remaining ingredients except peas. Heat to boiling. Reduce heat to medium-low; cover and cook 15 minutes or until potatoes are tender and turkey is no longer pink in center.

3 Stir in peas. Cover; cook 2 to 3 minutes, stirring occasionally, until peas are hot. Remove bay leaf.

1 Serving: Calories 390; Total Fat 7g (Saturated Fat 1.5g, Trans Fat 0g); Cholesterol 75mg; Sodium 940mg; Total Carbohydrate 47g (Dietary Fiber 7g) **Exchanges:** 2¹/₂ Starch, ¹/₂ Other Carbohydrate, 4 Very Lean Meat, ¹/₂ Fat **Carbohydrate Choices:** 3

budget smart

"Sweet potatoes are from the morning glory family and originated in the tropical areas of South America. They're available year-round and inexpensive, and they add a sweet touch to this tasty weeknight dinner for two."

★ **Best Budget Picks** (for more uses, see pages 314-15)

$2.91
per serving

Turkey Salad with Fruit

Prep Time: **20 Minutes** || Start to Finish: **2 Hours 20 Minutes** || **4 Servings**

1 container (6 oz) peach, orange or lemon yogurt (^{2}/$_3$ cup)

^{1}/$_4$ teaspoon ground ginger

10 oz cooked turkey or chicken, cut into ^{1}/$_2$-inch pieces (2 cups)

2 medium stalks celery, thinly sliced (1 cup)

1 medium green onion with top, cut into ^{1}/$_8$-inch slices

1 can (11 oz) mandarin orange segments, drained

1 can (8 oz) sliced water chestnuts, drained

1 cup seedless green grapes

4 cups mixed salad greens

1 In large bowl, mix yogurt and ginger. Stir in remaining ingredients except salad greens. Cover with plastic wrap; refrigerate at least 2 hours.

2 On 4 plates, arrange salad greens. Top greens with turkey salad.

1 Serving: Calories 270; Total Fat 6g (Saturated Fat 2g, Trans Fat 0g); Cholesterol 65mg; Sodium 135mg; Total Carbohydrate 29g (Dietary Fiber 4g) **Exchanges:** ^{1}/$_2$ Starch, ^{1}/$_2$ Fruit, ^{1}/$_2$ Other Carbohydrate, 1 Vegetable, 3 Very Lean Meat, 1 Fat **Carbohydrate Choices:** 2

Simple Swap: Substitute 2 cups cut-up cooked ham for the turkey.

budget smart

" Containers of fruit yogurt make great snacks—and here you use one to make a simple dressing for this turkey and fruit salad. Use whichever flavor you like best! "

$1.66
per serving

CHAPTER 2

Budget-Minded
Beef and Pork

Save Money on Meats

Save money and time with a few tips on getting the most from less expensive cut of meat:

- Use inexpensive cuts of meat like beef chuck, pork shoulder or stew meat in casseroles, soups and stews that call for cubed beef or pork, rather than the more expensive lean cuts. The meat will have ample time to tenderize as it cooks, and it will absorb the flavors of the other ingredients.

- Cook ground beef plain or with seasonings and diced onions or other diced vegetables; drain. Spoon the amount you'll use at one time into resealable freezer plastic bags or containers with lids; label and date. Freeze up to 3 months. Use in casseroles, chilies, skillet meals, sloppy joes, soups, spaghetti or tacos.

- Buy inexpensive ground beef, rather than the more expensive leaner packages. For recipes that call for browned ground beef, brown it as usual, drain it in a colander and then rinse it with hot water to remove remaining fat. You'll be left with very lean ground beef for your recipe, but at a cost-savings to you!

- Make extra cooked meatballs. Arrange in a single layer on a foil-lined cookie sheet; freeze. Transfer the number you'll use at one time into separate resealable freezer plastic bags or containers with lids; label and date. Use meatballs directly from the freezer in cooked recipes.

Meat Loaf

Prep Time: **20 Minutes** || Start to Finish: **1 Hour 25 Minutes** || **4 Servings**

★ **1 lb lean (at least 80%) ground beef**

1/4 **cup milk**

2 teaspoons Worcestershire sauce

1 teaspoon chopped fresh or 1/4 **teaspoon dried sage leaves**

1/4 **teaspoon salt**

1/4 **teaspoon ground mustard**

1/8 **teaspoon pepper**

1 clove garlic, finely chopped, or 1/8 **teaspoon garlic powder**

1 egg

2 slices bread, torn into small pieces

3 tablespoons chopped onion

1/3 **cup ketchup, chili sauce or barbecue sauce**

1 Heat oven to 350°F. In large bowl, mix all ingredients except ketchup.

2 In ungreased baking pan, spread beef mixture. Shape mixture into 8×4-inch loaf in pan. Spread ketchup over top.

3 Bake uncovered 50 to 60 minutes until meat and juices are no longer pink or until meat thermometer inserted in center of loaf reads 160°F and center of loaf is no longer pink.* Let stand 5 minutes; remove from pan.

*If you like bell pepper, onions and celery in your meat loaf, you may find that it may remain pink even though the beef is cooked to 160°F in the center. It's due to the natural nitrate content of these ingredients. So it is best to always check meat loaf with a thermometer to make sure it is thoroughly cooked.

1 Serving: Calories 290; Total Fat 15g (Saturated Fat 6g, Trans Fat 1g); Cholesterol 125mg; Sodium 560mg; Total Carbohydrate 15g (Dietary Fiber 0g) **Exchanges:** 1/2 Starch, 1/2 Other Carbohydrate, 3 Medium-Fat Meat **Carbohydrate Choices:** 1

Simple Swap: Substitute ground turkey for the ground beef. Bake about 60 minutes or until meat thermometer inserted in center of loaf reads 165°F.

budget smart

"Check your supermarket for ground meat labeled "meatloaf combination" (usually a blend of ground pork, veal and beef) especially if it's on sale. Use it instead of the ground beef for an Italian-style meat loaf."

★ **Best Budget Picks** (for more uses, pages 314–15)

$1.02
per serving

Fiesta Taco Casserole

Prep Time: **15 Minutes** || Start to Finish: **45 Minutes** || **4 Servings**

★ 1 lb lean (at least 80%) ground beef

★ 1 can (15 to 16 oz) spicy chili beans in sauce, undrained

1 cup chunky-style salsa

2 cups coarsely broken tortilla chips

$^3/_4$ cup sour cream

4 medium green onions, sliced ($^1/_4$ cup)

1 medium tomato, chopped ($^3/_4$ cup)

1 cup shredded Cheddar cheese (4 oz)

Shredded lettuce, if desired

Additional salsa, if desired

1 Heat oven to 350°F. In 10-inch skillet, cook beef over medium heat 8 to 10 minutes, stirring occasionally, until thoroughly cooked; drain. Stir in beans and 1 cup salsa. Heat to boiling, stirring occasionally.

2 In ungreased 2-quart casserole, place broken tortilla chips. Top with beef mixture. Spread with sour cream. Sprinkle with onions, tomato and cheese.

3 Bake uncovered 20 to 30 minutes or until hot and bubbly. Serve with lettuce and additional salsa.

1 Serving: Calories 650; Total Fat 38g (Saturated Fat 17g, Trans Fat 1.5g); Cholesterol 130mg; Sodium 1550mg; Total Carbohydrate 42g (Dietary Fiber 7g) **Exchanges:** 2 Starch, 1 Other Carbohydrate, 4$^1/_2$ Lean Meat, 4 Fat **Carbohydrate Choices:** 3

Lighten Up Fiesta Taco Casserole: Substitute ground turkey breast for the ground beef, and use reduced-fat sour cream and reduced-fat Cheddar cheese for 21 grams of fat and 520 calories per serving.

budget smart

" Mexican made easy! This family-pleasing taco bake uses staple ingredients like ground beef, salsa and canned beans, so you may already have some of these on hand. If not, stocking up on these foods is a good idea if you like Mexican flavors: Use any remaining ingredients in recipes like Beef and Bean Tortilla Bake (page 62) or Taco Supper Skillet (page 67). "

★ **Best Budget Picks** (for more uses, pages 314-15)

Beef and Bean Tortilla Bake

Prep Time: **20 Minutes** || Start to Finish: **55 Minutes** || **6 Servings**

★ **1 lb extra-lean (at least 90%) ground beef**

★ **1 can (15 oz) black beans, rinsed, drained**

★ **1 can (15 to 16 oz) pinto beans, rinsed, drained**

★ **1 can (14.5 oz) no-salt-added stewed tomatoes, undrained**

1 envelope (1 oz) 40%-less-sodium taco seasoning mix

²⁄₃ cup water

³⁄₄ cup shredded reduced-fat sharp Cheddar cheese (3 oz)

3 spinach-flavor flour tortillas (8 inch), cut in half, then cut crosswise into ¹⁄₂-inch-wide strips

1 Heat oven to 350°F. In 12-inch skillet, cook beef over medium heat 8 to 10 minutes, stirring occasionally, until brown; drain. Stir in black beans, pinto beans, tomatoes, taco seasoning mix and water. Cook 2 to 4 minutes, stirring occasionally, until heated through. Stir in ½ cup of the cheese.

2 In 8-inch square (2-quart) glass baking dish, spread 2 cups of the beef mixture. Top with half of the tortilla strips. Spoon half of the remaining beef mixture over tortilla strips. Add remaining tortilla strips; top with remaining beef mixture.

3 Bake uncovered about 30 minutes or until bubbly and heated through. Sprinkle with remaining ¼ cup cheese. Bake about 5 minutes longer or until cheese is melted. Cut into squares.

1 Serving: Calories 410; Total Fat 9g (Saturated Fat 3.5g, Trans Fat 0.5g); Cholesterol 45mg; Sodium 910mg; Total Carbohydrate 56g (Dietary Fiber 13g) **Exchanges:** 3 Starch, 1 Vegetable, 3 Very Lean Meat, 1 Fat **Carbohydrate Choices:** 3

$1.37 per serving

budget smart

"Mixing ground beef and beans is a great way to add more fiber to your meals without giving up the beef, plus it saves money. If you can't find spinach-flavor flour tortillas, substitute another flavor or use plain white."

Spinach and Beef Enchiladas

Prep Time: **25 Minutes** || Start to Finish: **1 Hour 10 Minutes** || **8 enchiladas**

★ 1 lb lean (at least 80%) ground beef

1 medium onion, chopped (½ cup)

1 box (9 oz) frozen spinach

1 can (4.5 oz) chopped green chiles, undrained

½ teaspoon ground cumin

½ teaspoon garlic-pepper blend

½ cup sour cream

2 cups shredded Colby-Monterey Jack cheese blend (8 oz)

1 can (10 oz) enchilada sauce

1 package (11.5 oz) flour tortillas (8 tortillas)

½ cup chunky-style salsa

1 Heat oven to 350°F. Spray 13×9-inch (3-quart) glass baking dish with cooking spray. In 12-inch nonstick skillet, cook beef and onion over medium-high heat 5 to 7 minutes, stirring occasionally, until beef is brown.

2 Stir in spinach; cook, stirring frequently, until thawed. Stir in green chiles, cumin, garlic-pepper blend, sour cream and 1 cup of the cheese.

3 Spread about 1 teaspoon enchilada sauce on each tortilla. Top each with about ½ cup beef mixture. Roll up tortillas; place seam sides down in baking dish. In small bowl, mix remaining enchilada sauce and the salsa; spoon over enchiladas. Sprinkle with remaining 1 cup cheese.

4 Spray sheet of foil with cooking spray; cover baking dish with foil. Bake 40 to 45 minutes or until thoroughly heated.

1 Enchilada: Calories 400; Total Fat 23g (Saturated Fat 11g, Trans Fat 0.5g); Cholesterol 70mg; Sodium 860mg; Total Carbohydrate 28g (Dietary Fiber 0g) **Exchanges:** 2 Starch, 2 High-Fat Meat, 1 Fat **Carbohydrate Choices:** 2

$1.65 per serving

budget smart

" Who can resist a hot, bubbly pan of enchiladas? And these are so easy to make! Buying ground beef in bulk will save you even more money—just remember to divide it into smaller portions before freezing so you can defrost just the amount you need. "

Beef and Kasha Mexicana

Prep Time: **10 Minutes** || Start to Finish: **25 Minutes** || **6 Servings (1⅓ cups each)**

★ 1 lb extra-lean (at least 90%) ground beef

1 small onion, chopped (½ cup)

1 cup uncooked buckwheat kernels or groats (kasha)

★ 1 can (14.5 oz) diced tomatoes, undrained

1 can (4.5 oz) chopped green chiles, undrained

1 package (1 oz) 40% less-sodium taco seasoning mix

2 cups frozen whole kernel corn (from 1-lb bag), thawed

1½ cups water

1 cup shredded reduced-fat Cheddar cheese (4 oz)

2 tablespoons chopped fresh cilantro, if desired

2 tablespoons sliced ripe olives, if desired

1 In 12-inch skillet, cook ground beef and onion over medium-high heat 5 to 7 minutes, stirring occasionally, until beef is thoroughly cooked; drain. Stir in kasha until kernels are moistened by beef mixture.

2 Stir in tomatoes, chiles, taco seasoning mix, corn and water. Heat to boiling. Cover; reduce heat to low. Simmer 5 to 7 minutes, stirring occasionally, until kasha is tender.

3 Sprinkle cheese over kasha mixture. Cover; cook 2 to 3 minutes or until cheese is melted. Sprinkle with cilantro and olives.

1 Serving: Calories 300; Total Fat 9g (Saturated Fat 3.5g, Trans Fat 0g); Cholesterol 50mg; Sodium 990mg; Total Carbohydrate 33g (Dietary Fiber 5g) **Exchanges:** 2 Starch, 2½ Lean Meat **Carbohydrate Choices:** 2

budget smart

" Trying to eat healthier but also looking to save money on dinner? Mixing ground meat with whole grains is a good way to do both. Here, kasha, a whole grain made from buckwheat, adds a delicious toasty flavor when mixed with ground beef, while also stretching the meat to make six servings. "

$1.81
per serving

Beefy Rice Skillet

Prep Time: **30 Minutes** || Start to Finish: **30 Minutes** || **4 Servings**

★ **1 lb lean (at least 80%) ground beef**

2$\frac{1}{2}$ cups hot water

$\frac{3}{4}$ cup ready-to-eat baby-cut carrots, cut lengthwise in half

1 tablespoon butter or margarine

$\frac{1}{4}$ teaspoon pepper

1 package (6.4 oz) four-cheese rice and pasta blend

1$\frac{1}{2}$ cups broccoli florets

$\frac{1}{2}$ cup cherry or grape tomatoes, cut in half

1 In 12-inch skillet, cook beef over medium-high heat 5 to 7 minutes, stirring occasionally, until thoroughly cooked; drain.

2 Stir water, carrots, butter, pepper, rice mixture and contents of seasoning packet into beef. Heat to boiling; reduce heat. Cover and cook about 15 minutes or until rice and carrots are almost tender, stirring occasionally.

3 Stir in broccoli. Cover and cook 5 minutes or until crisp-tender. Stir in tomatoes. Cook uncovered about 1 minute or until heated.

1 Serving: Calories 420; Total Fat 20g (Saturated Fat 9g, Trans Fat 1); Cholesterol 80mg; Sodium 690mg; Total Carbohydrate 35g (Dietary Fiber 2g) **Exchanges:** 2 Starch, 1 Vegetable, 2$\frac{1}{2}$ Medium-Fat Meat, 1 Fat **Carbohydrate Choices:** 2

budget smart

"This simple skillet dinner is a fast and frugal way to get kids to eat their fresh veggies! For extra savings, use $\frac{3}{4}$ cup chopped carrots instead of baby-cut and a chopped plum (Roma) tomato instead of cherry tomatoes. The prep time will increase only slightly."

$**1.54** per serving

Taco Supper Skillet

Prep Time: **30 Minutes** || Start to Finish: **30 Minutes** || **4 Servings**

★ ½ lb lean (at least 80%) ground beef

1 package (1 oz) taco seasoning mix

2¼ cups water

1½ cups uncooked wagon wheel pasta (5½ oz)

1½ cups frozen whole kernel corn (from 1-lb bag)

★ 1 can (15 oz) pinto or kidney beans, drained, rinsed

1 medium tomato, chopped (¾ cup)

½ cup sour cream

1 cup shredded Cheddar cheese (4 oz)

1 tablespoon chopped fresh chives, if desired

1 In 12-inch skillet, cook beef over medium-high heat 5 to 7 minutes, stirring frequently, until brown; drain.

2 Stir seasoning mix, water, uncooked pasta, corn, beans and tomato into beef. Heat to boiling; stir. Reduce heat to medium-low. Cover; cook 10 to 15 minutes, stirring occasionally, until pasta is desired doneness and most of the liquid has been absorbed.

3 Stir in sour cream. Remove from heat. Sprinkle with cheese and chives. Cover; let stand 2 to 3 minutes or until cheese is melted.

1 Serving: Calories 640; Total Fat 23g (Saturated Fat 12g, Trans Fat 1g); Cholesterol 85mg; Sodium 590mg; Total Carbohydrate 73g (Dietary Fiber 12g) **Exchanges:** 4½ Starch, ½ Other Carbohydrate, 3 Medium-Fat Meat, 1 Fat **Carbohydrate Choices:** 5

budget smart

" Family-favorite flavors combine with budget-smart ingredients in this hearty and quick skillet. The wagon wheel pasta is a really fun shape and perfect for holding the sauce, but you can substitute other short-cut pasta like farfalle or rotelle. "

$3.02 per serving

Easy Chili Mole

Prep Time: **30 Minutes** || Start to Finish: **30 Minutes** || **8 Servings (about 1 cup each)**

★ **1 lb extra-lean (at least 90%) ground beef**

1 medium onion, chopped (¹/₂ cup)

1 package (1.25 oz) Tex-Mex chili seasoning mix

★ **1 can (28 oz) diced tomatoes, undrained**

★ **1 can (28 oz) crushed tomatoes**

★ **1 can (15 oz) spicy chili beans, undrained**

1 oz unsweetened baking chocolate, coarsely chopped

8 soft corn tortillas (6 inch)

1 In 4-quart Dutch oven, cook beef and onion over medium heat, stirring occasionally, until beef is brown; drain.

2 Stir in seasoning mix, both tomatoes and beans. Heat to boiling over high heat. Reduce heat to low; cover and cook 15 minutes, stirring occasionally, to blend flavors. Stir in chocolate just until melted. Serve with tortillas.

1 Serving: Calories 270; Total Fat 8g (Saturated Fat 3g, Trans Fat 0g); Cholesterol 35mg; Sodium 830mg; Total Carbohydrate 32g (Dietary Fiber 7g) **Exchanges:** 1¹/₂ Starch, ¹/₂ Other Carbohydrate, 1 Vegetable, 1¹/₂ Lean Meat, ¹/₂ Fat **Carbohydrate Choices:** 2

budget smart

"If you've never tasted mole, you're in for a treat! Mole is a rich Mexican sauce flavored with a "secret" ingredient of unsweetened chocolate. This is the perfect way to use up any extra unsweetened chocolate you may have on hand from making brownies."

★ **Best Budget Picks** (for more uses, pages 314-15)

$1.20
per serving

Chili

Prep Time: **30 Minutes** || Start to Finish: **1 Hour 50 Minutes** || **4 Servings**

★ **1 lb lean (at least 80%) ground beef**

1 large onion, chopped (1 cup)

2 cloves garlic, finely chopped, or 1/4 teaspoon garlic powder

1 tablespoon chili powder

2 teaspoons chopped fresh or 1 teaspoon dried oregano leaves

1 teaspoon ground cumin

1/2 teaspoon salt

1/2 teaspoon red pepper sauce

★ **1 can (14.5 oz) diced tomatoes, undrained**

★ **1 can (15 to 16 oz) red kidney beans, undrained**

1 In 3-quart saucepan, cook beef, onion and garlic over medium heat 8 to 10 minutes, stirring occasionally, until beef is thoroughly cooked. Place strainer or colander in large bowl; line strainer with double thickness of paper towels. Pour beef mixture into strainer to drain. Return beef mixture to saucepan; discard paper towels and any juices in bowl.

2 Into beef, stir remaining ingredients except beans.

3 Heat mixture to boiling over high heat. Once mixture is boiling, reduce heat just enough so mixture bubbles gently. Cover; cook 1 hour, stirring occasionally.

4 Stir in beans. Heat to boiling over high heat. Once mixture is boiling, reduce heat just enough so mixture bubbles gently. Cook uncovered about 20 minutes, stirring occasionally, until desired thickness.

1 Serving: Calories 360; Total Fat 14g (Saturated Fat 5g, Trans Fat 1g); Cholesterol 70mg; Sodium 720mg; Total Carbohydrate 31g (Dietary Fiber 8g) **Exchanges:** 2 Starch, 3 Lean Meat, 1 Fat **Carbohydrate Choices:** 2

Lighten Up Chili: Use 1 lb lean ground turkey for the ground beef for chili with 7 grams of fat and 320 calories per serving.

Cincinnati-Style Chili: For each serving, spoon about ¾ cup beef mixture over 1 cup hot cooked spaghetti. Sprinkle each serving with ¼ cup shredded Cheddar cheese and 2 tablespoons chopped onion. Top with sour cream if desired.

budget smart

" There are as many different kinds of chili as there are states in America—and probably more! The Cincinnati-Style Chili variation, for example, serves the chili over spaghetti—making it a super kid-pleaser and a money-saver, too. Chili freezes well, so make a double batch the next time you see ground beef on sale. "

★ **Best Budget Picks** (for more uses, pages 314–15)

$1.37
per serving

Skillet Nacho Chili

Prep Time: **30 Minutes** || Start to Finish: **30 Minutes** || **4 Servings**

★ 1 lb lean (at least 80%) ground beef

1 medium onion, chopped (¹/₂ cup)

★ 1 can (19 oz) hearty tomato soup

★ 1 can (15 oz) spicy chili beans in sauce, undrained

1 can (4.5 oz) chopped green chiles, undrained

1 cup frozen whole kernel corn

1 cup shredded Cheddar cheese (4 oz)

2 cups corn chips

1 Spray 12-inch skillet with cooking spray; heat over medium-high heat. Cook beef and onion in skillet 5 to 7 minutes, stirring occasionally, until beef is thoroughly cooked and onion is tender; drain.

2 Stir soup, chili beans, green chiles and corn into beef mixture. Heat to boiling; reduce heat to medium. Cook 8 to 10 minutes, stirring occasionally, until sauce is slightly thickened and corn is cooked.

3 Sprinkle each serving with cheese. Serve with corn chips.

1 Serving: Calories 585; Total Fat 29g (Saturated Fat 11g, Trans Fat 1g); Cholesterol 95mg; Sodium 1790mg; Total Carbohydrate 45g (Dietary Fiber 8g) **Exchanges:** 3 Starch, 4 Medium-Fat Meat, 1 Fat **Carbohydrate Choices:** 3

Simple Swap: Substitute ground turkey for the ground beef.

budget smart

"This quick, easy and cheap-to-make chili is a big hit with kids. Have a bowl of regular or low-fat sour cream on the table in case the chili is too spicy for some eaters. Dairy quickly cuts spiciness."

$2.22 per serving

★ **Best Budget Picks** (for more uses, pages 314–15)

Grilled Hamburger Steaks with Roasted Onions

Prep Time: **25 Minutes** || Start to Finish: **25 Minutes** || **4 Servings**

★ 4 lean (at least 80%) ground beef patties (4 to 6 oz each)

2 tablespoons steak sauce

1 package (1 oz) onion soup mix (from 2-oz box)

2 large Bermuda or other sweet onions, cut in half, thinly sliced and separated (6 cups)

2 tablespoons packed brown sugar

1 tablespoon balsamic vinegar

Hamburger buns, if desired

1 Heat gas or charcoal grill. Cut 2 (12×8-inch) sheets of heavy-duty foil; spray with cooking spray. Brush beef patties with steak sauce; sprinkle with half of the soup mix (dry).

2 Place half of the onions on center of each foil sheet. Sprinkle with remaining soup mix, brown sugar and vinegar. Bring up 2 sides of foil over onions so edges meet. Seal edges, making tight ½-inch fold; fold again, allowing space on sides for heat circulation and expansion. Fold other sides to seal.

3 Place packets and beef patties on grill over medium heat. Cover grill; cook 10 to 15 minutes, turning patties and rotating packets ½ turn once or twice, until meat thermometer inserted in center of patties reads 160°F.

4 To serve, cut large X across top of each onion packet; carefully fold back foil to allow steam to escape. Serve onions over patties on hamburger buns.

1 Serving: Calories 320; Total Fat 13g (Saturated Fat 5g, Trans Fat 1g); Cholesterol 70mg; Sodium 790mg; Total Carbohydrate 30g (Dietary Fiber 4g) **Exchanges:** 1½ Starch, 1½ Vegetable, 2 Medium-Fat Meat, ½ Fat **Carbohydrate Choices:** 2

$1.59 per serving

budget smart

"A treat for all onion lovers, these burgers get a quick and inexpensive flavor kick from the delicious roasted onions, which caramelize in the sugar and balsamic vinegar."

Beef Stew

Prep Time: **30 Minutes** || Start to Finish: **3 Hours 30 Minutes** || **4 Servings**

1 tablespoon vegetable oil

1 lb boneless beef chuck, tip or round roast, trimmed of fat, cut into 1-inch cubes

3 cups water

1/2 teaspoon salt

1/8 teaspoon pepper

2 medium carrots, cut into 1-inch pieces

1 large unpeeled baking potato (russet or Idaho), cut into 1 1/2-inch pieces

1 medium green bell pepper, cut into 1-inch pieces

1 medium stalk celery, cut into 1-inch pieces

1 small onion, chopped (1/4 cup)

1 teaspoon salt

1 dried bay leaf

1/2 cup cold water

2 tablespoons all-purpose flour

1 In 12-inch skillet or 4-quart Dutch oven, heat oil over medium heat 1 to 2 minutes. Add beef; cook 10 to 15 minutes, stirring occasionally, until brown on all sides.

2 Remove skillet from heat, then add water, 1/2 teaspoon salt and the pepper. Heat to boiling over high heat. Once mixture is boiling, reduce heat just enough so mixture bubbles gently. Cover; cook 2 hours to 2 hours 30 minutes or until beef is almost tender.

3 Stir in remaining ingredients except cold water and flour. Cover; cook about 30 minutes longer or until vegetables are tender when pierced with a fork. Remove and discard bay leaf.

4 In tightly covered jar or container, shake cold water and flour; gradually stir into beef mixture. Heat to boiling, stirring constantly. Boil and stir 1 minute, until thickened.

1 Serving: Calories 350; Total Fat 17g (Saturated Fat 6g, Trans Fat 0.5g); Cholesterol 65mg; Sodium 980mg; Total Carbohydrate 25g (Dietary Fiber 4g) **Exchanges:** 1 1/2 Starch, 1 Vegetable, 2 1/2 Lean Meat, 1 1/2 Fat **Carbohydrate Choices:** 1 1/2

budget smart

Stews are great choices for budget-smart cooking because the best meat cuts for stew are often the least expensive, too. Beef chuck, tip and round roast are all fairly cheap cuts of beef and will cook into a tender and flavorful beef stew.

$2.06
per serving

Italian-Style Shepherd's Pie

Prep Time: **20 Minutes** || Start to Finish: **50 Minutes** || **4 Servings (1½ cups each)**

1 lb boneless beef sirloin steak, trimmed of fat, cut into 1-inch cubes

1 cup sliced onion (about 1 medium)

2 medium carrots, sliced (1 cup)

½ teaspoon seasoned salt

¼ teaspoon pepper

1½ cups sliced fresh mushrooms

1 jar (14 oz) tomato pasta sauce (any variety)

½ package (7.2-oz size) roasted garlic mashed potatoes (1 pouch)

1 cup hot water

⅔ cup milk

2 tablespoons butter or margarine

2 tablespoons shredded fresh Parmesan cheese

1 Heat oven to 375°F. Spray 2-quart casserole or 11×7-inch (2-quart) glass baking dish with cooking spray. Heat 12-inch nonstick skillet over medium-high heat. Add beef, onion and carrots to skillet; sprinkle with seasoned salt and pepper. Cook 3 to 5 minutes, stirring frequently, until beef is brown.

2 Stir in mushrooms and pasta sauce. Heat to boiling. Cook over medium heat 5 minutes, stirring occasionally. Spread in casserole.

3 Make potatoes as directed on package for 4 servings, using 1 pouch potatoes and seasoning, water, milk and butter. Spoon into 8 mounds around edge of hot beef mixture. Sprinkle cheese over all.

4 Bake uncovered 25 to 30 minutes or until bubbly and potatoes are light golden brown.

1 Serving: Calories 430; Total Fat 15g (Saturated Fat 6g, Trans Fat 0.5g); Cholesterol 80mg; Sodium 860mg; Total Carbohydrate 48g (Dietary Fiber 5g) **Exchanges:** 2 Starch, 1 Other Carbohydrate, 1 Vegetable, 3 Lean Meat, 1 Fat **Carbohydrate Choices:** 3

budget smart

" Thanks to instant potatoes, this extra-easy shepherd's pie is quick to prep and ready in under an hour! Sirloin steak is often on sale, but you can also use ground beef in this recipe for added savings. "

$2.81 per serving

★ **Best Budget Picks** (for more uses, pages 314–15)

Flank Steak with Smoky Honey Mustard Sauce

Prep Time: **30 Minutes** || Start to Finish: **30 Minutes** || **6 Servings**

Sauce

★ ¼ **cup honey mustard dressing**

1 **tablespoon frozen (thawed) orange juice concentrate**

1 **tablespoon water**

1 **small clove garlic, finely chopped**

1 **chipotle chile in adobo sauce (from 7-oz can), finely chopped**

Steak

1 **beef flank steak (about 1½ lb)**

6 **flour tortillas (8 inch; from 11.5-oz package)**

1 Heat gas or charcoal grill. In small bowl, mix sauce ingredients; reserve 2 tablespoons in separate bowl. Make cuts about ½ inch apart and ⅛ inch deep in diamond pattern in both sides of beef. Brush reserved sauce on both sides of beef.

2 Place beef on grill over medium heat. Cover grill; cook 17 to 20 minutes, turning once, until desired doneness. Cut beef across grain into thin slices. Serve with remaining sauce and tortillas.

1 Serving: Calories 360; Total Fat 16g (Saturated Fat 4.5g, Trans Fat 1.5g); Cholesterol 55mg; Sodium 460mg; Total Carbohydrate 22g (Dietary Fiber 0g) **Exchanges:** 1½ Starch, 4 Lean Meat, ½ Fat **Carbohydrate Choices:** 1½

budget smart

"For grilling steaks on the cheap, flank steak is one of your best bets. It's full of beefy flavor and less expensive than tenderloin or strip steak. To ensure the flank steak comes out tender and not chewy, score the meat before grilling as described in step 1. After grilling, slice it thinly across the grain or across the natural fibers in the meat. Leftover steak would be fantastic in sandwiches."

$3.09
per serving

Balsamic-Garlic Marinated Steak

Prep Time: **30 Minutes** || Start to Finish: **8 Hours 30 Minutes** || **6 Servings**

4 cloves garlic, finely chopped, or ¹/₂ teaspoon garlic powder

¹/₂ cup balsamic vinegar

¹/₄ cup chili sauce or ketchup

2 tablespoons packed brown sugar

2 tablespoons olive or vegetable oil

¹/₂ teaspoon Italian seasoning

¹/₄ teaspoon salt

¹/₄ teaspoon coarse ground pepper

1 boneless beef top round steak, 1 to 1¹/₂ inches thick (1¹/₂ lb)

1 In shallow glass dish or resealable food-storage plastic bag, mix garlic and remaining ingredients except beef. Add beef; turn to coat with marinade. Cover dish with plastic wrap or seal bag. Refrigerate at least 8 hours but no longer than 12 hours, turning beef occasionally.

2 Heat gas or charcoal grill. Remove beef from marinade, reserving the marinade.

3 Place beef on grill over medium heat. Cover grill; cook 12 to 18 minutes for medium-rare or 17 to 21 minutes for medium doneness, turning and brushing with marinade once or twice. Discard any remaining marinade. To serve, cut beef across grain into slices.

1 Serving: Calories 190; Total Fat 7g (Saturated Fat 1.5g, Trans Fat 0g); Cholesterol 65mg; Sodium 220mg; Total Carbohydrate 6g (Dietary Fiber 0g); **Exchanges:** ¹/₂ Other Carbohydrate, 3¹/₂ Very Lean Meat, 1 Fat **Carbohydrate Choices:** ¹/₂

budget smart

" Bewildered by all the vinegars available? Along with white and red wine vinegar, balsamic vinegar is one of the most useful choices. Created in the area of Modena, Italy, from grapes, it is rich with a dark molasses color and sweet taste. It's versatile enough to use in salad dressings, marinades, soups and stews, and sauces. "

$1.77
per serving

Szechuan Beef and Bean Sprouts

Prep Time: **20 Minutes** || Start to Finish: **30 Minutes** || **4 Servings (1¼ cups each)**

1 lb boneless beef eye of round steak, trimmed of fat

¼ cup reduced-sodium chicken broth

1 tablespoon reduced-sodium soy sauce

1 tablespoon Szechuan sauce

⅛ teaspoon crushed red pepper flakes

4 plum (Roma) tomatoes, cut into 8 pieces

2 cups fresh bean sprouts (4 oz)

1 tablespoon chopped fresh cilantro

1 Cut beef with grain into 2-inch strips; cut strips across grain into ⅛-inch slices. (Beef is easier to cut if partially frozen, 30 to 60 minutes.) In medium bowl, stir together broth, soy sauce, Szechuan sauce and pepper flakes. Stir in beef. Let stand 10 minutes.

2 Drain beef; reserve marinade. Heat 12-inch nonstick skillet over medium-high heat. Add half of the beef to skillet; cook and stir 2 to 3 minutes or until brown. Remove beef from skillet. Repeat with remaining beef. Return all beef to skillet.

3 Add reserved marinade, the tomatoes and bean sprouts to beef in skillet; stir-fry about 1 minute or until vegetables are warm. Sprinkle with cilantro.

1 Serving: Calories 200; Total Fat 6g (Saturated Fat 1.5g, Trans Fat 0g); Cholesterol 65mg; Sodium 430mg; Total Carbohydrate 6g (Dietary Fiber 1g) **Exchanges:** 1 Vegetable, 4 Very Lean Meat, 1 Fat **Carbohydrate Choices:** ½

budget smart

" Stir-fries are a great way to prepare inexpensive but tougher cuts of beef, such as eye and round, because the meat stays tender from being sliced thinly and cooked quickly. "

$1.76
per serving

Grilled Steak and Potato Salad

Prep Time: **30 Minutes** || Start to Finish: **30 Minutes** || **4 Servings**

³/₄ lb small red potatoes, cut in half

★ ²/₃ cup honey Dijon dressing and marinade

1 boneless beef top sirloin steak, ³/₄ inch thick (³/₄ lb)

¹/₄ teaspoon salt

¹/₄ teaspoon coarsely ground pepper

4 cups bite-size pieces romaine lettuce

2 medium tomatoes, cut into thin wedges

¹/₂ cup thinly sliced red onion

1 Heat gas or charcoal grill. In 2- or 2½-quart saucepan, place potatoes; add enough water to cover potatoes. Heat to boiling; reduce heat to medium. Cook uncovered 5 to 8 minutes or just until potatoes are tender.

2 Drain potatoes; place in medium bowl. Add 2 tablespoons of the dressing; toss to coat. Place potatoes in grill basket (grill "wok") if desired. Brush beef steak with 1 tablespoon of the dressing; sprinkle with salt and pepper.

3 Place beef and potatoes on grill. Cover grill; cook over medium heat 8 to 15 minutes, turning once, until beef is desired doneness and potatoes are golden brown. Cut beef into thin slices.

4 Among 4 plates, divide lettuce, tomatoes and onion. Top with beef and potatoes; drizzle with remaining dressing. Sprinkle with additional pepper if desired.

1 Serving: Calories 360; Total Fat 20g (Saturated Fat 4g, Trans Fat 0g); Cholesterol 35mg; Sodium 440mg; Total Carbohydrate 25g (Dietary Fiber 4g) **Exchanges:** ¹/₂ Starch, 1 Other Carbohydrate, 1 Vegetable, 2¹/₂ Lean Meat, 2¹/₂ Fat **Carbohydrate Choices:** 1¹/₂

budget smart

"Looking for a less expensive way to enjoy steak and potatoes? This dinner salad loaded with juicy steak slices and potatoes in a Dijon dressing fits the bill. Finishing the potatoes on the grill is optional but gives them a great grilled flavor."

$4.93
per serving

Fajita Salad

Prep Time: **20 Minutes** || Start to Finish: **20 Minutes** || **4 Servings**

³/₄ lb boneless lean beef sirloin steak

1 tablespoon canola oil

2 medium bell peppers, cut into strips

1 small onion, thinly sliced

4 cups bite-size pieces salad greens

★ ¹/₃ cup fat-free Italian dressing

¹/₄ cup plain fat-free yogurt

1 Cut beef across grain into bite-size strips. In 10-inch nonstick skillet, heat oil over medium-high heat. Add beef; cook about 3 minutes, stirring occasionally, until brown. Remove beef from skillet.

2 In same skillet, cook bell peppers and onion about 3 minutes, stirring occasionally, until bell peppers are crisp-tender. Stir in beef.

3 Place salad greens on serving platter. Top with beef mixture. In small bowl, mix dressing and yogurt; drizzle over salad.

1 Serving: Calories 280; Total Fat 17g (Saturated Fat 4g, Trans Fat 0g); Cholesterol 60mg; Sodium 230mg; Total Carbohydrate 9g (Dietary Fiber 2g) **Exchanges:** 1 Vegetable, 3 Lean Meat, 2 Fat **Carbohydrate Choices:** ¹/₂

budget smart

" Expensive taste doesn't have to be expensive if you make a little steak go a long way as in this 20-minute meal. "

$**4.62** per serving

★ **Best Budget Picks** (for more uses, pages 314–15)

Rosemary Pork Roast with Carrots

Prep Time: **15 Minutes** || Start to Finish: **1 Hour 55 Minutes** || **10 Servings**

Olive oil cooking spray

1 boneless pork center loin roast (about 2½ lb)

2 teaspoons dried rosemary leaves, crushed

1 teaspoon salt

¼ teaspoon pepper

2 lb ready-to-eat baby-cut carrots

1 large sweet onion, cut into 16 wedges

½ teaspoon garlic powder

1 Heat oven to 400°F. Spray 15×10×1-inch pan with olive oil cooking spray. Remove fat from pork. Spray pork with cooking spray; sprinkle with 1 teaspoon of the rosemary, ½ teaspoon of the salt and the pepper. Place in center of pan.

2 In large bowl, mix carrots, onion, garlic powder, the remaining teaspoon rosemary and ½ teaspoon salt. Arrange vegetable mixture around pork; spray vegetables with cooking spray.

3 Roast uncovered 1 hour to 1 hour 30 minutes or until meat thermometer inserted into center of pork reads 155°F and vegetables are tender. Remove from heat; cover with foil and let stand 10 minutes until thermometer reads 160°F. Slice pork; serve with vegetables.

1 Serving: Calories 240; Total Fat 10g (Saturated Fat 3.5g, Trans Fat 0g); Cholesterol 70mg; Sodium 340mg; Total Carbohydrate 10g (Dietary Fiber 3g) **Exchanges:** 2 Vegetable, 3 Lean Meat, ½ Fat **Carbohydrate Choices:** ½

budget smart

" Easy and impressive, this pork loin roast with carrots requires just a few simple seasonings, which lets the flavor of the meat stand out and keeps the grocery list short! Enjoy cold roast pork sandwiches the next day if there are any leftovers. "

$1.23 per serving

Pork Chops and Apples

Prep Time: **15 Minutes** || Start to Finish: **1 Hour** || **2 Servings**

1 medium unpeeled apple, such as Braeburn, Rome Beauty or Granny Smith, quartered

2 tablespoons packed brown sugar

¼ teaspoon ground cinnamon

2 pork rib chops, ½ to ¾ inch thick (about ¼ lb each)

1 Heat oven to 350°F. Cut each apple quarter into 3 or 4 wedges. Place wedges in 1½-quart casserole. Sprinkle with brown sugar and cinnamon.

2 Remove fat from pork chops, if necessary, and discard. Spray 8-inch or 10-inch skillet with cooking spray, and heat over medium heat 1 to 2 minutes. Cook pork chops in hot skillet about 5 minutes, turning once, until light brown.

3 Place pork in single layer on apples. Cover with lid or foil; bake about 45 minutes or until the pork is no longer pink in center and apples are tender when pierced with a fork. (For pork chops that are ¾ inch thick, meat thermometer inserted in center should read 160°F.)

1 Serving: Calories 260; Total Fat 9g (Saturated Fat 3g, Trans Fat 0g); Cholesterol 65mg; Sodium 45mg; Total Carbohydrate 23g (Dietary Fiber 2g) **Exchanges:** ½ Fruit, 1 Other Carbohydrate, 3 Lean Meat **Carbohydrate Choices:** 1½

budget smart

“ Pork chops and apples make a perfect pair in this easy dinner that's just enough for two. Nice side dish choices would be sautéed or steamed green beans or broccoli, along with mashed or baked potatoes. ”

$1.84
per serving

Speedy Pork Dinner

Prep Time: **20 Minutes** || Start to Finish: **50 Minutes** || **4 Servings**

4 pork loin or rib chops, ¹/₂ inch thick (1 to 1¹/₄ lb)

¹/₂ cup beef-flavored or chicken broth (from 32-oz carton)

3 medium potatoes, quartered

4 small carrots, cut into 1-inch pieces

2 medium onions, quartered

³/₄ teaspoon salt

¹/₄ teaspoon pepper

Chopped fresh parsley, if desired

1 Heat 12-inch nonstick skillet over medium-high heat. Cook pork in skillet about 5 minutes, turning once, until brown.

2 Add broth, potatoes, carrots and onions to skillet.

3 Sprinkle with salt and pepper. Heat to boiling; reduce heat. Cover and simmer about 30 minutes or until vegetables are tender and pork is no longer pink in center. Sprinkle with parsley.

1 Serving: Calories 290; Total Fat 9g (Saturated Fat 3g, Trans Fat 0g); Cholesterol 70mg; Sodium 640mg; Total Carbohydrate 28g (Dietary Fiber 4g) **Exchanges:** 1¹/₂ Starch, 1 Vegetable, 3 Lean Meat **Carbohydrate Choices:** 2

budget smart

"Once the veggies are prepped, this pork dinner comes together pretty quickly! The mix of budget-friendly winter vegetables cook alongside the chops to yield a one-dish meal."

$2.19 per serving

Barbecued Ribs

Prep Time: **15 Minutes** || Start to Finish: **2 Hours** || **6 Servings**

Ribs
4¹⁄₂ lb pork spareribs

Spicy Barbecue Sauce
¹⁄₃ cup butter or margarine

2 tablespoons white vinegar

2 tablespoons water

1 teaspoon granulated sugar

¹⁄₂ teaspoon garlic powder

¹⁄₂ teaspoon onion powder

¹⁄₂ teaspoon pepper

Dash of ground red pepper
    (cayenne)

1 Heat oven to 325°F. Cut ribs into 6 serving pieces. Place ribs, meaty sides down, in shallow roasting pan, about 13×9 inches.

2 Bake uncovered 1 hour.

3 Meanwhile, in 1-quart saucepan, heat sauce ingredients over medium heat, stirring frequently, until butter is melted. (Or microwave sauce ingredients in 1-cup microwavable measuring cup on High about 30 seconds or until butter is melted.)

4 Brush sauce over ribs, using pastry brush. Turn ribs over, using tongs. Brush meaty sides of ribs with sauce.

5 Bake uncovered about 45 minutes longer, brushing frequently with sauce, until ribs are tender and no longer pink next to bones. To serve any remaining sauce with ribs, heat sauce to boiling, stirring constantly, then continue to boil and stir 1 minute.

1 Serving: Calories 610; Total Fat 51g (Saturated Fat 21g, Trans Fat 0.5g); Cholesterol 190mg; Sodium 200mg; Total Carbohydrate 1g (Dietary Fiber 0g) **Exchanges:** 5¹⁄₂ High-Fat Meat, 1¹⁄₂ Fat **Carbohydrate Choices:** 0

budget smart

"The tangy barbecue sauce for these ribs takes just a few minutes to make from items you may already have in your pantry. If you want a spicier sauce, add a few dashes of your favorite hot sauce."

Country-Style Saucy Ribs: Use 3 lb pork country-style ribs; cut into 6 serving pieces if it is a rack of ribs. Place in 13×9-inch pan. Cover with foil; bake at 325°F for 2 hours; drain. Pour sauce over ribs. Bake uncovered about 30 minutes longer or until ribs are tender and no longer pink next to bones.

Slow Cooker Barbecued Ribs: Use 3½ lb spareribs and cut into 2- or 3-rib portions. Place ribs in 5- to 6-quart slow cooker. Sprinkle with ½ teaspoon salt and ¼ teaspoon pepper; add ½ cup water. Cover; cook on Low heat setting 8 to 9 hours or until tender. Remove ribs. Drain and discard liquid from slow cooker. Dip ribs into sauce to coat. Place ribs in slow cooker. Pour any remaining sauce over ribs. Cover; cook on Low heat setting 1 hour.

$2.53
per serving

Southwestern Grilled Pork Chops with Peach Salsa

Prep Time: **25 Minutes** || Start to Finish: **25 Minutes** || **4 Servings**

Salsa

3 ripe medium peaches, peeled, chopped (about 1½ cups)

¼ cup finely chopped red bell pepper

2 tablespoons finely chopped red onion

1 tablespoon chopped fresh cilantro

2 teaspoons packed brown sugar

2 teaspoons fresh lime juice

¼ teaspoon finely chopped serrano or jalapeño chile

Pork Chops

1 tablespoon chili powder

4 bone-in pork loin chops, ½ inch thick (4 oz each)

1 Heat gas or charcoal grill. In medium bowl, mix salsa ingredients; set aside.

2 Rub chili powder on both sides of each pork chop. Place pork on grill over medium heat. Cover grill; cook 6 to 9 minutes, turning once, until pork is no longer pink in center. Serve pork chops topped with salsa, or serve salsa on the side.

1 Serving: Calories 180; Total Fat 7g (Saturated Fat 2g, Trans Fat 0g); Cholesterol 50mg; Sodium 50mg; Total Carbohydrate 11g (Dietary Fiber 2g) **Exchanges:** 1 Other Carbohydrate, 2½ Lean Meat **Carbohydrate Choices:** 1

budget smart

" These restaurant-style pork chops are easy to grill up in your backyard, and the fresh peach salsa takes just minutes to make. Serve extra salsa with a bowl of tortilla chips, or spoon over baguette slices spread with cream cheese for an easy appetizer. "

$3.54
per serving

Cuban Pork Chops

Prep Time: **15 Minutes** || Start to Finish: **15 Minutes** || **4 Servings**

Cuban Rub
1 clove garlic

2 tablespoons grated lime peel

1 tablespoon cracked black pepper

1 tablespoon cumin seed

2 tablespoons olive or vegetable oil

½ teaspoon salt

Pork
4 boneless pork loin or rib chops, about 1 inch thick (about 2 lb), trimmed of fat

Garnish, if desired
Mango slices

1 Heat gas or charcoal grill. In small bowl, mix rub ingredients; rub evenly on both sides of pork.

2 Place pork on grill over medium heat. Cover grill; cook 8 to 10 minutes, turning frequently, until pork is no longer pink and meat thermometer inserted in center reads 160°F. Garnish with mango slices.

1 Serving: Calories 420; Total Fat 24g (Saturated Fat 7g, Trans Fat 0g); Cholesterol 140mg; Sodium 380mg; Total Carbohydrate 2g (Dietary Fiber 0g) **Exchanges:** 7 Lean Meat, 1 Fat **Carbohydrate Choices:** 0

budget smart

" Sometimes a quick rub is all it takes to jazz up the taste of pork chops! Try it on grilled chicken breasts for another Cuban-style dinner. "

$3.59 per serving

Pork Lo Mein

Prep Time: **25 Minutes** || Start to Finish: **25 Minutes** || **4 Servings**

½ lb boneless pork loin

2½ cups sugar snap peas

1½ cups ready-to-eat baby-cut carrots, cut lengthwise into ¼-inch sticks

½ package (9-oz size) refrigerated linguine, cut into 2-inch pieces

⅓ cup chicken broth

1 tablespoon soy sauce

2 teaspoons cornstarch

1 teaspoon sugar

2 teaspoons finely chopped gingerroot

2 to 4 cloves garlic, finely chopped

2 teaspoons canola oil

½ cup thinly sliced red onion

Toasted sesame seed, if desired (see page 34)

1 Trim fat from pork. Cut pork with grain into 2×1-inch strips; cut strips across grain into ⅛-inch slices (pork is easier to cut if partially frozen, about 1½ hours). Remove strings from peas.

2 In 3-quart saucepan, heat 2 quarts water to boiling. Add peas, carrots and linguine; heat to boiling. Boil 2 to 3 minutes or just until linguine is tender; drain.

3 In small bowl, mix broth, soy sauce, cornstarch, sugar, gingerroot and garlic.

4 In 12-inch nonstick skillet or wok, heat oil over medium-high heat. Add pork and onion; stir-fry about 2 minutes or until pork is no longer pink. Stir broth mixture; stir into pork mixture. Stir in peas, carrots and linguine. Cook 2 minutes, stirring occasionally. Sprinkle with sesame seed.

1 Serving: Calories 270; Total Fat 8g (Saturated Fat 2g, Trans Fat 0g); Cholesterol 35mg; Sodium 440mg; Total Carbohydrate 31g (Dietary Fiber 3g) **Exchanges:** 1 Starch, ½ Other Carbohydrate, 1 Vegetable, 2 Lean Meat, ½ Fat **Carbohydrate Choices:** 2

budget smart

Make your own Chinese takeout! Many common Chinese seasonings, like soy sauce and fresh gingerroot, are inexpensive and keep well. For other Chinese-style recipes that use similar seasonings, see Asian Hoisin Ribs (page 260) and Chicken Sesame Stir-Fry (page 42).

$2.43
per serving

Pork Fajita Wraps

Prep Time: **20 Minutes** || Start to Finish: **30 Minutes** || **4 Wraps**

¼ cup lime juice

1½ teaspoons ground cumin

¾ teaspoon salt

4 cloves garlic, finely chopped

½ lb pork tenderloin, cut into very thin slices

1 large onion, thinly sliced

3 medium bell peppers, thinly sliced

4 flour tortillas (8 inch)

1 In shallow glass or plastic dish, mix lime juice, cumin, salt and garlic. Stir in pork. Cover; refrigerate, stirring occasionally, at least 15 minutes but no longer than 24 hours.

2 Remove pork from marinade; reserve marinade. Heat 12-inch nonstick skillet over medium-high heat. Add pork; cook 3 minutes, stirring once. Stir in onion, bell peppers and marinade. Cook 5 to 8 minutes longer, stirring frequently, until onion and peppers are crisp-tender.

3 Place one-fourth of pork mixture on center of 1 tortilla. Fold one end of tortilla up about 1 inch over pork mixture; fold right and left sides over folded end, overlapping.

1 Wrap: Calories 260; Total Fat 6g (Saturated Fat 1.5g, Trans Fat 0.5g); Cholesterol 35mg; Sodium 770mg; Total Carbohydrate 34g (Dietary Fiber 3g) **Exchanges:** 2 Starch, 1 Vegetable, 1½ Lean Meat **Carbohydrate Choices:** 2

$2.78 per serving

budget smart

❝ Lime juice, cumin, garlic and bell pepper wrap up a bundle of flavor in these no-fuss "fajita-wiches." If you have chicken breasts on hand, it's fine to use those instead of the pork tenderloin, or use a ½-lb boneless pork chop. Just cut the meat into very thin slices before cooking. ❞

★ **Best Budget Picks** (for more uses, pages 314–15)

Ham Steak with Barbecued Baked Beans

Prep Time: **20 Minutes** || Start to Finish: **20 Minutes** || **4 Servings**

1 teaspoon vegetable oil

1 center-cut fully cooked ham steak (about 1 lb)

1 small green bell pepper, chopped (½ cup)

1 small onion, chopped (¼ cup)

★ 1 can (16 oz) baked beans

¼ cup barbecue sauce

1 In 12-inch nonstick skillet, heat oil over medium heat. Cook ham steak in oil 6 to 8 minutes, turning once, until browned and hot. Remove steak to deep serving platter; cover to keep warm.

2 In same skillet, cook bell pepper and onion over medium heat 2 to 4 minutes, stirring frequently, until crisp-tender. Stir in beans and barbecue sauce. Heat until bubbly. Pour beans over ham.

1 Serving: Calories 330; Total Fat 11g (Saturated Fat 3.5g, Trans Fat 0g); Cholesterol 65mg; Sodium 2100mg; Total Carbohydrate 30g (Dietary Fiber 7g) **Exchanges:** 1½ Starch, 1 Vegetable, 3 Lean Meat, ½ Fat **Carbohydrate Choices:** 2

budget smart

" Any leftover ham and beans would be great reheated and served with eggs and toast for a hearty breakfast. "

$2.37
per serving

Cheesy Scalloped Potatoes with Ham

Prep Time: **50 Minutes** || Start to Finish: **50 Minutes** || **6 Servings (1 cup each)**

2 tablespoons butter or margarine

1 clove garlic, finely chopped

2 lb round white potatoes (about 4 medium), peeled, thinly sliced

½ lb fully cooked ham, cut into ½-inch pieces (about 2 cups)

1 cup shredded American-Cheddar cheese blend (4 oz)

3 tablespoons all-purpose flour

¼ teaspoon pepper

1 pint (2 cups) half-and-half

1 In 4-quart Dutch oven, melt butter over medium heat. Cook garlic in butter 1 minute, stirring occasionally, until softened. Remove from heat. Stir in potatoes, ham, cheese, flour and pepper.

2 Pour half-and-half over potato mixture. Heat to boiling over medium-high heat; reduce heat to low. Cover and simmer about 30 minutes, stirring occasionally, until potatoes are tender.

1 Serving: Calories 430; Total Fat 24g (Saturated Fat 13g, Trans Fat 0.5g); Cholesterol 85mg; Sodium 850mg; Total Carbohydrate 34g (Dietary Fiber 3g) **Exchanges:** 2 Starch, 2 Medium-Fat Meat, 2½ Fat **Carbohydrate Choices:** 2

budget smart

" Cooked ham is so handy when you want to add meat to any dish—a little goes a long way! Check out the other recipes that also use cubed ham: Lemon-Basil Pasta with Ham (page 125), Ham and Wild Rice Soup (page 262) and Impossibly Easy Ham and Swiss Pie (page 303). "

$1.31
per serving

Bacon and Tomato Frittata

Prep Time: **20 Minutes** || Start to Finish: **20 Minutes** || **4 Servings**

1 carton (16 oz) fat-free egg product or 8 eggs

¼ teaspoon salt-free garlic-and-herb seasoning

¼ teaspoon salt

1 tablespoon canola oil

4 medium green onions, sliced (¼ cup)

2 large plum (Roma) tomatoes, sliced

½ cup shredded reduced-fat sharp Cheddar cheese (2 oz)

2 tablespoons real bacon pieces (from 2.8-oz package)

2 tablespoons reduced-fat sour cream

1 In medium bowl, mix egg product, garlic-and-herb seasoning and salt; set aside.

2 In 10-inch nonstick ovenproof skillet, heat oil over medium heat. Add onions; cook and stir 1 minute. Reduce heat to medium-low. Pour in egg mixture. Cook 6 to 9 minutes, gently lifting edges of cooked portions with spatula so that uncooked egg mixture can flow to bottom of skillet, until set.

3 Set oven control to broil. Top frittata with tomatoes, cheese and bacon. Broil with top 4 inches from heat 1 to 2 minutes or until cheese is melted. Top each serving with sour cream.

1 Serving: Calories 180; Total Fat 10g (Saturated Fat 4g, Trans Fat 0g); Cholesterol 20mg; Sodium 570mg; Total Carbohydrate 4g (Dietary Fiber 1g) **Exchanges:** 2½ Very Lean Meat, 2 Fat **Carbohydrate Choices:** 0

budget smart

" A frittata makes an easy and inexpensive weeknight meal ready to eat in 20 minutes. This version uses low-fat ingredients for a healthier take on frittatas. If you want a richer frittata, use regular cheese and sour cream. "

$1.06
per serving

Eggs and Sausage Skillet

Prep Time: **35 Minutes** || Start to Finish: **35 Minutes** || **6 Servings (1 cup each)**

1 package (12 oz) bulk reduced-fat pork sausage

4 oz fresh mushrooms, sliced (1½ cups)

3 cups frozen potatoes O'Brien (from 28-oz bag), thawed

½ teaspoon salt

⅛ teaspoon pepper

6 eggs

1 cup shredded Swiss cheese (4 oz)

1 large tomato, chopped (1 cup)

1 In 12-inch nonstick skillet, cook sausage over medium-high heat 5 to 7 minutes, stirring frequently, until no longer pink.

2 Stir mushrooms, potatoes, salt and pepper into sausage. Cook over medium heat about 8 minutes, stirring frequently, until potatoes begin to brown. Reduce heat to low.

3 Using back of spoon, make 6 indentations in potato mixture. Break 1 egg into each indentation. Cover and cook 8 to 10 minutes or until egg whites are set and yolks are beginning to thicken.

4 Sprinkle with cheese and tomato. Cover and cook 3 to 4 minutes or until cheese is melted.

1 Serving: Calories 310; Total Fat 16g (Saturated Fat 5g, Trans Fat 0g); Cholesterol 240mg; Sodium 670mg; Total Carbohydrate 21g (Dietary Fiber 3g) **Exchanges:** 1 Starch, 1 Vegetable, 2 High-Fat Meat, ½ Fat **Carbohydrate Choices:** 1½

budget smart

"Breakfast for dinner's a tried-and-true solution to the daily dinner dilemma. Look for bulk pork sausage on sale, and freeze any extra in 6-oz portions so you can defrost and use only the amount you need."

$1.52
per serving

CHAPTER 3

Penny-Pinching
Pasta and Pizza

Salads on the Side

Go beyond a bag of lettuce or a complete salad mix with one of these simple—and less expensive—taste sensations!

- **Hearts of Palm Salad:** Drain and slice canned or jarred hearts of palm; drizzle with your favorite vinaigrette dressing.

- **Cukes and Tomatoes Salad:** On a serving platter or individual salad plates, arrange cucumber chunks or slices with tomato wedges or slices. Sprinkle with salt and pepper; drizzle with your favorite dressing or add a splash of vinegar.

- **Mediterranean Vegetable Salad:** On a serving platter, arrange sliced tomatoes and sliced bell peppers; drizzle with your favorite vinaigrette dressing. Top with pitted kalamata olives or small whole pitted ripe olives; sprinkle with crumbled feta cheese.

- **Melon and Berries Salad with Vanilla Sauce:** On a serving platter, arrange sliced cantaloupe and honeydew melon; top with raspberries or blackberries. Mix together vanilla yogurt and milk until it has a saucy consistency; drizzle over fruit.

- **Sunny Lime Fruit Salad:** Drizzle a variety of cut-up fruits with thawed frozen lime-ade concentrate. Toss in poppy seed or slivered almonds if desired.

Chicken- and Spinach-Stuffed Shells

Prep Time: **30 Minutes** || Start to Finish: **1 Hour 10 Minutes** || **6 Servings (3 shells each)**

18 uncooked jumbo pasta shells (from 12- or 16-oz package)

2 cups frozen cut leaf spinach, thawed

1 egg, slightly beaten

5 oz cooked chicken or turkey, chopped (1 cup)

1 container (15 oz) whole-milk ricotta cheese or 2 cups cottage cheese

¼ cup grated Parmesan cheese

1 jar (26 oz) tomato pasta sauce

2 cups shredded Italian cheese blend (8 oz)

1 Heat oven to 350°F. Cook pasta shells as directed on package.

2 Meanwhile, place thawed spinach in strainer and squeeze with fingers to remove liquid. Place spinach on paper towels or clean kitchen towel and squeeze out any remaining liquid until spinach is dry.

3 In medium bowl, mix spinach, egg, chicken, ricotta cheese and Parmesan cheese. In strainer, drain pasta shells. Rinse with cool water; drain.

4 In 13×9-inch (3-quart) glass baking dish, spread 1 cup of the pasta sauce. Spoon about 2 tablespoons ricotta mixture into each pasta shell. Arrange shells, filled sides up, on sauce in baking dish. Spoon remaining sauce over stuffed shells.

5 Cover dish with foil. Bake 30 minutes. Carefully remove foil; sprinkle with Italian cheese blend. Bake uncovered 5 to 10 minutes longer or until cheese is melted.

1 Serving: Calories 580; Total Fat 27g (Saturated Fat 14g, Trans Fat 0.5g); Cholesterol 130mg; Sodium 1060mg; Total Carbohydrate 49g (Dietary Fiber 4g) **Exchanges:** 2 Starch, 1 Other Carbohydrate, 4 Medium-Fat Meat, 1 Fat **Carbohydrate Choices:** 3

budget smart

" If you don't have cooked chicken or turkey in your fridge, you could substitute chopped ham—or leave out meat altogether for a vegetarian version. It's important to get the spinach as dry as possible, so don't skip the towel-squeezing step. If the kids are around, they'd probably love to help you fill the cooked shells with the cheese mixture. "

$2.33
per serving

Super-Easy Chicken Manicotti

Prep Time: **15 Minutes** || Start to Finish: **1 Hour 20 Minutes** || **7 Servings**

1 jar (26 to 30 oz) tomato pasta sauce (any variety)

¾ cup water

1 teaspoon garlic salt

1½ lb uncooked chicken breast tenders (not breaded) (14 tenders)

14 uncooked manicotti pasta shells (8 oz)

2 cups shredded mozzarella cheese (8 oz)

Chopped fresh basil leaves, if desired

1 Heat oven to 350°F. In medium bowl, mix pasta sauce and water. In ungreased 13×9-inch (3-quart) glass baking dish, spread about one-third of the pasta sauce.

2 Sprinkle garlic salt on chicken. Insert chicken into uncooked manicotti shells, stuffing from each end of shell to fill if necessary. Place shells on pasta sauce in baking dish. Pour remaining pasta sauce evenly over shells, covering completely. Cover tightly with foil.

3 Bake about 1 hour or until shells are tender. Sprinkle with cheese. Bake uncovered about 5 minutes longer or until cheese is melted. Sprinkle with basil.

1 Serving: Calories 450; Total Fat 13g (Saturated Fat 5g, Trans Fat 0g); Cholesterol 75mg; Sodium 1130mg; Total Carbohydrate 48g (Dietary Fiber 3g) **Exchanges:** 3 Starch, 4 Lean Meat **Carbohydrate Choices:** 3

budget smart

" This is probably the easiest manicotti recipe you'll ever see. It's only slightly more work (and a bit cheaper) to start with uncooked boneless skinless chicken breasts instead of tenders; slice them into 1¼-inch strips before using. Be sure to wash your hands thoroughly after handling the raw chicken. "

$1.84
per serving

Chicken Alfredo

Prep Time: **30 Minutes** || Start to Finish: **30 Minutes** || **6 Servings**

8 oz uncooked linguine

2 teaspoons butter or margarine

2 tablespoons finely chopped shallot

1 clove garlic, finely chopped

1 pint (2 cups) fat-free half-and-half

3 tablespoons all-purpose flour

1/2 cup reduced-fat sour cream

1/4 cup shredded fresh Parmesan cheese

1/2 teaspoon salt

1/8 teaspoon white pepper

1 1/4 lb chicken breast strips for stir-fry

1 jar (7 oz) roasted red bell peppers, drained, thinly sliced

1/3 cup shredded fresh Parmesan cheese

2 tablespoons chopped fresh parsley

1 In 4-quart Dutch oven, cook linguine as directed on package. Drain; rinse with hot water. Return to Dutch oven to keep warm.

2 Meanwhile, in 2-quart saucepan, melt butter over medium heat. Add shallot and garlic; cook and stir 1 minute. In medium bowl, beat half-and-half and flour with wire whisk; add to saucepan. Heat to boiling, stirring frequently. Beat in sour cream with wire whisk. Reduce heat to low; cook 1 to 2 minutes or until heated. Remove from heat; stir in 1/4 cup cheese, the salt and pepper.

3 Heat 12-inch nonstick skillet over medium-high heat. Add chicken; cook about 5 minutes, stirring frequently, until no longer pink in center.

4 Add chicken, bell peppers and sauce to linguine; stir to mix. Cook over low heat until hot. Garnish each serving with cheese and parsley.

1 Serving: Calories 430; Total Fat 12g (Saturated Fat 6g, Trans Fat 0g); Cholesterol 80mg; Sodium 710mg; Total Carbohydrate 47g (Dietary Fiber 2g) **Exchanges:** 2 Starch, 1 Other Carbohydrate, 4 Very Lean Meat, 1 1/2 Fat **Carbohydrate Choices:** 3

budget smart

" Don't be intimidated by the long list of ingredients—many are kitchen staples with plenty of uses, so you'll get a lot of mileage from any extras. To streamline this list, substitute foods you already have—slice your own strips from 1 1/4 lb chicken breasts, use black pepper instead of white or cut up a red bell pepper instead of using the jarred roasted peppers. "

$2.51
per serving

Bow Ties with Chicken and Asparagus

Prep Time: **25 Minutes** || Start to Finish: **25 Minutes** || **6 Servings (1½ cups each)**

4 cups uncooked bow-tie (farfalle) pasta (8 oz)

1 lb fresh asparagus spears

1 tablespoon canola oil

★ 1 lb boneless skinless chicken breasts, cut into 1-inch pieces

1 package (8 oz) sliced fresh mushrooms (3 cups)

2 cloves garlic, finely chopped

★ 1 cup fat-free chicken broth with 33% less sodium

1 tablespoon cornstarch

4 medium green onions, sliced (¼ cup)

2 tablespoons chopped fresh basil leaves

Salt, if desired

¼ cup finely shredded Parmesan cheese (1 oz)

1 Cook and drain pasta as directed on package, omitting salt.

2 Meanwhile, break off tough ends of asparagus as far down as stalks snap easily. Wash asparagus; cut into 1-inch pieces.

3 In 12-inch nonstick skillet, heat oil over medium-high heat. Add chicken; cook 2 minutes, stirring occasionally. Stir in asparagus, mushrooms and garlic. Cook 6 to 8 minutes, stirring occasionally, until chicken is no longer pink in center and vegetables are tender.

4 In small bowl, gradually stir broth into cornstarch. Stir in onions and basil. Stir cornstarch mixture into chicken mixture. Cook and stir 1 to 2 minutes or until thickened and bubbly. Season with salt. Toss with pasta. Sprinkle with cheese.

1 Serving: Calories 320; Total Fat 7g (Saturated Fat 2g, Trans Fat 0g); Cholesterol 50mg; Sodium 210mg; Total Carbohydrate 37g (Dietary Fiber 3g) **Exchanges:** 2 Starch, 1 Vegetable, 2½ Very Lean Meat, 1 Fat **Carbohydrate Choices:** 2½

budget smart

" If you don't want to buy fresh basil just for this recipe, you could use parsley instead, or use up the remaining basil by making pesto (see page 136). "

★ **Best Budget Picks** (for more uses, see pages 314–15)

$2.51
per serving

Turkey Pasta Primavera

Prep Time: **20 Minutes** || Start to Finish: **20 Minutes** || **4 Servings**

1 package (9 oz) refrigerated fettuccine or linguine

★ 2 tablespoons Italian dressing

1 bag (1 lb) frozen broccoli, carrots and cauliflower, thawed, drained

2 cups cut-up cooked turkey or chicken

1 teaspoon salt

2 large tomatoes, seeded, chopped (2 cups)

1/4 cup freshly grated Parmesan cheese

2 tablespoons chopped fresh parsley

1 Cook and drain fettuccine as directed on package.

2 Meanwhile, in 10-inch skillet, heat dressing over medium-high heat. Cook vegetable mixture in dressing, stirring occasionally, until crisp-tender.

3 Stir turkey, salt and tomatoes into vegetables. Cook about 3 minutes or just until turkey is hot. Spoon turkey mixture over fettuccine. Sprinkle with cheese and parsley.

1 Serving: Calories 400; Total Fat 12g (Saturated Fat 3g, Trans Fat 0g); Cholesterol 65mg; Sodium 980mg; Total Carbohydrate 44g (Dietary Fiber 6g) **Exchanges:** 2 Starch, 2 Vegetable, 3½ Lean Meat **Carbohydrate Choices:** 2½

budget smart

"Here's a quick, easy and healthy pasta for a busy weeknight. *Primavera* is Italian for "spring-style," and any dish labeled primavera includes plenty of vegetables. For an even less expensive version, substitute 9 oz of dried pasta for the fresh; it'll take just a little longer to cook."

★ **Best Budget Picks** (for more uses, see pages 314–15)

$3.18
per serving

Overnight Rotini Bake

Prep Time: **20 Minutes** || Start to Finish: **9 Hours 15 Minutes** || **8 Servings (1¼ cups each)**

★ 1½ lb lean (at least 80%) ground beef

1 large onion, chopped (1 cup)

1 large bell pepper, chopped (1 cup)

2 large cloves garlic, finely chopped

★ 1 can (28 oz) crushed tomatoes, undrained

2 cups hot water

1 envelope (1 oz) onion soup mix (from 2-oz package)

1 teaspoon Italian seasoning

3 cups uncooked rotini or fusilli pasta (9 oz)

1½ cups shredded Italian cheese blend or mozzarella cheese (6 oz)

1 Spray 13×9-inch (3-quart) glass baking dish with cooking spray. In 4-quart Dutch oven, cook beef, onion, bell pepper and garlic over medium-high heat 5 to 7 minutes, stirring occasionally, until beef is thoroughly cooked; drain. Stir in tomatoes, water, soup mix (dry), Italian seasoning and pasta. Spoon into baking dish.

2 Cover tightly with foil; refrigerate at least 8 hours but no longer than 24 hours.

3 Heat oven to 375°F. Bake covered 45 minutes. Sprinkle with cheese. Bake uncovered about 10 minutes longer or until cheese is melted and casserole is bubbly.

1 Serving: Calories 390; Total Fat 16g (Saturated Fat 7g, Trans Fat TK); Cholesterol 60mg; Sodium 610mg; Total Carbohydrate 35g (Dietary Fiber 3g) **Exchanges:** 2 Starch, 1 Vegetable, 3 Medium-Fat Meat **Carbohydrate Choices:** 2

Simple Swap: Substitute ground turkey for the ground beef.

budget smart

" This overnight recipe is well worth the wait for a bubbly, cheesy pasta casserole! And the advance planning pays off with plenty of leftovers. Or make two pans and you're all set for the neighborhood block party. "

★ **Best Budget Picks** (for more uses, see pages 314–15)

Spicy Parmesan Meatballs with Angel Hair Pasta

Prep Time: **50 Minutes** || Start to Finish: **50 Minutes** || **4 Servings**

¾ cup Fiber One® cereal

★ 1 lb extra-lean (at least 90%) ground beef

¼ cup shredded Parmesan cheese (1 oz)

¾ teaspoon Italian seasoning

¼ teaspoon garlic powder

1 can (8 oz) tomato sauce

★ 1 can (14.5 oz) diced tomatoes with green pepper and onion, undrained

⅛ teaspoon ground red pepper (cayenne)

6 oz uncooked whole wheat angel hair (capellini) or other long pasta

Additional shredded Parmesan cheese, if desired

1 to 2 tablespoons chopped fresh parsley, if desired

1 Place cereal in resealable food-storage plastic bag; seal bag and finely crush with rolling pin or meat mallet (or finely crush in food processor).

2 In large bowl, mix cereal, beef, ¼ cup cheese, the Italian seasoning, garlic powder and ¼ cup of the tomato sauce until well blended (reserve remaining tomato sauce for sauce). Shape into 16 (1½-inch) meatballs.

3 Spray 12-inch skillet with cooking spray. Cook meatballs in skillet over medium heat 8 to 10 minutes, turning occasionally, until browned. Drain if necessary. Add remaining tomato sauce, tomatoes and red pepper to skillet; turn meatballs to coat.

4 Cover; cook over medium-low heat 15 to 20 minutes, stirring sauce and turning meatballs occasionally, until meatballs are thoroughly cooked and no longer pink in center.

5 Meanwhile, cook and drain pasta as directed on package. Serve meatballs over pasta. Top each serving with additional Parmesan cheese and parsley.

1 Serving: Calories 460; Total Fat 12g (Saturated Fat 5g, Trans Fat 0.5g); Cholesterol 75mg; Sodium 950mg; Total Carbohydrate 54g (Dietary Fiber 10g) **Exchanges:** 2½ Starch, 1 Other Carbohydrate, 3½ Lean Meat **Carbohydrate Choices:** 3½

budget smart

❝ When you get to the bottom of a box of cereal and there's only crushed bits left, use them in this healthful meatball and whole-grain pasta dinner! You can also use regular angel hair or substitute other long pasta like spaghetti. ❞

$1.42
per serving

Mexi Shells

Prep Time: **15 Minutes** || Start to Finish: **55 Minutes** || **6 Servings**

18 uncooked jumbo pasta shells

★ 4 cans (8 oz each) no-salt-added tomato sauce

2 tablespoons all-purpose flour

1 teaspoon chili powder

3 teaspoons ground cumin

★ ¾ lb extra-lean (at least 90%) ground beef

1 small onion, chopped (¼ cup)

1 tablespoon chopped fresh cilantro

1 can (4.5 oz) chopped green chiles, drained

★ 1 can (15 or 16 oz) chili beans in sauce, undrained

1 cup shredded part-skim mozzarella cheese (4 oz)

1 Heat oven to 350°F. Cook pasta shells as directed on package.

2 Meanwhile, in medium bowl, mix tomato sauce, flour, chili powder and 2 teaspoons of the cumin; set aside.

3 In 2-quart saucepan, cook beef and onion over medium heat 8 to 10 minutes, stirring occasionally, until beef is brown; drain. Stir in remaining 1 teaspoon cumin, the cilantro, green chiles and chili beans.

4 Drain pasta shells. In ungreased 13×9-inch glass baking dish, spread 1 cup of the tomato sauce mixture. Spoon about 1½ tablespoons beef mixture into each pasta shell. Place filled sides up on sauce in dish. Pour remaining tomato sauce mixture over shells. Sprinkle with cheese.

5 Cover with foil and bake 30 minutes. Uncover and let stand 10 minutes before serving.

1 Serving: Calories 380; Total Fat 10g (Saturated Fat 4.5g, Trans Fat 0g); Cholesterol 70mg; Sodium 1020mg; Total Carbohydrate 46g (Dietary Fiber 7g) **Exchanges:** 3 Starch, 2½ Very Lean Meat, ½ Fat **Carbohydrate Choices:** 3

budget smart

"These deeply delicious stuffed shells have a Mexican accent, thanks to the cumin, chili powder, cilantro and green chiles. Serve these with a lightly dressed salad."

$1.63
per serving

★ **Best Budget Picks** (for more uses, see pages 314-15)

Chile-Sausage Pasta

Prep Time: **25 Minutes** || Start to Finish: **25 Minutes** || **5 Servings (1½ cups each)**

2½ cups uncooked bow-tie (farfalle) pasta (5 oz)

¾ lb mild Italian sausage links, cut into 1-inch pieces

★ 1 can (14.5 oz) diced tomatoes and mild green chiles, undrained

1 can (8 oz) tomato sauce

★ 1 can (15 oz) pinto beans, drained, rinsed

Chopped fresh cilantro or parsley, if desired

1 Cook and drain pasta as directed on package.

2 Meanwhile, in 12-inch nonstick skillet, cook sausage over medium heat 8 to 10 minutes, stirring occasionally, until no longer pink. Stir in tomatoes and tomato sauce. Reduce heat to medium-low. Cover; cook 5 minutes, stirring occasionally.

3 Stir in beans and pasta. Cook uncovered 3 to 5 minutes, stirring occasionally, until thoroughly heated. Sprinkle with cilantro.

1 Serving: Calories 410; Total Fat 14g (Saturated Fat 4.5g, Trans Fat 0g); Cholesterol 40mg; Sodium 1090mg; Total Carbohydrate 49g (Dietary Fiber 10g) **Exchanges:** 2½ Starch, ½ Other Carbohydrate, 1 Vegetable, 1½ High-Fat Meat **Carbohydrate Choices:** 3

$1.25 per serving

budget smart

" Ready in less than 30 minutes, this straightforward pasta will delight, and there's an extra serving for a lunch tomorrow. If anyone in your group likes spicy food, put a bottle of hot sauce on the table. "

Italian Sausage with Tomatoes and Penne

Prep Time: **25 Minutes** || Start to Finish: **25 Minutes** || **4 Servings**

3 cups uncooked penne pasta (9 oz)

1 lb uncooked Italian sausage links, cut crosswise into 1/4-inch slices

1/2 cup beef broth

1 medium yellow summer squash, cut lengthwise in half, then cut crosswise into 1/4-inch slices

2 cups grape or cherry tomatoes, cut lengthwise in half

1/4 cup chopped fresh or 1 tablespoon dried basil leaves

6 green onions, cut into 1/2-inch pieces (1/2 cup)

2 tablespoons olive or vegetable oil

1 Cook and drain pasta as directed on package.

2 Meanwhile, spray 12-inch skillet with cooking spray; heat over medium-high heat. Cook sausage in skillet 4 to 6 minutes, stirring frequently, until brown. Stir in broth; reduce heat to medium. Cover and cook 5 minutes.

3 Stir in squash, tomatoes and 2 tablespoons of the basil. Heat to boiling; reduce heat to low. Cover and simmer 5 minutes, stirring occasionally. Stir in onions. Simmer uncovered 1 minute.

4 Toss pasta, oil and remaining 2 tablespoons basil. Divide pasta among individual bowls. Top with sausage mixture.

1 Serving: Calories 590; Total Fat 31g (Saturated Fat 9g, Trans Fat 0); Cholesterol 120mg; Sodium 920mg; Total Carbohydrate 51g (Dietary Fiber 4g) **Exchanges:** 3 Starch, 1 Vegetable, 2 High-Fat Meat, 5 Fat **Carbohydrate Choices:** 3 1/2

budget smart

"Grape and cherry tomatoes can sometimes be expensive, so feel free to substitute any kind of chopped fresh tomatoes here, or use canned drained tomatoes. Either way, this summertime pasta dish is juicy, meaty and satisfying."

$2.68
per serving

Mac 'n Cheese Shells with Sausage

Prep Time: **25 Minutes** || Start to Finish: **25 Minutes** || **4 Servings (1½ cups each)**

3 cups reduced-sodium chicken broth (from 32-oz carton)

2 cups uncooked small pasta shells (8 oz)

1½ cups frozen baby sweet peas

½ lb smoked sausage, cut in half lengthwise, then cut into ½-inch pieces

2 cups shredded American-Cheddar cheese blend (8 oz)

3 tablespoons grated Parmesan cheese, if desired

1 In 3-quart saucepan, heat broth to boiling over medium-high heat. Add pasta; heat to boiling. Boil 6 minutes; do not drain. Reduce heat. Stir in peas and sausage. Cover and simmer 3 to 5 minutes or until pasta is tender. Remove from heat.

2 Add American-Cheddar cheese; toss gently until cheese is melted. Sprinkle with Parmesan cheese.

1 Serving: Calories 570; Total Fat 25g (Saturated Fat 14g, Trans Fat 0.5g); Cholesterol 90mg; Sodium 1370mg; Total Carbohydrate 53g (Dietary Fiber 5g) **Exchanges:** 3½ Starch, 3 High-Fat Meat, 2 Fat **Carbohydrate Choices:** 3½

budget smart

"Frozen peas are not only cheaper than fresh, they're often sweeter since they're usually frozen very soon after being harvested. Keep some on hand to add color and springtime flavor to everything from pasta and rice to meat."

$1.84 per serving

Ham and Cheese Ziti

Prep Time: **30 Minutes** || Start to Finish: **55 Minutes** || **8 Servings (1⅓ cups each)**

1 package (16 oz) ziti pasta
    (5 cups)

½ cup butter or margarine

2 cloves garlic, finely chopped

½ cup all-purpose flour

1 teaspoon salt

4 cups milk

1 teaspoon Dijon mustard

4 cups shredded Colby cheese
    (16 oz)

8 oz sliced cooked deli ham,
    cut into thin strips

⅔ cup grated Parmesan cheese

1 Heat oven to 350°F. Cook and drain pasta as directed on package.

2 Meanwhile, melt butter in 4-quart saucepan or Dutch oven over low heat. Cook garlic in butter 30 seconds, stirring frequently. Stir in flour and salt, using wire whisk. Cook over medium heat, stirring constantly, until mixture is smooth and bubbly.

3 Gradually stir in milk. Heat to boiling, stirring constantly. Boil and stir 1 minute. Stir in mustard and Colby cheese. Cook, stirring occasionally, until cheese is melted. Stir pasta and ham into cheese sauce. Pour pasta mixture into ungreased 13×9-inch (3-quart) glass baking dish. Sprinkle with Parmesan cheese.

4 Bake uncovered 20 to 25 minutes or until bubbly.

1 Serving: Calories 715; Total Fat 38g (Saturated Fat 23g, Trans Fat 1g); Cholesterol 120mg; Sodium 1290mg; Total Carbohydrate 58g (Dietary Fiber 2g) **Exchanges:** 4 Starch, 3 Fat **Carbohydrate Choices:** 4

budget smart

" This is a cheese lover's dream dish. You can substitute cooked sausage, turkey or chicken for the sliced ham if that's what you have on hand. "

$1.73
per serving

Lemon-Basil Pasta with Ham

Prep Time: **30 Minutes** || Start to Finish: **30 Minutes** || **4 Servings**

2 cups uncooked rotini pasta
  (6 oz)

2 cups 1-inch pieces asparagus
  spears

1 cup diced cooked ham

1 tablespoon grated lemon peel

1 clove garlic, finely chopped

¼ cup olive or vegetable oil

½ cup sliced fresh basil leaves

½ cup shredded Swiss cheese
  (2 oz)

1 Cook and drain pasta as directed on package, adding asparagus during last 3 to 4 minutes of cooking.

2 Return pasta mixture to saucepan. Stir in ham, lemon peel, garlic and oil. Cook over medium heat, stirring occasionally, until hot. Stir in basil. Sprinkle with cheese.

1 Serving: Calories 410; Total Fat 22g (Saturated Fat 6g, Trans Fat 0g); Cholesterol 35mg; Sodium 710mg; Total Carbohydrate 37g (Dietary Fiber 4g) **Exchanges:** 2 Starch, 1 Vegetable, 1½ Lean Meat, 3 Fat **Carbohydrate Choices:** 2½

budget smart

❝ If you don't have fresh basil, use ⅓ cup chopped fresh parsley and add 1 teaspoon dried basil leaves. Ham, asparagus and Swiss cheese are natural partners, and the lemon zest brings them together in this toothsome, cost-conscious dish. ❞

$2.00 per serving

Florentine Tuna Tetrazzini

Prep Time: **20 Minutes** || Start to Finish: **1 Hour 5 Minutes** || **4 Servings (1½ cups each)**

1 package (9 oz) refrigerated linguine, cut into thirds

★ 1 can (10¾ oz) condensed cream of celery soup

1 box (10 oz) frozen creamed spinach, thawed

¾ cup milk

2 cans (6 oz each) albacore tuna in water, drained

¼ cup sliced drained roasted red bell peppers (from 7-oz jar)

¼ cup Italian-style dry bread crumbs

2 tablespoons grated Parmesan cheese

1 tablespoon butter or margarine, melted

1 Heat oven to 350°F. Spray 8-inch square (2-quart) glass baking dish with cooking spray. Cook and drain linguine as directed on package.

2 In baking dish, mix soup, spinach and milk. Stir in tuna, bell peppers and linguine. In small bowl, mix bread crumbs, cheese and butter; sprinkle over tuna mixture.

3 Bake uncovered 40 to 45 minutes or until bubbly around edges and top is golden brown.

1 Serving: Calories 540; Total Fat 14g (Saturated Fat 5g, Trans Fat 1g); Cholesterol 45mg; Sodium 1220mg; Total Carbohydrate 69g (Dietary Fiber 5g) **Exchanges:** 4 Starch, ½ Other Carbohydrate, 1 Vegetable, 3½ Lean Meat **Carbohydrate Choices:** 4

Simple Swap: Chopped pimientos make a good substitution for the roasted red bell peppers.

budget smart

"If it says "Florentine," chances are there's spinach involved. To make this recipe truly "straight-from-the-pantry," substitute dried linguine for the fresh."

★ **Best Budget Picks** (for more uses, see pages 314-15)

$2.55
per serving

Linguine with Tuna and Tomatoes

Prep Time: **20 Minutes** || Start to Finish: **20 Minutes** || **Servings: 4 (1½ cups each)**

8 oz uncooked linguine

½ cup crumbled feta cheese
(2 oz)

2 cups cherry tomatoes,
quartered, or coarsely
chopped tomatoes

1 can (12 oz) water-packed
white tuna, drained, flaked

2 tablespoons chopped fresh
parsley

2 tablespoons olive, canola
or soybean oil

1 clove garlic, finely chopped

¼ teaspoon salt

1 In 3-quart saucepan, cook linguine to desired doneness as directed on package. Drain; return to saucepan.

2 Reserve 2 tablespoons of the feta cheese for garnish. Add remaining feta cheese and remaining ingredients to linguine; toss to mix. Sprinkle with reserved feta cheese.

1 Serving: Calories 440; Total Fat 12g (Saturated Fat 3.5g, Trans Fat 0g); Cholesterol 35mg; Sodium 780mg; Total Carbohydrate 54g (Dietary Fiber 4g) **Exchanges:** 3 Starch, 1 Vegetable, 2½ Lean Meat, ½ Fat **Carbohydrate Choices:** 3½

budget smart

" This tasty pasta comes together in a jiffy. Think of it as a kind of inside-out tuna noodle casserole, but lighter and more flavorful. In a pinch, use canned diced tomatoes instead of fresh, but the fresh cherry tomatoes add a nice punch of fresh flavor. "

$1.89 per serving

Scampi with Fettuccine

Prep Time: **20 Minutes** || Start to Finish: **20 Minutes** || **4 Servings**

8 oz uncooked regular or spinach fettuccine

2 tablespoons olive or vegetable oil

1½ lb uncooked deveined peeled medium shrimp, thawed if frozen, tail shells removed

2 medium green onions, thinly sliced (2 tablespoons)

2 cloves garlic, finely chopped

1 tablespoon chopped fresh or ½ teaspoon dried basil leaves

1 tablespoon chopped fresh parsley

2 tablespoons lemon juice

¼ teaspoon salt

Grated Parmesan cheese, if desired

1 Cook and drain fettuccine as directed on package. Meanwhile, in 10-inch skillet, heat oil over medium heat. Cook remaining ingredients in oil 2 to 3 minutes, stirring frequently, until shrimp are pink; remove from heat.

2 Toss fettuccine with shrimp mixture in skillet. Sprinkled with Parmesan cheese.

1 Serving: Calories 380; Total Fat 10g (Saturated Fat 1.5g, Trans Fat 0g); Cholesterol 290mg; Sodium 670mg; Total Carbohydrate 38g (Dietary Fiber 2g) **Exchanges:** 2½ Starch, 3½ Very Lean Meat, 1½ Fat **Carbohydrate Choices:** 2½

budget smart

" Treat yourself to a scampi dinner at home—ready in only 20 minutes! Medium shrimp are often less expensive per pound than large or jumbo (which also means more shrimps for everyone). "

$4.15 per serving

Fettuccine Alfredo

Prep Time: **30 Minutes** || Start to Finish: **30 Minutes** || **4 Servings**

8 oz uncooked fettuccine

½ cup butter or margarine

½ cup whipping cream

¾ cup grated Parmesan cheese

½ teaspoon salt

Dash of pepper

Chopped fresh parsley,
   if desired

1 Cook and drain pasta as directed on package.

2 Meanwhile, in 2-quart saucepan, heat butter and whipping cream over low heat, stirring constantly, until butter is melted. Stir in cheese, ½ teaspoon salt and dash of pepper until mixture is smooth.

3 Pour sauce over hot fettuccine, and stir until fettuccine is well coated. Sprinkle with parsley.

1 Serving: Calories 580; Total Fat 41g (Saturated Fat 24g, Trans Fat 1.5g); Cholesterol 155mg; Sodium 760mg; Total Carbohydrate 39g (Dietary Fiber 2g) **Exchanges:** 2½ Starch, 1 Lean Meat, 7 Fat **Carbohydrate Choices:** 2½

Lighten Up Fettuccine Alfredo: For 24 grams of fat and 440 calories per serving, decrease butter to ⅓ cup and substitute fat-free half-and-half for the whipping cream.

Chicken Fettuccine Alfredo: In step 2, stir in 2 cups chopped cooked chicken or turkey with the cheese.

budget smart

"Fettuccine Alfredo is simple to make and delightfully rich. If you want to pick up a nice hunk of Parmesan to freshly grate, this is the recipe for it—it really shows off the flavor of the cheese. Pregrated Parmesan costs less and cuts down on prep, so choose what works best for you."

80¢
per serving

Tagliatelle Pasta with Asparagus and Gorgonzola Sauce

Prep Time: **25 Minutes** || Start to Finish: **25 Minutes** || **4 Servings**

1 lb asparagus

8 oz uncooked tagliatelle pasta or fettuccine

2 tablespoons olive or vegetable oil

4 medium green onions, sliced (¼ cup)

¼ cup chopped fresh parsley

1 clove garlic, finely chopped

1 cup crumbled Gorgonzola cheese (4 oz)

½ teaspoon freshly cracked pepper

1 Break off tough ends of asparagus as far down as stalks snap easily. Cut asparagus into 1-inch pieces. Cook pasta as directed on package, adding asparagus during last 5 minutes of cooking; drain.

2 Meanwhile, in 12-inch skillet, heat oil over medium-high heat. Cook onions, parsley and garlic in oil about 5 minutes, stirring occasionally, until onions are tender. Reduce heat to medium.

3 Add pasta, asparagus and cheese to mixture in skillet. Cook about 3 minutes, tossing gently, until cheese is melted and pasta is evenly coated. Sprinkle with pepper.

1 Serving: Calories 370; Total Fat 17g (Saturated Fat 7g, Trans Fat 0g); Cholesterol 70mg; Sodium 640mg; Total Carbohydrate 40g (Dietary Fiber 3g) **Exchanges:** 2 Starch, ½ Other Carbohydrate, 1 Vegetable, 1 High-Fat Meat, 1½ Fat **Carbohydrate Choices:** 2½

budget smart

"Gorgonzola, an Italian blue cheese, is a natural match for the asparagus, and it shows in this luscious pasta dish. If the price of Gorgonzola is steep at your supermarket, any blue cheese could be substituted and will be delicious as well."

$2.12
per serving

Penne with Spicy Sauce

Prep Time: **30 Minutes** || Start to Finish: **30 Minutes** || **6 Servings**

1 package (16 oz) penne pasta

★ 1 can (28 oz) Italian-style peeled whole tomatoes, undrained

2 tablespoons olive or vegetable oil

2 cloves garlic, finely chopped

1 teaspoon crushed red pepper flakes

2 tablespoons chopped fresh parsley

1 tablespoon tomato paste (from 6-oz can)

$\frac{1}{2}$ cup freshly grated or shredded Parmesan cheese

1 Cook and drain pasta as directed on package. Meanwhile, in food processor or blender, place tomatoes with juice. Cover; process until coarsely chopped.

2 In 12-inch skillet, heat oil over medium-high heat. Cook garlic, red pepper flakes and parsley in oil about 5 minutes, stirring frequently, until garlic just begins to turn golden. Stir in chopped tomatoes and tomato paste. Heat to boiling; reduce heat. Cover; simmer about 10 minutes, stirring occasionally, until slightly thickened.

3 Add pasta and ¼ cup of the cheese to mixture in skillet. Cook about 3 minutes, tossing gently, until pasta is evenly coated. Sprinkle with remaining ¼ cup cheese.

1 Serving: Calories 400; Total Fat 9g (Saturated Fat 2.5g, Trans Fat 0g); Cholesterol 5mg; Sodium 640mg; Total Carbohydrate 66g (Dietary Fiber 6g) **Exchanges:** 4 Starch, 1 Vegetable, 1½ Fat **Carbohydrate Choices:** 4½

budget smart

❝ If you don't think you'll use the remaining tomato paste anytime soon, here's a great way to store it: Scoop tablespoon-size dollops onto a cookie sheet lined with waxed paper; freeze until firm. Place in a freezer container or resealable freezer plastic bag. Now you can defrost and use a tablespoon at a time as you need it! ❞

★ **Best Budget Picks** (for more uses, see pages 314–15)

86¢
per serving

Rigatoni with Basil Pesto

Prep Time: **30 Minutes** || Start to Finish: **30 Minutes** || **4 Servings**

Rigatoni
3 cups uncooked rigatoni pasta (8 oz)

Basil Pesto
1 cup firmly packed fresh basil leaves

2 cloves garlic

⅓ cup grated Parmesan cheese

⅓ cup olive or vegetable oil

2 tablespoons pine nuts or walnut pieces

Additional grated Parmesan cheese, if desired

1 Cook pasta as directed on package.

2 Meanwhile, in food processor or blender, place the basil leaves, garlic, cheese, oil and pine nuts. Cover and process, stopping occasionally to scrape sides, until smooth.

3 Drain pasta. Place in large serving bowl or back in Dutch oven. Immediately pour pesto over hot pasta, and toss until pasta is well coated. Serve with additional grated Parmesan cheese.

1 Serving: Calories 470; Total Fat 25g (Saturated Fat 4.5g, Trans Fat 0g); Cholesterol 5mg; Sodium 135mg; Total Carbohydrate 50g (Dietary Fiber 3g) **Exchanges:** 3½ Starch, 4½ Fat **Carbohydrate Choices:** 3

Simple Swap (Cilantro Pesto): Substitute ¾ cup firmly packed fresh cilantro leaves and ¼ cup firmly packed fresh parsley leaves for the fresh basil.

Simple Swap (Spinach Pesto): Substitute 1 cup firmly packed fresh spinach leaves and ¼ cup firmly packed fresh basil leaves (or 2 tablespoons dried basil leaves) for the 1 cup fresh basil.

budget smart

" Store-bought pesto may be convenient, but it's also convenient (and cheaper) to have homemade pesto stored in your freezer. For freezing, in step 2 process everything but the cheese, scrape into a freezer container and store in the freezer up to 6 months. Thaw in the refrigerator and add the cheese just before serving. Pine nuts also keep well tightly sealed in the freezer, so if you bought a large package of nuts, you can store the remainder for up to 2 years to use as needed. "

$1.68
per serving

Asian Noodle Bowl

Prep Time: **25 Minutes** || Start to Finish: **25 Minutes** || **4 Servings**

1/4 cup barbecue sauce

2 tablespoons hoisin sauce or barbecue sauce

1 tablespoon peanut butter

Dash of ground red pepper (cayenne), if desired

1 tablespoon vegetable oil

1 small onion, cut into thin wedges

1/4 cup chopped red bell pepper

2 cups fresh broccoli florets or 2 cups frozen (thawed) broccoli florets

1/2 cup water

1 package (10 oz) Chinese noodles (curly)

1 can (14 to 15 oz) baby corn nuggets, drained

1/4 cup salted peanuts, coarsely chopped

1 In small bowl, mix barbecue sauce, hoisin sauce, peanut butter and ground red pepper; set aside.

2 In 12-inch skillet, heat oil over medium heat 1 to 2 minutes. Add onion and bell pepper. Cook 2 minutes, stirring frequently. Stir in broccoli and water. Cover with lid; cook 2 to 4 minutes, stirring occasionally, until broccoli is crisp-tender.

3 Meanwhile, cook and drain noodles as directed on package.

4 While noodles are cooking, stir corn and sauce mixture into vegetable mixture. Cook uncovered 3 to 4 minutes, stirring occasionally, until mixture is hot and bubbly.

5 Divide noodles among 4 individual serving bowls. Spoon vegetable mixture over noodles. Sprinkle with peanuts.

1 Serving: Calories 520; Total Fat 13g (Saturated Fat 2g, Trans Fat 0g); Cholesterol 0mg; Sodium 590mg; Total Carbohydrate 83g (Dietary Fiber 8g) **Exchanges:** 4 Starch, 1 Other Carbohydrate, 1 Vegetable, 1/2 High-Fat Meat, 1 1/2 Fat **Carbohydrate Choices:** 5 1/2

budget smart

" Once the vegetables and sauce are prepped, this dish comes together quickly. To avoid waste, serve the remaining 3/4 red bell pepper cut into strips with a dip as a quick appetizer. If you're using fresh broccoli, buy a whole broccoli rather than precut florets. It's usually cheaper per pound and you can use the stem, peeled and sliced into 1/4-inch slices, with the florets. "

$1.76
per serving

Gemelli with Fresh Green and Yellow Wax Beans

Prep Time: **25 Minutes** ‖ Start to Finish: **1 Hour 25 Minutes** ‖ **6 Servings**

2 cups uncooked gemelli pasta
(8 oz)

4 oz fresh green beans, cut into
2-inch pieces (1 cup)

4 oz fresh yellow wax beans,
cut into 2-inch pieces (1 cup)

1 pint (2 cups) grape or cherry
tomatoes, halved

¼ cup vegetable oil

¼ cup tarragon vinegar or
white wine vinegar

½ teaspoon salt

¾ cup shaved Parmesan cheese
(3 oz)

¼ teaspoon freshly ground
black pepper

1 Cook pasta as directed on package, adding green and yellow beans for last 5 minutes of cooking time; drain. Rinse with cold water to cool; drain well.

2 In large bowl, mix pasta, beans and tomatoes.

3 In small bowl, beat oil, vinegar and salt with wire whisk until well blended; stir into pasta mixture. Stir in ½ cup of the cheese. Cover; refrigerate at least 1 hour to blend flavors.

4 Just before serving, stir salad; top with remaining ¼ cup cheese and sprinkle with pepper.

1 Serving: Calories 320; Total Fat 14g (Saturated Fat 4g, Trans Fat 0g); Cholesterol 10mg; Sodium 580mg; Total Carbohydrate 37g (Dietary Fiber 3g) **Exchanges:** 2 Starch, 1 Vegetable, ½ Medium-Fat Meat, 2 Fat **Carbohydrate Choices:** 2½

budget smart

"This refreshing and inexpensive springtime pasta dish would make a side dish at a barbecue or a nice lunch. Use frozen peas instead of one or both of the beans if you want."

84¢
per serving

Spinach Pasta Salad

Prep Time: **30 Minutes** || Start to Finish: **30 Minutes** || **6 Servings**

3 cups uncooked bow-tie (farfalle) pasta (6 oz)

1 small tomato, quartered

½ cup basil pesto

¼ teaspoon salt

¼ teaspoon pepper

4 cups bite-size pieces spinach leaves

2 medium carrots, thinly sliced (1 cup)

1 small red onion, thinly sliced

1 can (14 oz) quartered artichoke hearts, drained, rinsed

1 Cook and drain pasta as directed on package. Rinse with cold water; drain.

2 Meanwhile, in food processor or blender, place tomato, pesto, salt and pepper. Cover; process 30 seconds.

3 Toss pasta, pesto mixture and remaining ingredients.

1 Serving: Calories 290; Total Fat 12g (Saturated Fat 2.5g, Trans Fat 0g); Cholesterol 0mg; Sodium 560mg; Total Carbohydrate 35g (Dietary Fiber 6g) **Exchanges:** 1½ Starch, ½ Other Carbohydrate, 1 Vegetable, 2½ Fat **Carbohydrate Choices:** 2

budget smart

" This vegetarian pasta salad is brimming with flavors! If you bought a large container of pesto, why not double the recipe to use it up? The leftovers will be great cold. "

$1.34 per serving

Mom's Macaroni and Cheese

Prep Time: **10 Minutes** || Start to Finish: **40 Minutes** || **5 Servings**

1½ cups uncooked elbow macaroni (5 oz)

2 tablespoons butter or margarine

1 small onion, chopped (¼ cup)

¼ cup all-purpose flour

½ teaspoon salt

¼ teaspoon pepper

1¾ cups milk

6 oz American cheese loaf (from 8-oz package), cut into ½-inch cubes

1 Heat oven to 375°F. Cook and drain pasta as directed on package.

2 Meanwhile, in 3-quart saucepan, melt butter over medium heat. Add onion. Cook about 2 minutes, stirring occasionally, until onion is softened. Stir in flour, salt and pepper. Cook 1 to 2 minutes, stirring constantly, until smooth and bubbly. Remove from heat. Stir in milk with wire whisk. Return saucepan to medium heat and heat to boiling, stirring constantly. Continue boiling and stirring 1 minute.

4 Remove saucepan from heat again. Stir in cheese until melted and smooth. Stir macaroni into cheese sauce.

5 Into ungreased 1½-quart casserole, spoon macaroni mixture. Bake uncovered about 30 minutes or until bubbly and light brown.

1 Serving: Calories 360; Total Fat 18g (Saturated Fat 11g, Trans Fat 0.5g); Cholesterol 50mg; Sodium 810mg; Total Carbohydrate 35g (Dietary Fiber 2g) **Exchanges:** 1½ Starch, 1 Other Carbohydrate, 1½ High-Fat Meat, 1 Fat **Carbohydrate Choices:** 2

budget smart

"Everybody loves macaroni and cheese! The boxed kind may be a budget pantry staple, but this simple homemade version is a lot more delicious, and still pretty economical at $.63 per serving. If you want to replicate the traditional orange color, use the yellow cheese loaf rather than white. To give this a crunchy crust, sprinkle crushed corn flake cereal or similar cereal on top for the last 15 minutes of baking."

63¢
per serving

Fresh Mozzarella and Tomato Pizza

Prep Time: **35 Minutes** || Start to Finish: **3 Hours 15 Minutes** || **8 Servings**

Italian-Style Pizza Dough (see recipe below)

4 oz fresh mozzarella cheese, well drained

2 plum (Roma) tomatoes, thinly sliced

¼ teaspoon salt

Fresh cracked pepper to taste

¼ cup thin strips fresh basil leaves

1 tablespoon chopped fresh oregano leaves

1 tablespoon small capers, if desired

1 tablespoon extra-virgin or regular olive oil

1 Make Italian-Style Pizza Dough.

2 Move oven rack to lowest position. Heat oven to 425°F. Grease cookie sheet or 12-inch pizza pan with oil. Press dough into 12-inch circle on cookie sheet or pat in pizza pan, using floured fingers. Press dough from center to edge so edge is slightly thicker than center.

3 Cut cheese into ¼-inch slices. Place cheese on dough to within ½ inch of edge. Arrange tomatoes on cheese. Sprinkle with salt, pepper, 2 tablespoons of the basil, the oregano and capers. Drizzle with oil.

4 Bake about 20 minutes or until crust is golden brown and cheese is melted. Sprinkle with remaining 2 tablespoons basil.

1 Serving: Calories 140; Total Fat 5g (Saturated Fat 2g, Trans Fat 0g); Cholesterol 10mg; Sodium 300mg; Total Carbohydrate 17g (Dietary Fiber 1g) **Exchanges:** 1 Starch, 1 Fat **Carbohydrate Choices:** 1

38¢ per serving

Italian-Style Pizza Dough: In large bowl, dissolve 1 packet regular or quick active dry yeast (2¼ teaspoons). Stir in ¾ cup all-purpose flour, 1 teaspoon extra-virgin or regular olive oil, ½ teaspoon salt and ½ teaspoon sugar. Stir in enough additional flour to make dough easy to handle. Place dough on lightly floured surface. Knead about 10 minutes or until smooth and springy. Grease large bowl with oil. Place dough in bowl, turning dough to grease all sides. Cover and let rise in warm place 20 minutes. Gently push fist into dough to deflate. Cover and refrigerate at least 2 hours but no longer than 48 hours. (If dough should double in size during refrigeration, gently push fist into dough to deflate.)

White Bean and Spinach Pizza

Prep Time: **15 Minutes** || Start to Finish: **25 Minutes** || **8 Servings**

2 cups water

$1/2$ cup sun-dried tomato halves (not oil-packed)

1 can (15 to 16 oz) great northern or navy beans, drained, rinsed

2 medium cloves garlic, finely chopped

1 package (14 oz) prebaked original Italian pizza crust (12 inch)

$1/4$ teaspoon dried oregano leaves

1 cup firmly packed spinach leaves, shredded

$1/2$ cup shredded Colby–Monterey Jack cheese blend (2 oz)

1 Heat oven to 425°F. Heat water to boiling. In small bowl, pour enough boiling water over dried tomatoes to cover. Let stand 10 minutes; drain. Cut into thin strips; set aside.

2 In food processor, place beans and garlic. Cover; process until smooth.

3 Place pizza crust on ungreased cookie sheet. Spread beans over pizza crust. Sprinkle with oregano, tomatoes, spinach and cheese. Bake 8 to 10 minutes or until cheese is melted.

1 Serving: Calories 240; Total Fat 6g (Saturated Fat 3g, Trans Fat 0g); Cholesterol 10mg; Sodium 370mg; Total Carbohydrate 36g (Dietary Fiber 4g) **Exchanges:** 2$1/2$ Starch, $1/2$ Lean Meat, $1/2$ Fat **Carbohydrate Choices:** 2$1/2$

budget smart

" Give this super-quick pizza a try and you may come to love white beans. Cut into smaller slices, this would make a great budget-friendly appetizer for a party. "

$1.14
per serving

Mexican Chicken Pizza with Cornmeal Crust

Prep Time: **20 Minutes** || Start to Finish: **40 Minutes** || **6 Servings**

1½ cups all-purpose flour

1 tablespoon sugar

1¼ teaspoons regular active dry yeast

¼ teaspoon coarse (kosher or sea) salt

¾ cup warm water

1 tablespoon olive oil

⅓ cup yellow cornmeal

Additional cornmeal

1½ cups Mexican cheese blend (6 oz)

★ 1½ cups shredded cooked chicken breast

★ 1 can (14.5 oz) organic fire roasted or plain diced tomatoes, drained

½ medium yellow bell pepper, chopped (½ cup)

¼ cup sliced green onions (4 medium)

¼ cup chopped fresh cilantro

1 Heat oven to 450°F. In medium bowl, stir together ¾ cup of the flour, the sugar, yeast and salt. Stir in warm water and oil. Beat with electric mixer on high speed 1 minute. Stir in ⅓ cup cornmeal and remaining ¾ cup flour to make a soft dough.

2 On lightly floured surface, knead dough until smooth and elastic, about 5 minutes. Cover and let rest 10 minutes.

3 Spray large cookie sheet with cooking spray; sprinkle with additional cornmeal. On cookie sheet, press dough into 4×10-inch rectangle; prick with fork. Bake 8 to 10 minutes or until edges just begin to turn brown.

4 Sprinkle with ½ cup of the cheese blend. Top with chicken, tomatoes and bell pepper. Sprinkle with remaining 1 cup cheese. Bake 6 to 8 minutes longer or until cheese is melted and edges are golden brown. Sprinkle with green onions and cilantro.

1 Serving: Calories 340; Total Fat 13g (Saturated Fat 6g, Trans Fat 0g); Cholesterol 55mg; Sodium 360mg; Total Carbohydrate 35g (Dietary Fiber 2g) **Exchanges:** 2 Starch, 1 Vegetable, 2 Lean Meat, 1 Fat **Carbohydrate Choices:** 2

budget smart

❝ This hurry-up homemade technique makes it easy to save by making your pizza instead of ordering delivery—it's ready in 40 minutes! ❞

★ **Best Budget Picks** (for more uses, see pages 314-15)

$1.44
per serving

Barbecue Pizza Wedges

Prep Time: **10 Minutes** || Start to Finish: **20 Minutes** || **4 Servings (3 wedges each)**

1 package (10 oz) prebaked
   Italian pizza crusts (6 inch)

¼ cup barbecue sauce

½ cup chopped cooked chicken

1 tablespoon chopped red onion

1 cup finely shredded
   mozzarella cheese (4 oz)

6 cherry tomatoes, thinly sliced
   (⅓ cup)

1 Heat gas or charcoal grill for indirect cooking as directed by manufacturer. Top pizza crusts with remaining ingredients in order given.

2 Place pizzas on grill for indirect cooking over medium heat. Cover grill; cook 8 to 10 minutes, rotating pizzas occasionally, until cheese is melted and pizzas are hot. Cut each into 6 wedges.

1 Serving: Calories 340; Total Fat 11g (Saturated Fat 6g, Trans Fat 0g); Cholesterol 40mg; Sodium 690mg; Total Carbohydrate 40g (Dietary Fiber 2g) **Exchanges:** 2 Starch, ½ Other Carbohydrate, 2 Lean Meat, 1 Fat **Carbohydrate Choices:** 2½

budget smart

" Grilled pizza is easy to make, especially with smaller-size crusts like these. If you're looking for other ways to use barbecue sauce, try Large-Crowd Sloppy Joes (page 254), Three-Bean Beer Pot (page 272) and Cowboy Casserole (page 300). "

$1.68
per serving

Canadian Bacon–Whole Wheat Pizza

Prep Time: **15 Minutes** || Start to Finish: **55 Minutes** || **8 Servings**

1 package regular active or fast-acting dry yeast

1 cup warm water (105°F to 115°F)

2½ cups whole wheat flour

3 tablespoons olive oil

½ teaspoon salt

1 tablespoon whole-grain cornmeal

1 can (8 oz) pizza sauce

2 cups finely shredded Italian mozzarella and Parmesan cheese blend (8 oz)

1 package (6 oz) sliced Canadian bacon, cut into fourths

1 small green bell pepper, chopped (½ cup)

1 In medium bowl, dissolve yeast in warm water. Stir in flour, 2 tablespoons of the oil and the salt. Beat vigorously with spoon 20 strokes. Let dough rest 20 minutes.

2 Move oven rack to lowest position. Heat oven to 425°F. Grease cookie sheet with remaining 1 tablespoon oil; sprinkle with cornmeal. Pat dough into 12×10-inch rectangle on cookie sheet, using floured fingers; pinch edges to form ½-inch rim.

3 Spread pizza sauce over crust. Top with cheese, bacon and bell pepper. Bake 15 to 20 minutes or until edge of crust is golden brown.

1 Serving: Calories 320; Total Fat 14g (Saturated Fat 6g, Trans Fat 0g); Cholesterol 35mg; Sodium 750mg; Total Carbohydrate 32g (Dietary Fiber 5g) **Exchanges:** 1 Starch, 1 Other Carbohydrate, 2 Medium-Fat Meat, ½ Fat **Carbohydrate Choices:** 2

budget smart

"What a treat! You don't often find Canadian bacon on pizza, but it's delicious, and a 6-oz package won't stretch your wallet too far. You can also use sliced ham in place of the Canadian bacon."

$1.49
per serving

CHAPTER 4

Vegetarian Meals
with Value

Vegetarian Kid-Pleasers

Many vegetables, grains, legumes and nut products are less expensive per pound than meat, poultry, fish and seafood, so a vegetarian meal can be very easy on your budget, but will it please the whole family? Here's a list of vegetarian meals that are sure to please the kids!

- Baked regular potatoes or sweet potatoes topped with cheese sauce, cheese, meatless chili, canned dried beans, salsa, pesto or vegetables

- Cheese or vegetable pizza

- Eggs, any style, served plain or with vegetables or cheese

- Grilled cheese sandwiches with soup

- Macaroni and cheese

- Meatless chili

- Pancakes, waffles and French toast

- Pasta, cheese-filled ravioli or cheese-filled tortellini topped with pasta sauce, or pasta tossed with olive oil or melted butter and grated or shredded cheese; serve plain or add vegetables or beans

- Quesadillas filled with foods like cheese, beans or vegetables

- Soy-protein burgers, hot dogs and "chicken" nuggets

- Tacos filled with foods like shredded lettuce, tomatoes, beans, cheese, guacamole and salsa

- Vegetable stir-fry with rice or pasta

- Wraps or burritos—fill flour tortillas with foods like shredded lettuce, cabbage or carrots, chopped vegetables, rice, beans, cheese, peanut sauce, peanut butter and jelly, salsa or leftovers

- Yogurt parfaits—layer yogurt, granola or slightly crushed cereal, and fresh fruit

Sage and Garlic Vegetable Bake

Prep Time: **25 Minutes** || Start to Finish: **1 Hour 40 Minutes** || **4 Servings (2 cups each)**

1 medium butternut squash, peeled, cut into 1-inch pieces (3 cups)

2 medium parsnips, peeled, cut into 1-inch pieces (2 cups)

★ 2 cans (14 oz each) stewed tomatoes, undrained

2 cups frozen cut green beans

1/2 cup coarsely chopped onion

1/2 cup uncooked quick-cooking barley

1/2 cup water

1 teaspoon dried sage leaves

1/2 teaspoon seasoned salt

2 cloves garlic, finely chopped

1 Heat oven to 375°F. In ungreased 3-quart casserole, mix all ingredients, breaking up large pieces of tomatoes.

2 Cover and bake 1 hour to 1 hour 15 minutes or until vegetables and barley are tender.

1 Serving: Calories 250; Total Fat 1g (Saturated Fat 0g, Trans Fat 0g); Cholesterol 0mg; Sodium 730mg; Total Carbohydrate 60g (Dietary Fiber 11g) **Exchanges:** 2½ Starch, 1 Other Carbohydrate, 1 Vegetable **Carbohydrate Choices:** 3

budget smart

" Butternut squash plays a starring role in this fall vegetable casserole. If you've never bought a whole squash, you'll be amazed at how inexpensive they can be. It takes a few minutes to peel the skin and scoop out the stringy center, but as a bonus you get all the seeds, which you can roast just like pumpkin seeds! "

★ **Best Budget Picks** (for more uses, see pages 314–15)

$2.55
per serving

Green Chile, Egg and Potato Bake

Prep Time: **20 Minutes** || Start to Finish: **1 Hour 30 Minutes** || **8 Servings**

3 cups frozen diced hash brown potatoes (from 2-lb bag), thawed

$1/2$ cup frozen whole kernel corn, thawed

$1/4$ cup chopped roasted red bell peppers (from 7-oz jar)

1 can (4.5 oz) chopped green chiles, undrained

$1\frac{1}{2}$ cups shredded Colby-Monterey Jack cheese (6 oz)

10 eggs

$1/2$ cup small curd cottage cheese

$1/2$ teaspoon dried oregano leaves

$1/4$ teaspoon garlic powder

4 medium green onions, chopped ($1/4$ cup)

1 Heat oven to 350°F. Spray 11x7-inch (2-quart) glass baking dish with cooking spray. In baking dish, layer potatoes, corn, bell peppers, chiles and 1 cup of the shredded cheese.

2 In medium bowl, beat eggs, cottage cheese, oregano and garlic powder with wire whisk until well blended. Slowly pour over potato mixture. Sprinkle with onions and remaining $1/2$ cup cheese.

3 Cover and bake 30 minutes. Uncover and bake about 30 minutes longer or until knife inserted in center comes out clean. Let stand 5 to 10 minutes before cutting.

1 Serving: Calories 270; Total Fat 14g (Saturated Fat 7g, Trans Fat 0g); Cholesterol 285mg; Sodium 530mg; Total Carbohydrate 20g (Dietary Fiber 2g) **Exchanges:** $1/2$ Starch, $1\frac{1}{2}$ Medium-Fat Meat, 1 Fat **Carbohydrate Choices:** 1

budget smart

" This "egg"-cellent Mexican-style bake will be the hit of your next brunch! If you're looking for other ways to use the rest of the jarred roasted red bell peppers, try Chicken Linguine Alfredo (page 110), Florentine Tuna Tetrazzini (page 126), Peppered Pork Pitas (page 206) and Turkey and Roasted Red Pepper Sandwich (page 212). "

Curry Lentil and Brown Rice Casserole

Prep Time: **30 Minutes** || Start to Finish: **1 Hour 50 Minutes** || **4 Servings (1½ cups each)**

1 medium dark-orange sweet potato, peeled, cut into ½- to ¾-inch pieces (2 cups)

¾ cup dried lentils (6 oz), sorted, rinsed

½ cup uncooked natural whole-grain brown rice

½ cup chopped red bell pepper

½ cup raisins

2½ cups water

2 tablespoons soy sauce

2 teaspoons curry powder

2 tablespoons slivered almonds, if desired

1 Heat oven to 375°F. In ungreased 2- or 2½-quart casserole, mix all ingredients except almonds.

2 Cover and bake 1 hour to 1 hour 15 minutes or until rice and lentils are tender. Uncover and stir mixture. Let stand 5 minutes before serving. Sprinkle with almonds.

1 Serving: Calories 270; Total Fat 1.5g (Saturated Fat 0g, Trans Fat 0g); Cholesterol 0mg; Sodium 470mg; Total Carbohydrate 63g (Dietary Fiber 12g) **Exchanges:** 2 Starch, 2 Other Carbohydrate, 1 Very Lean Meat **Carbohydrate Choices:** 3½

budget smart

"Mild, hearty lentils and brown rice get zing from the curry power and a touch of sweetness from the raisins. Cut the remaining red bell pepper into strips and serve them with ranch dressing to satisfy any hungry mouths while the casserole is baking."

$1.14
per serving

Spanish Rice Bake

Prep Time: **20 Minutes** || Start to Finish: **1 Hour 25 Minutes** || **4 Servings (1 cup each)**

2 tablespoons canola oil

1 cup uncooked long-grain brown rice

1 medium onion, chopped (¹/₂ cup)

1 small green bell pepper, chopped (¹/₂ cup)

1 cup frozen whole kernel corn (from 1-lb bag), thawed, drained

★ 1 can (10 ³/₄ oz) condensed tomato soup

2¹/₂ cups boiling water

1 tablespoon chopped fresh cilantro, if desired

1 teaspoon chili powder

¹/₄ teaspoon salt

1¹/₂ cups shredded reduced fat Colby–Monterey Jack cheese blend (6 oz)

1 Heat oven to 375°F. Spray 2-quart casserole with cooking spray. In 10-inch skillet, heat oil over medium heat. Cook brown rice, onion and bell pepper in oil 6 to 8 minutes, stirring frequently, until rice is light brown and onion is tender. Stir in corn.

2 In casserole, mix remaining ingredients except cheese. Stir in rice mixture and 1 cup of the cheese.

3 Cover; bake 20 minutes. Stir mixture. Cover; bake about 30 minutes longer or until rice is tender. Stir mixture; sprinkle with remaining ½ cup cheese. Bake uncovered 2 to 3 minutes or until cheese is melted. Let stand 10 minutes before serving.

1 Serving: Calories 460; Total Fat 18g (Saturated Fat 6g, Trans Fat 0g); Cholesterol 20mg; Sodium 960mg; Total Carbohydrate 59g (Dietary Fiber 8g) **Exchanges:** 3 Starch, 1 Other Carbohydrate, 1 High-Fat Meat, 1¹/₂ Fat **Carbohydrate Choices:** 4

budget smart

"Jazz it up! If you've got 'em, offer sides of salsa, sour cream and chopped avocado or guacamole. How about crushed red pepper flakes, too?"

$1.50
per serving

Rice and Bean Bake

Prep Time: **10 Minutes** || Start to Finish: **1 Hour 15 Minutes** || **4 Servings (1²/₃ cups each)**

1 cup uncooked regular long-grain rice

1¹/₂ cups boiling water

1 tablespoon vegetable or chicken bouillon granules

1¹/₂ teaspoons chopped fresh or ¹/₂ teaspoon dried marjoram leaves

1 medium onion, chopped (¹/₂ cup)

★ 1 can (15 to 16 oz) kidney beans, undrained

1 box (9 oz) frozen baby lima beans, thawed, drained

¹/₂ cup shredded Cheddar cheese (2 oz)

1 Heat oven to 350°F. In ungreased 2-quart casserole, mix all ingredients except cheese.

2 Cover and bake 1 hour to 1 hour 5 minutes or until liquid is absorbed; stir. Sprinkle with cheese.

1 Serving: Calories 430; Total Fat 6g (Saturated Fat 3.5g, Trans Fat 0g); Cholesterol 15mg; Sodium 1330mg; Total Carbohydrate 80g (Dietary Fiber 12g) **Exchanges:** 5 Starch, ¹/₂ Other Carbohydrate, 1 Very Lean Meat **Carbohydrate Choices:** 4¹/₂

budget smart

"Gotta love canned and frozen beans—they're healthy, cheap and convenient! This easy rice and bean bake, for example, requires only 10 minutes of prep work, then dinner's in the oven."

83¢
per serving

★ **Best Budget Picks** (for more uses, see pages 314–15)

Asparagus Risotto

Prep Time: **45 Minutes** || Start to Finish: **45 Minutes** || **5 Servings (1¼ cups each)**

3 cups vegetable broth or reduced-sodium chicken broth (from 32-oz carton)

3 cups water

1 tablespoon olive or canola oil

1 medium onion, chopped (½ cup)

¼ cup shredded carrot

2 cloves garlic, finely chopped

¼ cup dry white wine, vegetable broth or reduced-sodium chicken broth (from 32-oz carton)

1 package (12 oz) uncooked Arborio or other short-grain rice

½ teaspoon coarse (kosher or sea) salt

1 box (9 oz) frozen asparagus cuts, thawed

2 tablespoons pine nuts, toasted*

2 oz shredded Parmesan cheese (½ cup)

1 In 3- to 4-quart saucepan, heat broth and water to boiling. Reduce heat; simmer while preparing risotto.

2 In 10-inch skillet, heat oil over medium heat. Cook and stir onion, carrot and garlic in oil 2 to 3 minutes or until onion and carrot are tender. Stir in wine; cook 1 minute or until wine boils. Stir in rice, salt and 1 cup simmering liquid. Cook until liquid is absorbed into rice, stirring frequently. Continue to add liquid, 1 cup at a time, cooking until liquid is absorbed, stirring frequently.

3 When 4 cups liquid have been absorbed, stir in asparagus. Test rice for doneness, and continue adding ½ cup liquid at a time until rice is tender but still firm and creamy (process takes 15 to 20 minutes).

4 Remove skillet from heat. Stir in pine nuts and cheese. Serve immediately.

*To toast pine nuts: In ungreased heavy skillet, cook over medium-low heat 5 to 7 minutes, stirring frequently until browning begins, then stirring constantly until golden brown.

1 Serving: Calories 360; Total Fat 8g (Saturated Fat 2.5g, Trans Fat 0g); Cholesterol 10mg; Sodium 760mg; Total Carbohydrate 58g (Dietary Fiber 1g) **Exchanges:** 3 Starch, ½ Other Carbohydrate, 1 Vegetable, 1½ Fat **Carbohydrate Choices:** 4

budget smart

"If you spot a sale on fresh asparagus, use it instead of frozen. To use fresh, cut 9 oz fresh asparagus into 1-inch pieces. In a separate pot of boiling water, boil the asparagus pieces uncovered 4 to 6 minutes or until crisp-tender. Drain, then substitute them for the frozen asparagus in step 3."

$1.73 per serving

Farmers' Market Barley Risotto

Prep Time: **1 Hour 15 Minutes** || Start to Finish: **1 Hour 15 Minutes** || **4 Servings (1½ cups each)**

1 tablespoon olive oil

1 medium onion, chopped (½ cup)

1 medium bell pepper, coarsely chopped (1 cup)

2 cups chopped fresh mushrooms (4 oz)

1 cup frozen whole kernel corn

1 cup uncooked pearl barley

¼ cup dry white wine or chicken broth

2 cups roasted vegetable stock or chicken broth

3 cups water

1½ cups grape tomatoes, cut in half (if large, cut into quarters)

⅔ cup shredded Parmesan cheese

3 tablespoons chopped fresh or 1 teaspoon dried basil leaves

½ teaspoon pepper

1 In 4-quart Dutch oven, heat oil over medium heat. Cook onion, bell pepper, mushrooms and corn in oil about 5 minutes, stirring frequently, until onion is crisp-tender. Add barley, stirring about 1 minute to coat.

2 Stir in wine and ½ cup of the vegetable stock. Cook 5 minutes, stirring frequently, until liquid is almost absorbed. Repeat with remaining stock and 3 cups water, adding ½ to ¾ cup of stock or water at a time and stirring frequently, until absorbed.

3 Stir in tomatoes, ⅓ cup of the cheese, the basil and pepper. Cook until hot. Sprinkle with remaining ⅓ cup cheese.

1 Serving: Calories 370; Total Fat 9g (Saturated Fat 4g, Trans Fat 0g); Cholesterol 15mg; Sodium 820mg; Total Carbohydrate 56g (Dietary Fiber 11g) **Exchanges:** 2½ Starch, ½ Other Carbohydrate, 2 Vegetable, ½ Medium-Fat Meat, 1 Fat **Carbohydrate Choices:** 4

$2.06 per serving

budget smart

" Here's a farmers' market shopping secret: Many farmers will give a discount near the end of the day to help sell off remaining food. It's the perfect time to snag those pricey heirloom tomatoes, which you could substitute for the grape tomatoes in this risotto (use 1½ cups roughly chopped tomatoes). "

Vegetable Curry with Couscous

Prep Time: **25 Minutes** || Start to Finish: **25 Minutes** || **4 Servings**

1 tablespoon vegetable oil

1 medium red bell pepper, cut into thin strips

¼ cup vegetable or chicken broth

1 tablespoon curry powder

1 teaspoon salt

1 bag (1 lb) frozen broccoli, carrots and cauliflower (or other combination)

½ cup raisins

⅓ cup chutney

2 cups hot cooked couscous or rice

¼ cup chopped peanuts

1 In 12-inch skillet, heat oil over medium-high heat. Cook bell pepper in oil 4 to 5 minutes, stirring frequently, until tender.

2 Stir in broth, curry powder, salt and vegetables. Heat to boiling. Boil about 4 minutes, stirring frequently, until vegetables are crisp-tender.

3 Stir in raisins and chutney. Serve over couscous. Sprinkle with peanuts.

1 Serving: Calories 330; Total Fat 9g (Saturated Fat 1.5g, Trans Fat 0g); Cholesterol 0mg; Sodium 730mg; Total Carbohydrate 53g (Dietary Fiber 7g) **Exchanges:** 3 Starch, 2 Vegetable, ½ Fat **Carbohydrate Choices:** 3½

budget smart

" This vegetable curry is equally good over couscous or rice, so use whichever you prefer or have on hand! Try using any extra chutney in sandwiches instead of mayo or mustard. "

$2.59
per serving

Couscous, Corn and Lima Bean Sauté

Prep Time: **20 Minutes** || Start to Finish: **25 Minutes** || **8 Servings (1¼ cups each)**

1 tablespoon butter or margarine

1 large onion, chopped (1 cup)

1 clove garlic, finely chopped

1 box (12 oz) whole wheat couscous

1 box (9 oz) frozen whole kernel corn, thawed

2 boxes (9 oz each) frozen baby lima beans, thawed

2 cups water

1 tablespoon chopped fresh or 1 teaspoon dried thyme leaves

1 teaspoon salt

⅓ cup slivered almonds, toasted*

1 In 12-inch skillet, melt butter over medium-high heat. Add onion and garlic; cook about 2 minutes, stirring occasionally, until onion is crisp-tender.

2 Stir in remaining ingredients except almonds. Heat to boiling over high heat. Remove from heat; let stand 5 minutes. Fluff before serving. Sprinkle with almonds.

*To toast almonds, sprinkle in ungreased heavy skillet. Cook over medium heat 5 to 7 minutes, stirring frequently until almonds begin to brown, then stirring constantly until light brown.

1 Serving: Calories 390; Total Fat 6g (Saturated Fat 1.5g, Trans Fat 0g); Cholesterol 5mg; Sodium 470mg; Total Carbohydrate 69g (Dietary Fiber 11g) **Exchanges:** 4 Starch, 2 Vegetable, ½ Fat **Carbohydrate Choices:** 4½

Simple Swap: If you're not partial to lima beans, substitute frozen shelled edamame.

budget smart

" Couscous is cheap, versatile and quick to prepare, making it a great pantry staple to keep on hand for last-minute meals, like this 25-minute veggie sauté. "

$1.35
per serving

Quinoa with Black Beans

Prep Time: **30 Minutes** || Start to Finish: **30 Minutes** || **4 Servings (1 cup each)**

1 cup uncooked quinoa

2 cups vegetable or chicken broth

★ 1 cup black beans (from 15-oz can), drained, rinsed

1/2 cup frozen whole kernel corn, thawed

1 small tomato, chopped (1/2 cup)

1/4 cup chopped fresh cilantro

4 medium green onions, chopped (1/4 cup)

1 tablespoon fresh lime juice

1 clove garlic, finely chopped

1/4 teaspoon salt

1 Rinse quinoa thoroughly by placing in a fine-mesh strainer and holding under cold running water until water runs clear; drain well.

2 In 2-quart saucepan, heat broth to boiling. Add quinoa; reduce heat to low. Cover; simmer 15 to 20 minutes or until liquid is absorbed.

3 Fluff quinoa with fork. Stir in remaining ingredients. Cook uncovered about 3 minutes, stirring occasionally, until thoroughly heated.

1 Serving: Calories 260; Total Fat 3.5g (Saturated Fat 0.5g, Trans Fat 0g); Cholesterol 0mg; Sodium 660mg; Total Carbohydrate 45g (Dietary Fiber 8g) **Exchanges:** 3 Starch, 1/2 Lean Meat **Carbohydrate Choices:** 3

budget smart

" Go whole-grain with quinoa, pronounced "KEEN-wa." A nutty tasting whole grain, quinoa contains all the amino acids, making it a complete protein like meat. That makes it a great grain to use in vegetarian dishes when you want some protein. Leftovers would make an easy lunch for tomorrow. "

★ **Best Budget Picks** (for more uses, see pages 314–15)

$1.02
per serving

Southwestern Bean Skillet

Prep Time: **20 Minutes** || Start to Finish: **20 Minutes** || **4 Servings**

1 cup fresh corn kernels or frozen whole kernel corn

2 tablespoons chopped fresh cilantro

$\frac{1}{2}$ teaspoon salt

1 small green bell pepper, chopped ($\frac{1}{2}$ cup)

1 small onion, chopped ($\frac{1}{4}$ cup)

★ 1 can (15 oz) chili beans in sauce, undrained

★ 1 can (15 oz) black beans, drained, rinsed

1 cup shredded Cheddar–Monterey Jack cheese blend with jalapeño peppers (4 oz)

2 medium tomatoes, chopped ($1\frac{1}{2}$ cups)

1 In 12-inch skillet, mix all ingredients except cheese and tomatoes. Heat to boiling; reduce heat. Cover and simmer 5 minutes.

2 Uncover and simmer 5 to 10 minutes, stirring occasionally, until vegetables are tender. Stir in cheese and tomatoes until cheese is melted.

1 Serving: Calories 425; Total Fat 11g (Saturated Fat 6g, Trans Fat 0g); Cholesterol 30mg; Sodium 1660mg; Total Carbohydrate 57g (Dietary Fiber 13g) **Exchanges:** 3 Starch, 2 Vegetable, 1 Fat **Carbohydrate Choices:** 4

budget smart

" This super-easy skillet dish is also super-fast. Going with beans really cuts down on the cost and gives you a fiber boost! Serve with white or yellow rice flavored with additional chopped fresh cilantro if you have any remaining. "

★ **Best Budget Picks** (for more uses, see pages 314–15)

$2.20
per serving

Vegetables and Tofu Skillet Supper

Prep Time: **45 Minutes** || Start to Finish: **45 Minutes** || **4 Servings**

2 tablespoons olive or vegetable oil

1/2 cup coarsely chopped red onion

4 or 5 small red potatoes, sliced (2 cups)

1 cup frozen cut green beans (from 12-oz bag)

1/2 teaspoon Italian seasoning

1/2 teaspoon garlic salt

1/2 package (14-oz size) firm tofu, cut into 1/2-inch cubes

2 plum (Roma) tomatoes, thinly sliced

1 Hard-Cooked Egg, chopped

1 In 12-inch skillet, heat oil over medium-high heat. Cook onion in oil 2 minutes, stirring frequently. Stir in potatoes; reduce heat to medium-low. Cover and cook 10 to 12 minutes, stirring occasionally, until potatoes are tender.

2 Stir in green beans, Italian seasoning and garlic salt. Cover and cook 6 to 8 minutes, stirring occasionally, until beans are tender and potatoes are light golden brown.

3 Stir in tofu and tomatoes. Cook 3 to 5 minutes, stirring occasionally and gently, just until hot. Sprinkle each serving with egg.

1 Serving: Calories 230; Total Fat 9g (Saturated Fat 1.5g, Trans Fat 0g); Cholesterol 55mg; Sodium 330mg; Total Carbohydrate 31g (Dietary Fiber 5g) **Exchanges:** 2 Starch, 1 Fat **Carbohydrate Choices:** 2

Hard-Cooked Egg: In saucepan, place eggs in single layer. Add cold water to at least 1 inch above eggs. Cover and heat to boiling. Remove from heat; let stand covered 15 minutes. Drain. Immediately place eggs in cold water with ice cubes, or run cold water over eggs until completely cooled. To remove shell, crackle it by tapping gently all over, roll between hands to loosen. Peel, starting at large end. If shell is hard to peel, hold egg in cold water while peeling.

budget smart

❝This delicious main course is low-calorie and low-cost. Add a fresh touch by sprinkling each serving with a little chopped cilantro or chives if you have some. Serve any leftovers for a tasty lunch the next day.❞

$1.00 per serving

Spicy Chipotle–Peanut Noodle Bowls

Prep Time: **30 Minutes** || Start to Finish: **30 Minutes** || **4 Servings**

½ cup creamy peanut butter

½ cup apple juice

2 tablespoons soy sauce

2 chipotle chiles in adobo sauce (from 7-oz can), seeded, chopped

1 teaspoon adobo sauce from can of chiles

¼ cup chopped fresh cilantro

4 cups water

2 medium carrots, cut into julienne strips (1½ × ¼ × ¼ inch)

1 medium red bell pepper, cut into julienne strips (1½ × ¼ × ¼ inch)

1 package (8 to 10 oz) Chinese curly noodles

2 tablespoons chopped peanuts

1 In small bowl, mix peanut butter, apple juice, soy sauce, chiles and adobo sauce until smooth. Stir in cilantro.

2 In 2-quart saucepan, heat water to boiling. Add carrots and bell pepper; cook 1 minute. Remove carrots and bell pepper from water with slotted spoon. Add noodles to water; cook and drain as directed on package.

3 Toss noodles with peanut butter mixture; divide noodles among 4 bowls. Top with carrots and bell pepper. Sprinkle with peanuts.

1 Serving: Calories 500; Total Fat 20g (Saturated Fat 4g, Trans Fat 0g); Cholesterol 0mg; Sodium 800mg; Total Carbohydrate 62g (Dietary Fiber 7g) **Exchanges:** 3½ Starch, 2 Vegetable, ½ High-Fat Meat, 3 Fat **Carbohydrate Choices:** 4

budget smart

" Put peanut butter to work for dinner with these lightly spicy peanut noodles. They're also good cold, so consider making a double batch and having some for lunch. "

$1.72
per serving

Garden Vegetable Spaghetti

Prep Time: **25 Minutes** || Start to Finish: **25 Minutes** || **6 Servings**

1 package (16 oz) spaghetti

2 tablespoons olive or
    vegetable oil

2 medium carrots, sliced (1 cup)

1 medium onion, diced (½ cup)

2 medium zucchini, cut into
    ½-inch slices (4 cups)

2 cloves garlic, finely chopped

3 medium tomatoes, cut into
    1-inch pieces

½ cup frozen sweet peas
    (from 12-oz bag), cooked
    and drained

1 tablespoon chopped fresh or
    1 teaspoon dried basil leaves

½ teaspoon salt

¼ teaspoon pepper

⅔ cup grated Parmesan cheese

1 Cook and drain spaghetti as directed on package.

2 Meanwhile, in 10-inch skillet, heat oil over medium-high heat. Cook carrots, onion, zucchini and garlic in oil, stirring frequently, until vegetables are crisp-tender.

3 Stir in remaining ingredients except cheese; cook until hot. Serve vegetable mixture over spaghetti. Sprinkle with cheese.

1 Serving: Calories 440; Total Fat 10g (Saturated Fat 3g, Trans Fat 0g); Cholesterol 10mg; Sodium 430mg; Total Carbohydrate 71g (Dietary Fiber 7g) **Exchanges:** 4 Starch, 2 Vegetable, 1½ Fat **Carbohydrate Choices:** 5

Simple Swap: Substitute 1 small eggplant (about 12 oz), peeled and diced (3½ cups), for the zucchini.

budget smart

"Chock full of vegetables, this pasta dish is like summer in a bowl! If you don't have basil, try parsley or thyme."

$1.85
per serving

Spaghetti with Squash

Prep Time: **35 Minutes** || Start to Finish: **35 Minutes** || **6 Servings**

1 medium spaghetti squash
(about 3 lb)

4 oz uncooked spaghetti,
broken in half

¼ cup chopped fresh parsley

2 tablespoons grated Parmesan
cheese

2 tablespoons butter or
margarine, melted

1 tablespoon chopped fresh or
1 teaspoon dried oregano
leaves

½ teaspoon garlic salt

1 Prick squash with fork; place on microwavable paper towel in microwave oven. Microwave on High 8 minutes; turn squash over. Microwave 8 to 11 minutes longer or until tender. Let stand 10 minutes.

2 Meanwhile, cook and drain spaghetti as directed on package; return spaghetti to saucepan.

3 Cut squash lengthwise in half; remove seeds and fibers. Reserve one half for another use. From other half, remove spaghetti-like strands with 2 forks; reserve shell. Add squash and remaining ingredients to spaghetti in saucepan; toss. Return spaghetti mixture to squash shell to serve.

1 Serving: Calories 170; Total Fat 5g (Saturated Fat 2.5g, Trans Fat 0g); Cholesterol 10mg; Sodium 260mg; Total Carbohydrate 28g (Dietary Fiber 4g) **Exchanges:** 2 Starch, 1 Fat **Carbohydrate Choices:** 2

$1.71
per serving

budget smart

" If you've never tried spaghetti squash, you're in for a fun surprise: once cooked, it separates into yellow spaghetti-like strands! It's a fun way to add vegetables to your pasta, and like all winter squash it costs little per pound. The remaining squash would make a great side dish to any roast or stewed meat, maybe with some grated Parmesan cheese on top. "

Cheese Enchiladas

Prep Time: **20 Minutes** || Start to Finish: **45 Minutes** || **4 Servings**

$\frac{1}{3}$ **cup chopped green bell pepper**

1 clove garlic, finely chopped, or $\frac{1}{8}$ teaspoon garlic powder

1 tablespoon chili powder

1$\frac{1}{2}$ teaspoons chopped fresh or $\frac{1}{2}$ teaspoon dried oregano leaves

$\frac{1}{4}$ **teaspoon ground cumin**

1 can (15 oz) tomato sauce

1 medium onion, chopped ($\frac{1}{2}$ cup)

2 cups shredded Monterey Jack cheese (8 oz)

1 cup shredded Cheddar cheese (4 oz)

$\frac{1}{2}$ **cup sour cream**

2 tablespoons chopped fresh parsley, if desired

$\frac{1}{4}$ **teaspoon pepper**

8 corn tortillas (5 or 6 inch)

Additional sour cream and chopped green onions, if desired

1 Heat oven to 350°F.

2 In medium bowl, mix bell pepper, garlic, chili powder, oregano, cumin and tomato sauce; set aside. In large bowl, mix onion, Monterey Jack cheese, Cheddar cheese, $\frac{1}{2}$ cup sour cream, the parsley and pepper.

3 Place 2 tortillas between dampened microwavable paper towels or microwavable plastic wrap; microwave on High 15 to 20 seconds to soften. Immediately spoon about $\frac{1}{3}$ cup of the cheese mixture down one side of each softened tortilla to within 1 inch of edge. Roll tortilla around filling; place seam side down in ungreased 11×7-inch glass (2-quart) baking dish. Repeat with remaining tortillas and cheese mixture.

4 Pour tomato sauce mixture over tortillas. Bake uncovered about 25 minutes or until hot and bubbly. Garnish with additional sour cream and chopped green onions.

1 Serving: Calories 560; Total Fat 34g (Saturated Fat 21g, Trans Fat 1g); Cholesterol 100mg; Sodium 1090mg; Total Carbohydrate 36g (Dietary Fiber 6g) **Exchanges:** 2 Starch, $\frac{1}{2}$ Other Carbohydrate, 3 High-Fat Meat, 1$\frac{1}{2}$ Fat **Carbohydrate Choices:** 2$\frac{1}{2}$

Beef Enchiladas: Add 1$\frac{1}{2}$ cups shredded or chopped cooked beef. In step 3, spoon about 2 tablespoons beef over the cheese mixture on each tortilla.

Chicken Enchiladas: Add 1$\frac{1}{2}$ cups shredded or chopped cooked chicken or turkey. In step 3, spoon about 2 tablespoons chicken over the cheese mixture on each tortilla.

budget smart

"If your family loves Mexican food, add these cheese enchiladas to your repertoire of budget-friendly meals. The uncooked enchiladas can be prepared up to 24 hours ahead of time and refrigerated, covered, until you're ready to bake them. You can spice up the flavor by adding a finely chopped stemmed and seeded jalapeño chile or two."

$1.86
per serving

Chipotle and Black Bean Burritos

Prep Time: **20 Minutes** || Start to Finish: **20 Minutes** || 4 Servings

2 tablespoons vegetable oil

1 large onion, chopped (1 cup)

6 cloves garlic, finely chopped, or ³/₄ teaspoon garlic powder

★ 1 can (15 oz) black beans, drained, rinsed and mashed

2 to 3 chipotle chiles in adobo sauce (from a 7-oz can), drained, finely chopped (2 teaspoons)

4 flour tortillas (8 or 10 inch)

1 cup shredded mozzarella cheese (4 oz)

1 large tomato, chopped (1 cup)

Chunky-style salsa, if desired

Sour cream, if desired

1 In 10-inch nonstick skillet, heat oil over medium-high heat. Add onion and garlic; cook 6 to 8 minutes, stirring occasionally, until onion is tender. Stir in mashed beans and chiles. Cook, stirring frequently, until hot.

3 Place ¼ of the bean mixture on center of each tortilla. Top with cheese and tomato.

4 Fold one end of each tortilla up about 1 inch over filling; fold right and left sides over folded end, overlapping. Fold remaining end down. Place seam side down on serving platter or plate. Spoon on salsa and dollop of sour cream.

1 Serving: Calories 450; Total Fat 17g (Saturated Fat 6g, Trans Fat 0.5g); Cholesterol 15mg; Sodium 820mg; Total Carbohydrate 56g (Dietary Fiber 12g) **Exchanges:** 3 Starch, ¹/₂ Other Carbohydrate, 1¹/₂ Medium-Fat Meat, 1¹/₂ Fat **Carbohydrate Choices:** 4

budget smart

“Many vegetarian dishes are naturally cost friendly and these 20-minute burritos are no exception!”

$1.64
per serving

Veggie Quesadillas

Prep Time: **15 Minutes** || Start to Finish: **20 Minutes** || **4 Servings (1 quesadilla each)**

1 cup shredded zucchini

1 small tomato, seeded, chopped (½ cup)

1 tablespoon chopped fresh or 1 teaspoon dried oregano leaves

½ teaspoon garlic-pepper blend

8 whole wheat flour tortillas (8 inch)

2 cups shredded Italian cheese blend (8 oz)

Tomato pasta sauce or marinara sauce, heated, if desired

1 Heat oven to 350°F. In medium bowl, mix zucchini, tomato, oregano and garlic-pepper blend.

2 On ungreased large cookie sheet, place 4 tortillas. Sprinkle ½ cup of the cheese evenly over each of the 4 tortillas. Spoon ¼ of the vegetable mixture over cheese. Top with remaining tortillas.

3 Bake about 6 minutes or until hot and cheese is melted. Cut each quesadilla into wedges. Serve with pasta sauce.

1 Serving: Calories 300; Total Fat 16g (Saturated Fat 10g, Trans Fat 0.5g); Cholesterol 40mg; Sodium 680mg; Total Carbohydrate 20g (Dietary Fiber 4g) **Exchanges:** 1½ Starch, 2 Medium-Fat Meat, ½ Fat **Carbohydrate Choices:** 1

budget smart

" These quesadillas are easy to double or triple for a thrifty and quick party appetizer. Use a pizza wheel or kitchen scissors to cut them into wedges. "

$1.90
per serving

Italian Frittata with Vinaigrette Tomatoes

Prep Time: **10 Minutes** || Start to Finish: **30 Minutes** || **6 Servings**

1 can (14 oz) vegetable or chicken broth

³/₄ cup uncooked bulgur wheat

1 medium zucchini, sliced, slices cut in half crosswise (1¹/₂ cups)

1 cup sliced fresh mushrooms (3 oz)

1 small red bell pepper, chopped (¹/₂ cup)

1 small onion, chopped (¹/₄ cup)

¹/₂ teaspoon dried oregano leaves

¹/₂ teaspoon dried basil leaves

6 eggs

¹/₃ cup fat-free (skim) milk

¹/₄ teaspoon salt

¹/₄ teaspoon pepper

¹/₂ cup shredded mozzarella cheese (2 oz)

3 medium plum (Roma) tomatoes, chopped, drained (1 cup)

★ 2 tablespoons balsamic vinaigrette dressing

1 In 12-inch nonstick skillet, heat broth to boiling over high heat. Stir in bulgur; reduce heat to low. Top bulgur evenly with zucchini, mushrooms, bell pepper and onion. Sprinkle with oregano and basil. Cover; cook 12 minutes. Fluff bulgur with spatula, mixing with vegetables.

2 Meanwhile, in medium bowl, beat eggs, milk, salt and pepper with wire whisk until well blended.

3 Pour egg mixture evenly over bulgur mixture. Increase heat to medium-low. Cover; cook 5 minutes. Remove cover; sprinkle with cheese. Cook uncovered 5 to 7 minutes or until sharp knife inserted in center of egg mixture comes out clean.

4 Meanwhile, in medium microwavable bowl, mix tomatoes and dressing. Microwave uncovered on High 30 seconds to blend flavors.

5 Cut frittata into wedges (bulgur will form a "crust" on the bottom; use spatula to lift wedge out of skillet). Top with tomato mixture.

1 Serving: Calories 230; Total Fat 10g (Saturated Fat 3.5g, Trans Fat 0g); Cholesterol 215mg; Sodium 560mg; Total Carbohydrate 20g (Dietary Fiber 4g) **Exchanges:** 1 Other Carbohydrate, 1 Vegetable, 1¹/₂ Very Lean Meat, 2 Fat **Carbohydrate Choices:** 1

budget smart

❝ Eggs for dinner! Eggs are a tasty, easy and inexpensive alternative to meat. Here they're used in a 30-minute veggie frittata with a delicious whole-grain "crust" made of bulgur. Bulgur is one of the fastest whole grains to prepare (see "Cooking Grains—At a Glance" on page 11), and can be served instead of rice or couscous. ❞

★ **Best Budget Picks** (for more uses, see pages 314–15)

$1.16
per serving

Peppers Stuffed with Broccoli, Beans and Rice

Prep Time: **20 Minutes** || Start to Finish: **30 Minutes** || **2 Servings**

2 large bell peppers, cut in half lengthwise, seeded

²/₃ cup water

¹/₂ cup uncooked instant brown rice

1 cup chopped fresh broccoli

2 tablespoons chopped onion

★ ¹/₂ cup canned red beans, drained, rinsed

¹/₃ cup chunky-style salsa

¹/₄ cup shredded reduced-fat Cheddar cheese (1 oz)

2 tablespoons chopped fresh cilantro

1 In 8- or 9-inch square microwavable dish, place peppers, cut sides down. Cover dish with plastic wrap, folding back one edge or corner ¼ inch to vent steam. Microwave on High about 4 minutes or until tender.

2 Meanwhile, in 1-quart saucepan, heat water to boiling over high heat. Stir in rice, broccoli and onion. Reduce heat to low; cover and simmer about 10 minutes or until water is absorbed. Stir in beans and salsa.

3 Spoon hot rice mixture into pepper halves. Place filled sides up in microwavable dish. Sprinkle each pepper half with 1 tablespoon of the cheese.

4 Cover dish with plastic wrap, folding back one edge or corner ¼ inch to vent steam. Microwave on High about 1 minute or until cheese is melted. Sprinkle with cilantro. Let stand 1 to 2 minutes before serving.

1 Serving: Calories 260; Total Fat 2.5g (Saturated Fat 1g, Trans Fat 0g); Cholesterol 0mg; Sodium 430mg; Total Carbohydrate 46g (Dietary Fiber 8g) **Exchanges:** 2 Starch, ¹/₂ Other Carbohydrate, 2 Vegetable, ¹/₂ Lean Meat **Carbohydrate Choices:** 3

budget smart

"These stuffed peppers make a quick meal for two. Feel free to use any red or green salsa you have on hand. You could also substitute parsley for the cilantro."

$3.42 per serving

★ **Best Budget Picks** (for more uses, see pages 314–15)

Grilled Veggie Burger and Roasted Pepper Sandwiches

Prep Time: **10 Minutes** || Start to Finish: **25 Minutes** || **4 Sandwiches**

1 package (10-oz) frozen meatless soy-protein burgers (4 burgers)

¹/₂ teaspoon salt

4 slices (³/₄ oz each) mozzarella cheese

4 whole-grain sandwich buns, split

¹/₄ cup roasted-garlic mayonnaise

1 cup roasted bell peppers

1 medium tomato, sliced

1 Heat coals or gas grill for direct heat. Sprinkle burgers with salt.

2 Cover and grill burgers 4 to 6 inches from medium heat 8 to 10 minutes, turning once or twice, until thoroughly heated. Top each burger with cheese. Cover and grill about 1 minute or just until cheese is melted.

3 Spread cut sides of buns with garlic mayonnaise. Thinly slice roasted bell peppers. Layer tomato, burger and bell peppers in each bun.

1 Sandwich: Calories 450; Total Fat 24g (Saturated Fat 6g, Trans Fat 0g); Cholesterol 20mg; Sodium 1190mg; Total Carbohydrate 38g (Dietary Fiber 4g) **Exchanges:** 2 Starch, 1 Vegetable, 2 Medium-Fat Meat, 2¹/₂ Fat **Carbohydrate Choices:** 2¹/₂

Simpe Swap: If you can't find roasted-garlic mayonnaise, just add a teaspoon of garlic powder or minced garlic to ¼ cup regular mayonnaise.

budget smart

"If you have the odds and ends of partially used bell peppers in your fridge, use them in this veggie burger sandwich. You don't even have to roast them! Just chop roughly and scatter on top of each burger."

$2.62 per serving

Veggie and Bean Burgers

Prep Time: **10 Minutes** || Start to Finish: **25 Minutes** || **4 sandwiches**

¼ cup uncooked instant rice

¼ cup boiling water

½ cup broccoli florets

2 oz fresh mushrooms (about 4 medium)

½ small red bell pepper, cut up

★ 1 can (15 to 16 oz) garbanzo beans, rinsed, drained

1 egg

1 clove garlic

½ teaspoon seasoned salt

1 teaspoon instant chopped onion

⅓ cup Italian-style dry bread crumbs

3 tablespoons vegetable oil

4 whole wheat hamburger buns, split

Toppings (Cheddar cheese slices, lettuce, sliced tomato, sliced onion and mayonnaise), if desired

1 In medium bowl, stir rice and boiling water. Cover and let stand 5 minutes. Drain if necessary.

2 Meanwhile, in food processor, place broccoli, mushrooms and bell pepper. Cover and process, using quick on-and-off motions, to finely chop vegetables (do not puree). Stir vegetables into rice.

3 Add beans, egg, garlic and seasoned salt to food processor. Cover and process until smooth. Stir bean mixture, onion and bread crumbs into vegetable mixture.

4 Using about ½ cup vegetable mixture for each patty, shape into four ½-inch-thick patties.

5 In 10-inch nonstick skillet, heat oil over medium-high heat. Cook patties in oil 8 to 10 minutes, turning once, until brown and crisp. Serve on buns with toppings.

1 Sandwich: Calories 460; Total Fat 16g (Saturated Fat 2.5g, Trans Fat 0g); Cholesterol 55mg; Sodium 540mg; Total Carbohydrate 61g (Dietary Fiber 9g) **Exchanges:** 3½ Starch, 2 Vegetable, 2 Fat **Carbohydrate Choices:** 4

Veggie and Bean "Meatballs": Heat oven to 400°F. Generously spray 15×10×1-inch pan with cooking spray. Shape vegetable mixture into 16 balls; place in pan. Generously spray tops of balls with cooking spray. Bake about 20 minutes or until crisp. Serve with pasta sauce (any flavor) or cheese sauce.

budget smart

"It's easier to make your own veggie burgers than you think and a lot cheaper than store-bought! These take only 25 minutes from start to finish."

$1.32 per serving

★ **Best Budget Picks** (for more uses, see pages 314-15)

Red Bean and Rice Cakes

Prep Time: **20 Minutes** || Start to Finish: **45 Minutes** || **8 Servings**

½ cup uncooked regular long-grain white rice

1 cup water

1 cup Fiber One® cereal

★ 2 cans (15 to 16 oz each) red or kidney beans, drained, rinsed

1 small onion, finely chopped (¼ cup)

¼ cup diced green bell pepper

1 egg or 2 egg whites, beaten

1 tablespoon chili powder

1 teaspoon ground cumin

¼ teaspoon ground red pepper (cayenne)

Salad greens, if desired

½ cup chunky-style salsa

1 Cook rice in water as directed on package. Meanwhile, place cereal in resealable food-storage plastic bag; seal bag and crush with rolling pin or meat mallet (or crush in food processor).

2 In large bowl, place beans; mash with potato masher or fork. Stir in onion, bell pepper, cooked rice, egg, 2 tablespoons of the cereal, the chili powder, cumin and red pepper. Shape into 8 patties; coat patties completely with remaining cereal.

3 Spray 10-inch skillet with cooking spray. Cook 4 patties in skillet over medium heat about 10 minutes, turning once, until brown. Remove patties from skillet. Cover and keep warm while cooking remaining patties.

4 Serve patties on salad greens; top with salsa.

1 Serving: Calories 210; Total Fat 1.5g (Saturated Fat 0g, Trans Fat 0g); Cholesterol 25mg; Sodium 300mg; Total Carbohydrate 40g (Dietary Fiber 10g) **Exchanges:** 2 Starch, ½ Other Carbohydrate, ½ Very Lean Meat **Carbohydrate Choices:** 2½

51¢ per serving

budget smart

" Don't have salsa or greens on hand? Serve these covered with warmed tomato sauce and sprinkled with shredded Cheddar or other cheese. "

Vegetarian Chili

Prep Time: **40 Minutes** || Start to Finish: **40 Minutes** || **6 Servings**

2 medium unpeeled white or red potatoes, cut into $\frac{1}{2}$-inch cubes

1 medium onion, chopped ($\frac{1}{2}$ cup)

1 small bell pepper (any color), chopped

★ 1 can (15 to 16 oz) garbanzo beans, drained, rinsed

★ 1 can (15 to 16 oz) kidney beans, drained, rinsed

★ 2 cans (14.5 oz each) diced tomatoes, undrained

1 can (8 oz) tomato sauce

1 tablespoon chili powder

1 teaspoon ground cumin

1 medium zucchini, cut into $\frac{1}{2}$-inch slices, then cut in half

1 In 4-quart Dutch oven, place all ingredients except zucchini. Heat to boiling over high heat, stirring occasionally.

2 Once chili is boiling, reduce heat just enough so chili bubbles gently. Cover; cook 10 minutes.

3 Stir zucchini into chili. Cover; cook 5 to 7 minutes longer, stirring occasionally, until potatoes and zucchini are tender when pierced with fork.

1 Serving: Calories 280; Total Fat 2.5g (Saturated Fat 0g, Trans Fat 0g); Cholesterol 0mg; Sodium 650mg; Total Carbohydrate 51g (Dietary Fiber 12g) **Exchanges:** 2$\frac{1}{2}$ Starch, $\frac{1}{2}$ Other Carbohydrate, 1 Vegetable, $\frac{1}{2}$ Very Lean Meat **Carbohydrate Choices:** 3$\frac{1}{2}$

budget smart

"With all the flavors from the beans, vegetables and spices in this vegetarian chili, you won't miss the beef one bit! Leftovers are possibly even more delicious the next day."

★ **Best Budget Picks** (for more uses, see pages 314–15)

$1.40
per serving

Lentil-Tofu Soup

Prep Time: **30 Minutes** || Start to Finish: **30 Minutes** || **2 Servings (about 1¼ cups each)**

1 tablespoon canola oil

1 small onion, chopped (¼ cup)

1½ teaspoons curry powder

½ teaspoon ground cumin

1 clove garlic, finely chopped

⅓ cup dried lentils, sorted, rinsed

2½ cups fat-free vegetable broth with ⅓ less sodium (from 32-oz carton)

4 oz firm tofu (from 12-oz package)

¾ cup coarsely chopped fresh broccoli

2 tablespoons chopped fresh parsley

1 In 2-quart saucepan, heat oil over medium heat. Add onion, curry powder, cumin and garlic; cook, stirring occasionally, 4 to 6 minutes or until onion is tender. Stir in lentils and broth. Heat to boiling. Reduce heat; cover and simmer 10 minutes.

2 Meanwhile, cut tofu into ½-inch pieces.

3 Stir tofu, broccoli and parsley into simmering lentil mixture. Cook over medium heat about 5 to 8 minutes, stirring occasionally, until broccoli is crisp-tender.

1 Serving: Calories 270; Total Fat 10g (Saturated Fat 1g, Trans Fat 0g); Cholesterol 0mg; Sodium 370mg; Total Carbohydrate 31g (Dietary Fiber 7g) **Exchanges:** 2 Starch, 1½ Medium-Fat Meat **Carbohydrate Choices:** 2

budget smart

" Sometimes it's nice not to have any leftovers! This soup makes just enough for two (or just one if you want a second helping), so you're using up only the amount of ingredients you really need. "

$1.86
per serving

Mediterranean Couscous Salad

Prep Time: **20 Minutes** || Start to Finish: **1 Hour 20 Minutes** || **5 Servings (1½ cup each)**

1 cup vegetable or chicken broth (from 32-oz carton)

¾ cup uncooked couscous

3 medium plum (Roma) tomatoes, cubed (1 cup)

1 small unpeeled cucumber, cubed (1 cup)

½ cup halved pitted kalamata olives

4 medium green onions, chopped (¼ cup)

¼ cup chopped fresh or 1 tablespoon dried dill weed

2 tablespoons lemon juice

2 tablespoons olive or vegetable oil

⅛ teaspoon salt

2 tablespoons crumbled feta cheese

1 In 2-quart saucepan, heat broth to boiling. Stir in couscous; remove from heat. Cover; let stand 5 minutes.

2 In large bowl, place tomatoes, cucumber, olives, onions and dill weed. Stir in couscous.

3 In small bowl, beat lemon juice, oil and salt with wire whisk until well blended; pour over vegetable mixture and toss. Cover; refrigerate 1 hour to blend flavors.

4 Just before serving, sprinkle with cheese.

1 Serving: Calories 380; Total Fat 16g (Saturated Fat 3g, Trans Fat 0g); Cholesterol 5mg; Sodium 790mg; Total Carbohydrate 49g (Dietary Fiber 5g) **Exchanges:** 2½ Starch, ½ Other Carbohydrate, 1 Vegetable, 3 Fat **Carbohydrate Choices:** 3

budget smart

❝ What a refreshing and economical dish for a summer party—or, even better, a picnic! Be sure to add the crumbled feta cheese just before serving to preserve its tangy flavor. ❞

$2.41
per serving

Lo Mein Noodle Salad

Prep Time: **20 Minutes** || Start to Finish: **20 Minutes** || **6 Servings (1½ cups each)**

Salad

1 package (8 oz) lo mein noodles

1 bag (10 oz) frozen shelled edamame (green) soybeans

1 large red bell pepper, chopped (1½ cups)

4 medium green onions, sliced (¼ cup)

Dressing

⅓ cup rice vinegar

⅓ cup peanut butter

¼ cup soy sauce

2 tablespoons packed brown sugar

2 tablespoons vegetable oil

¼ teaspoon crushed red pepper flakes

1 Break lo mein noodles into thirds. Cook as directed on package. Rinse with cold water; drain.

2 Cook edamame as directed on bag; drain.

3 In medium bowl, place bell pepper, onions, noodles and edamame.

4 In small bowl, beat dressing ingredients with wire whisk until well blended. Spoon over noodle mixture; toss to coat. Serve immediately, or cover and refrigerate until serving time.

1 Serving: Calories 400; Total Fat 15g (Saturated Fat 2.5g, Trans Fat 0g); Cholesterol 0mg; Sodium 820mg; Total Carbohydrate 48g (Dietary Fiber 6g) **Exchanges:** 2 Starch, 1 Other Carbohydrate, 1 Vegetable, 1 High-Fat Meat, 1 Fat **Carbohydrate Choices:** 3

budget smart

" Here's a fun use for the peanut butter in your pantry—a cold noodle salad that's healthy and not at all costly. It's a great dish to serve either at room temperature or chilled. "

$1.30 per serving

Hearty Soybean and Cheddar Pasta Salad

Prep Time: **20 Minutes** || Start to Finish: **1 Hour 30 Minutes** || **6 Servings**

Dressing

3 tablespoons canola or olive oil

1/4 cup red wine vinegar

1 teaspoon Italian seasoning

1/2 teaspoon salt

1/4 teaspoon pepper

1/4 teaspoon garlic powder

Salad

1 cup uncooked penne pasta (3 oz)

1 box (10 oz) frozen soybeans (about 2 cups)

2 large tomatoes, coarsely chopped (2 cups)

1 medium cucumber, coarsely chopped (1 cup)

2 small yellow bell peppers, coarsely chopped (1 cup)

3 oz Cheddar cheese, cut into 1/2-inch cubes (3/4 cup)

1 In small bowl, beat all dressing ingredients with wire whisk until well mixed.

2 Cook and drain pasta as directed on package. Rinse with cold water; drain.

3 Meanwhile, cook soybeans as directed on package. Rinse with cold water; drain.

4 In large bowl, toss pasta, soybeans, remaining salad ingredients and dressing. Cover and refrigerate at least 1 hour before serving.

1 Serving: Calories 270; Total Fat 15g (Saturated Fat 4g, Trans Fat 0g); Cholesterol 15mg; Sodium 350mg; Total Carbohydrate 22g (Dietary Fiber 4g) **Exchanges:** 1 Starch, 1 Vegetable, 1 Medium-Fat Meat, 2 Fat **Carbohydrate Choices:** 1½

budget smart

" Frozen green soybeans (also called edamame) are a handy and healthy snack on their own, very high in protein and fiber, and quite inexpensive. They're sold in and out of their pods. For this recipe, you'd want them out of the pod. They're used as a tasty centerpiece in this cheesy veggie pasta salad. "

$2.00
per serving

CHAPTER 5

Save on
Sandwiches and Soups

"Souper" Soup Toppers

It's easy to make your own terrific toppers for soups, stews and chilies.

EASY CHEESE BISCUITS
Heat oven to 450°F. Mix 1 cup Original Bisquick® mix, 1/2 cup milk and 1/4 cup shredded cheddar cheese until soft dough forms; beat vigorously 20 seconds. Drop dough by 6 to 8 spoonfuls about 2 inches apart onto ungreased cookie sheet. Bake 6 to 8 minutes or until golden brown.

SEASONED CROUTONS
Cut dry (not hard) bread into 1/2-inch cubes, and toss with olive oil to lightly coat (or spread one side of dry bread with softened butter or margarine, and cut into 1/2-inch cubes). Sprinkle with grated Parmesan cheese and Italian seasoning, or your favorite herbs or seasoning. Cook in ungreased skillet over medium heat 4 to 7 minutes, stirring frequently, until golden brown.

TORTILLA STRIPS
Heat oven to 375°F. Brush 4 small corn or flour tortillas with melted butter or margarine. Sprinkle with chili powder, if desired. Cut each tortilla into 2 1/2-inch strips or 12 wedges, or cut into shapes with cookie cutters. Place in single layer on 2 ungreased cookie sheets. Bake 6 to 8 minutes or until light brown and crisp. Cool slightly.

French Dip Sandwiches

Prep Time: **5 Minutes** || Start to Finish: **3 Hours 5 Minutes** || **10 Sandwiches**

1 boneless beef chuck roast (3 lb)

1 clove garlic, finely chopped, or ⅛ teaspoon garlic powder

1 can (14 oz) beef broth

1½ cups water

⅓ cup soy sauce

1 teaspoon dried rosemary leaves

1 teaspoon dried thyme leaves

1 dried bay leaf

3 or 4 peppercorns

2 loaves (1 lb each) French bread

1 Heat oven to 325°F. Place beef in ovenproof 4-quart Dutch oven.

2 In medium bowl, mix remaining ingredients except bread. Pour mixture over beef.

3 Cover; bake 2 to 3 hours or until beef is tender.

4 Carefully remove Dutch oven from oven. Remove beef from Dutch oven and place on cutting board. Cover with foil to keep warm. Skim any fat from surface of cooking juices, using spoon. Remove bay leaf and peppercorns. Cut beef, across the grain, into thin slices. Heat cooking juices to boiling. Spoon juices into individual bowls for dipping.

5 Cut each loaf of bread into 5 pieces, each about 4 inches long; cut pieces horizontally in half. Fill bread with beef. Serve sandwiches with juices for dipping.

1 Sandwich: Calories 500; Total Fat 19g (Saturated Fat 7g, Trans Fat 1.5g); Cholesterol 80mg; Sodium 1080mg; Total Carbohydrate 46g (Dietary Fiber 2g) **Exchanges:** 3 Starch, 3½ Medium-Fat Meat **Carbohydrate Choices:** 3

Slow Cooker French Dip Sandwiches: Prepare as directed in steps 1 and 2—except place beef roast in 3½- to 4-quart slow cooker. Cover; cook on Low heat setting 7 to 8 hours. Continue as directed in step 4.

budget smart

" This succulent sandwich was invented in Los Angeles in the early 1900s. Serving the broth alongside meant the tip of the sandwich could be dipped just before taking a bite so it wouldn't get soggy. It was often served with spicy mustard, which you might like to add as well. Because the meat is cooked for so long, an inexpensive beef cut like chuck roast is ideal; it will be tender and delicious when done. "

$1.92
per serving

Italian Steak Sandwiches

Prep Time: **20 Minutes** || Start to Finish: **20 Minutes** || **4 Sandwiches**

1 tablespoon butter or margarine

1 medium onion, thinly sliced

4 beef cube steaks (about 1½ lb)

½ teaspoon salt

¼ teaspoon pepper

¼ cup basil pesto

4 kaiser buns, split (toasted in oven if desired)

4 slices (about ¾ oz each) mozzarella cheese

1 medium tomato, thinly sliced

1 In 12-inch nonstick skillet, melt butter over medium-high heat. Cook onion in butter 3 to 4 minutes, stirring frequently, until tender; push to side of skillet.

2 Add beef steaks to skillet; sprinkle with salt and pepper. Cook 5 to 8 minutes, turning once, for medium doneness (160°F).

3 Spread pesto on cut sides of buns. Layer steaks, cheese, onion and tomato in buns.

1 Sandwich: Calories 600; Total Fat 29g (Saturated Fat 11g, Trans Fat 1.5g); Cholesterol 95mg; Sodium 880mg; Total Carbohydrate 32g (Dietary Fiber 2g) **Exchanges:** 2 Starch, 6½ Very Lean Meat, 5 Fat **Carbohydrate Choices:** 2

budget smart

" Shorten your shopping list! If you don't have pesto, use mayonnaise, bottled Russian salad dressing or vinaigrette instead, if you have one of those ingredients on hand. "

$3.52
per serving

★ **Best Budget Picks** (for more uses, see pages 314-15)

Grilled Barbecued Beef and Bean Burgers

Prep Time: **25 Minutes** || Start to Finish: **25 Minutes** || **5 Sandwiches**

★ ½ lb extra-lean (at least 90%) ground beef

★ 1 can (15 to 16 oz) great northern beans, drained, rinsed

¼ cup finely crushed saltine crackers (about 7 squares)

2 tablespoons barbecue sauce

¼ teaspoon pepper

1 egg

5 teaspoons barbecue sauce

5 whole-grain burger buns or sandwich buns, split

Leaf lettuce, sliced tomatoes and sliced onions, if desired

1 Heat gas or charcoal grill. In large bowl, mix beef, beans, cracker crumbs, 2 tablespoons barbecue sauce, the pepper and egg. Shape mixture into 5 patties, about ½ inch thick.

2 Carefully brush canola or soybean oil on grill rack. Place patties on grill over medium heat. Cover grill; cook 5 minutes. Turn patties; spread each patty with 1 teaspoon barbecue sauce. Cook covered 6 to 8 minutes longer or until meat thermometer inserted in center of patties reads 160°F.

3 Place patties in buns with lettuce, tomatoes and onions.

1 Sandwich: Calories 320; Total Fat 7g (Saturated Fat 2.5g, Trans Fat 0.5g); Cholesterol 70mg; Sodium 610mg; Total Carbohydrate 43g (Dietary Fiber 7g) **Exchanges:** 2 Starch, 1 Other Carbohydrate, 2 Lean Meat **Carbohydrate Choices:** 3

budget smart

"Mixing beans and crackers with the ground beef not only saves you money, but they make these burgers healthier by adding fiber and decreasing the amount of fat. Don't press on the burgers while they grill; that way they'll retain all their juices and come out tender and juicy! If you like, toast the split buns right on the grill."

$1.08 per serving

Broiled Dijon Burgers

Prep Time: **20 Minutes** || Start to Finish: **20 Minutes** || **6 Sandwiches**

1 egg

2 tablespoons milk

2 teaspoons Dijon mustard

¼ teaspoon salt

⅛ teaspoon pepper

1 cup soft bread crumbs (about 2 slices bread)

1 small onion, finely chopped (¼ cup)

★ 1 lb extra-lean (at least 90%) ground beef

6 100% whole wheat burger buns, split, toasted

1 Set oven control to broil. Spray broiler pan rack with cooking spray.

2 In medium bowl, mix egg, milk, mustard, salt and pepper. Stir in bread crumbs and onion. Stir in beef. Shape mixture into 6 patties, each about ½ inch thick.

3 Place patties on rack in broiler pan. Broil with tops about 5 inches from heat for about 10 minutes for medium, turning once, until meat thermometer inserted in center reads 160°F. Serve burgers on buns.

1 Sandwich: Calories 270; Total Fat 9g (Saturated Fat 3g, Trans Fat 1g); Cholesterol 85mg; Sodium 470mg; Total Carbohydrate 25g (Dietary Fiber 3g) **Exchanges:** 1½ Starch, 2½ Lean Meat **Carbohydrate Choices:** 1½

budget smart

"Use whatever mustard you have on hand—even honey mustard would be good in these healthful, whole-grain burgers. The soft bread crumbs and onion stretch the meat without detracting from the beefy flavor. Avoid overmixing the beef mixture for a tender, juicier burger."

★ **Best Budget Picks** (for more uses, see pages 314–15)

$1.03
per serving

Italian Sausage Burgers

Prep Time: **10 Minutes** || Start to Finish: **25 Minutes** || **6 Sandwiches**

★ **1 lb lean (at least 80%) ground beef**

½ lb bulk mild or hot Italian sausage

2 tablespoons Italian-style dry bread crumbs

6 slices (¾ oz each) mozzarella cheese

12 slices Italian bread, ½ inch thick

½ cup sun-dried tomato mayonnaise

1 cup shredded lettuce

1 medium tomato, thinly sliced

1 Heat coals or gas grill for direct heat. In large bowl, mix beef, sausage and bread crumbs. Shape mixture into 6 patties, about ½ inch thick and 3½ inches in diameter.

2 Cover and grill patties 4 to 6 inches from medium heat 12 to 15 minutes, turning once, until meat thermometer inserted in center reads 160°F. Top patties with cheese. Cover and grill about 1 minute longer or until cheese is melted. Add bread slices to side of grill for last 2 to 3 minutes of grilling, turning once, until lightly toasted.

3 Spread toasted bread with mayonnaise; top 6 bread slices with lettuce, tomato and patties. Top with remaining bread slices.

1 Sandwich: Calories 490; Total Fat 31g (Saturated Fat 10g, Trans Fat 1g); Cholesterol 85mg; Sodium 750mg; Total Carbohydrate 25g (Dietary Fiber 2g) **Exchanges:** 1½ Starch, 3½ High-Fat Meat, 1 Fat **Carbohydrate Choices:** 1½

budget smart

" If you don't have sun-dried tomato mayonnaise, you can make your own: Combine ⅓ cup mayonnaise with about 2 tablespoons chopped sun-dried tomatoes. Regular mayonnaise works just fine as well. Be sure to use lean ground beef here, since the bulk sausage already contributes the fat needed to make the burgers juicy. "

$1.91
per serving

Peppered Pork Pitas

Prep Time: **20 Minutes** || Start to Finish: **20 Minutes** || **4 Sandwiches**

1/3 cup mayonnaise or salad dressing

2 tablespoons milk

2 cloves garlic, finely chopped

1 lb boneless pork loin chops, cut into thin bite-size strips

1 tablespoon olive or vegetable oil

1 teaspoon coarsely ground pepper

1 jar (7 oz) roasted red bell peppers, drained, sliced

4 pita fold breads (7 inch)

1 In small bowl, mix mayonnaise, milk and garlic; set aside.

2 In medium bowl, mix pork, oil and pepper. Heat 12-inch skillet over medium-high heat. Cook pork in skillet 5 to 6 minutes, stirring occasionally, until pork is lightly browned on outside and no longer pink in center. Stir in bell peppers; heat until warm.

3 Heat pita folds as directed on package. Lightly spread one side of each pita fold with garlic mixture. Spoon pork mixture over each; fold up.

1 Sandwich: Calories 550; Total Fat 27g (Saturated Fat 6g, Trans Fat 0g); Cholesterol 75mg; Sodium 520mg; Total Carbohydrate 44g (Dietary Fiber 2g) **Exchanges:** 3 Starch, 3 Lean Meat, 3 Fat **Carbohydrate Choices:** 3

budget smart

"Pork loin chops are lean and tender. You could also use boneless pork shoulder, which may be less expensive, especially if you find it on sale. Either way, freezing the meat for 15 minutes will make it easier to slice."

$3.72
per serving

Bacon and Onion Cheese Sandwiches

Prep Time: **25 Minutes** || Start to Finish: **25 Minutes** || **4 Sandwiches**

4 slices bacon, cut into ½-inch pieces

1 medium onion, thinly sliced

8 slices (¾ oz each) Cheddar cheese

8 slices Vienna bread, ½ inch thick

1 In 12-inch nonstick skillet, cook bacon over medium heat about 4 minutes, stirring occasionally, until almost cooked.

2 Add onion to skillet. Cook 2 to 3 minutes, turning occasionally, until tender. Remove bacon and onion from skillet. Reserve 1 tablespoon drippings in skillet.

3 To make each sandwich, layer bacon, onion and cheese between 2 bread slices. Place 2 sandwiches in drippings in skillet. Cover; cook over medium-low heat 3 to 5 minutes, turning once, until bread is crisp and golden brown and cheese is melted. Repeat with remaining sandwiches.

1 Sandwich: Calories 350; Total Fat 19g (Saturated Fat 10g, Trans Fat 0.5g); Cholesterol 55mg; Sodium 730mg; Total Carbohydrate 27g (Dietary Fiber 2g) **Exchanges:** 2 Starch, 1½ High-Fat Meat, 1 Fat **Carbohydrate Choices:** 2

budget smart

" The secret to this dressed-up twist on grilled cheese is to cook the sandwiches in the bacon drippings, which makes them deliciously crisp and brown. This recipe is very adaptable—try using other kinds of cheese or bread based on what you have on hand. "

$1.04
per serving

Caesar Chicken Paninis

Prep Time: **30 Minutes** || Start to Finish: **30 Minutes** || **4 Sandwiches**

★ **4 boneless skinless chicken breasts (about 1¼ lb)**

4 hard rolls (about 5×3 inches), split

4 slices red onion

1 large tomato, sliced

★ **⅓ cup Caesar dressing**

¼ cup shredded Parmesan cheese (1 oz)

4 leaves romaine lettuce

1 Between pieces of plastic wrap or waxed paper, place each chicken breast smooth side down; gently pound with flat side of meat mallet or rolling pin until about ¼ inch thick.

2 Spray 8- or 10-inch skillet with cooking spray; heat over medium-high heat. Cook chicken in skillet 10 to 15 minutes, turning once, until chicken is no longer pink in center. Remove chicken from skillet; keep warm.

3 In skillet, place rolls, cut sides down. Cook over medium heat about 2 minutes or until toasted. Place lettuce on bottom halves of rolls. Top with chicken, onion, tomato, dressing, cheese, lettuce and tops of rolls.

1 Sandwich: Calories 500; Total Fat 20g (Saturated Fat 4.5g, Trans Fat 1g); Cholesterol 90mg; Sodium 750mg; Total Carbohydrate 37g (Dietary Fiber 3g) **Exchanges:** 2 Starch, 1 Vegetable, 4½ Very Lean Meat, 3½ Fat **Carbohydrate Choices:** 2½

$2.62 per serving

budget smart

"Skip the local sandwich joint and make your own chicken Caesar paninis at home. Not only will you save a ton of money, you'll ensure the sandwich is freshly made, with crisp lettuce and juicy chicken."

★ **Best Budget Picks** (for more uses, see pages 314-15)

Grilled Italian Turkey Burgers

Prep Time: **30 Minutes** || Start to Finish: **30 Minutes** || **2 Sandwiches**

½ lb ground turkey breast

3 tablespoons tomato pasta sauce

1 tablespoon finely chopped red onion

2 slices (1 oz each) mozzarella cheese, cut in half

½ baguette (8 inches), cut into two 4-inch pieces

2 lettuce leaves

2 slices red onion

Additional tomato pasta sauce, if desired

1 Heat gas or charcoal grill. In medium bowl, mix turkey, 3 tablespoons pasta sauce and chopped onion. Shape mixture into 2 patties, each about ¾ inch thick and the approximate shape of the baguette pieces.

2 Carefully brush grill rack with canola oil. Place patties on grill. Cover grill; cook over medium heat 12 to 15 minutes, turning once, until thermometer inserted in center of patties reads 165°F. Top patties with cheese. Cover grill; cook about 1 minute longer or until cheese is melted.

3 Cut baguette pieces in half horizontally. Place lettuce leaves on bottom halves; top with burgers and onion slices. Top with remaining baguette halves. Serve with additional pasta sauce.

1 Sandwich: Calories 450; Total Fat 15g (Saturated Fat 6g, Trans Fat 1g); Cholesterol 90mg; Sodium 710mg; Total Carbohydrate 40g (Dietary Fiber 3g) **Exchanges:** 2 Starch, ½ Other Carbohydrate, 4½ Very Lean Meat, 2½ Fat **Carbohydrate Choices:** 2½

$1.96 per serving

budget smart

" Ground turkey is naturally lighter than beef, and often cheaper to boot. Avoid overmixing the ground turkey with other ingredients for a lighter textured burger. "

Turkey and Roasted Red Pepper Sandwich

Prep Time: **25 Minutes** || Start to Finish: **25 Minutes** || **6 Servings**

1 loaf (16 oz) French bread

1 lb thinly sliced cooked turkey

1 jar (7 oz) roasted red bell
  peppers, drained

8 slices (about 1 oz each)
  pepper Jack cheese

1 Heat gas or charcoal grill. Cut 30×18-inch sheet of heavy-duty foil. Cut bread in half horizontally. Layer turkey, peppers and cheese on bottom half of bread. Cover with top half. Place sandwich on center of foil.

2 Bring up 2 sides of foil over sandwich so edges meet. Seal edges, making tight ½-inch fold; fold again, allowing space for heat circulation and expansion. Fold other sides to seal.

3 Place packet on grill over low heat. Cover grill; cook 10 to 13 minutes, rotating packet ½ turn after 5 minutes, until sandwich is toasted and cheese is melted.

4 To serve, carefully fold back foil to allow steam to escape. Cut sandwich into 6 pieces.

1 Serving: Calories 470; Total Fat 18g (Saturated Fat 8g, Trans Fat 1g); Cholesterol 100mg; Sodium 780mg; Total Carbohydrate 41g (Dietary Fiber 2g) **Exchanges:** 2½ Starch, 4 Lean Meat, 1 Fat **Carbohydrate Choices:** 3

budget smart

"This sandwich couldn't be much easier! Pack them into lunches for the whole family to avoid that costly trip to the sandwich counter at lunch time. Pack a snack or dessert and piece of fruit along with them, and you won't be tempted to hit the vending machines either!"

$1.80
per serving

Lemon-Pepper Fish Fillet Sandwiches

Prep Time: **15 Minutes** || Start to Finish: **15 Minutes** || **4 Sandwiches**

2 tablespoons whole-grain yellow cornmeal

2 tablespoons all-purpose flour

1 teaspoon seasoned salt

½ teaspoon lemon-pepper seasoning

1 tablespoon canola oil

2 walleye fillets (about 6 oz each), each cut crosswise in half

¼ cup tartar sauce

4 100% whole wheat or rye sandwich buns, toasted

1 cup shredded lettuce

1 In shallow bowl, mix cornmeal, flour, seasoned salt and lemon-pepper seasoning.

2 In 12-inch nonstick skillet, heat oil over medium-high heat. Coat fish fillets with flour mixture. Cook in oil 4 to 6 minutes, turning once, until fish flakes easily with fork.

3 Spread tartar sauce on cut sides of toasted buns. Layer lettuce and fish fillets in buns.

1 Sandwich: Calories 330; Total Fat 14g (Saturated Fat 2g, Trans Fat 0g); Cholesterol 50mg; Sodium 930mg; Total Carbohydrate 29g (Dietary Fiber 2g) **Exchanges:** 1½ Starch, ½ Other Carbohydrate, 2 Very Lean Meat, 2½ Fat **Carbohydrate Choices:** 2

budget smart

" If you can't find walleye, you can substitute other medium-textured white fish fillets like hake, flounder or catfish. It's fine to buy what's on sale, but make sure the fish is fresh (the flesh should be shiny, firm and elastic and spring back when touched). Frozen fillets should be tightly wrapped and frozen solid with little or no ice crystals, or dark or dry spots that may indicate freezer burn. "

$2.45
per serving

Tuna Salad Sandwiches

Prep Time: **15 Minutes** || Start to Finish: **15 Minutes** || **4 Sandwiches**

2 cans (6 oz each) tuna in water, drained

1 medium stalk celery, chopped (½ cup)

1 small onion, chopped (¼ cup)

½ cup mayonnaise or salad dressing

1 teaspoon lemon juice

¼ teaspoon salt

¼ teaspoon pepper

8 slices bread

1 In medium bowl, mix all ingredients except bread.

2 Spread tuna mixture on 4 bread slices. Top with remaining bread slices.

1 Sandwich: Calories 410; Total Fat 24g (Saturated Fat 4g, Trans Fat 0g); Cholesterol 30mg; Sodium 870mg; Total Carbohydrate 29g (Dietary Fiber 1g) **Exchanges:** 2 Starch, 2 Very Lean Meat, 4 Fat **Carbohydrate Choices:** 2

Lighten Up Tuna Salad Sandwiches: Use fat-free mayonnaise for a tuna salad sandwich with 3 grams of fat and 240 calories.

Chicken Salad Sandwiches: Substitute 1½ cups chopped cooked chicken or turkey for the tuna. Omit the lemon juice.

Egg Salad Sandwiches: Substitute 6 Hard-Cooked Eggs (page 172), chopped, for the tuna. Omit the lemon juice.

Ham Salad Sandwiches: Substitute 1½ cups chopped cooked ham for the tuna. Omit the salt and pepper. Substitute 1 teaspoon yellow mustard for the lemon juice.

$1.01 per serving

budget smart

" A week of "brown-bagging" sandwiches like these will really make a dent in your food budget if you've been hitting the sandwich counter a lot recently at lunch time. All the versions are easy and quick. Make sure to store the sandwiches in the fridge. "

Veggie Focaccia Sandwiches

Prep Time: **20 Minutes** || Start to Finish: **20 Minutes** || **4 Sandwiches**

½ medium yellow bell pepper, cut into ½-inch strips

½ medium green bell pepper, cut into ½-inch strips

1 small onion, cut into ¼-inch slices

★ 2 tablespoons balsamic vinaigrette or Italian dressing

1 round focaccia bread (8 inch), cut into 4 wedges

2 tablespoons chopped fresh basil leaves

½ cup shredded mozzarella cheese (2 oz)

2 plum (Roma) tomatoes

1 Spray 8- or 10-inch skillet with cooking spray; heat over medium-high heat. Add bell peppers, onion and vinaigrette to the skillet. Cook 4 to 5 minutes, stirring occasionally, until peppers are crisp-tender; remove from heat.

2 Split each focaccia wedge horizontally. Spoon ¼ of vegetable mixture onto each bottom half of focaccia wedge; sprinkle with basil and cheese. Top with tomatoes and tops of focaccia wedges.

1 Sandwich: Calories 280; Total Fat 12g (Saturated Fat 3g, Trans Fat 0g); Cholesterol 10mg; Sodium 660mg; Total Carbohydrate 35g (Dietary Fiber 2g) **Exchanges:** 2 Starch, 1 Vegetable, 2 Fat **Carbohydrate Choices:** 2

Lighten Up Veggie Focaccia Sandwiches: Use fat-free balsamic vinaigrette to reduce the fat to 9 grams and the calories to 250 per serving.

budget smart

"Try making these Italian-style sandwiches in summertime, when many of the ingredients will be at their peak of flavor—and probably cheaper as well. To save even more money, substitute 1 whole green bell pepper for the ½ green and ½ yellow bell peppers."

★ **Best Budget Picks** (for more uses, see pages 314–15)

$1.74
per serving

Grilled Mushroom-Pepper Whole Wheat Sandwiches

Prep Time: **30 Minutes** || Start to Finish: **30 Minutes** || **4 Sandwiches**

4 medium fresh portabella mushroom caps (3½ to 4 inch)

4 slices red onion (½ inch thick)

2 tablespoons reduced-fat mayonnaise or salad dressing

★ 2 teaspoons reduced-fat balsamic vinaigrette

8 slices whole wheat bread

4 slices (¾ oz each) reduced-fat mozzarella cheese

8 strips (2×1 inch) roasted red bell pepper (from 7-oz jar), patted dry

8 large basil leaves

1 Heat closed medium-size contact grill for 5 minutes.

2 Place mushrooms on grill. Close grill; cook 4 to 5 minutes or until slightly softened. Remove mushrooms from grill. Place onion on grill. Close grill; cook 4 to 5 minutes or until slightly softened. Remove onion from grill.

3 In small bowl, mix mayonnaise and vinaigrette; spread over bread slices. Top 4 bread slices with mushrooms, cheese, onion, bell pepper and basil. Top with remaining bread, mayonnaise sides down.

4 Place 2 sandwiches on grill. Close grill; cook 2 to 3 minutes or until sandwiches are golden brown and toasted. Repeat with remaining 2 sandwiches.

1 Sandwich: Calories 340; Total Fat 9g (Saturated Fat 2.5g, Trans Fat 0.5g); Cholesterol 10mg; Sodium 660mg; Total Carbohydrate 50g (Dietary Fiber 7g) **Exchanges:** 2 Starch, 1 Other Carbohydrate, 1 Vegetable, 1 Medium-Fat Meat, ½ Fat **Carbohydrate Choices:** 3

budget smart

" Most everything tastes better grilled, and portabella mushrooms are no exception! This recipe uses only 2 teaspoons vinaigrette, but there are plenty of other uses for it beyond dressing a salad. Try the Feta-Topped Chicken (page 28) and the Italian Frittata with Vinaigrette Tomatoes (page 182) for some ideas. "

★ **Best Budget Picks** (for more uses, see pages 314–15)

$1.44
per serving

Italian Chicken Noodle Soup

Prep Time: **30 Minutes** ‖ Start to Finish: **30 Minutes** ‖ **6 Servings (1½ cups each)**

1 tablespoon olive or canola oil

★ ½ lb boneless skinless chicken breasts, cut into ½-inch pieces

1 medium onion, chopped (½ cup)

★ 2 cans (14 oz each) chicken broth

2 cups water

3 medium carrots, sliced (1½ cups)

2 cups fresh broccoli florets

1½ cups uncooked medium egg noodles

1 teaspoon dried basil leaves

½ teaspoon garlic-pepper blend

¼ cup shredded Parmesan cheese (1 oz)

1 In 4-quart saucepan, heat oil over medium heat. Add chicken; cook 4 to 6 minutes, stirring occasionally, until no longer pink in center. Stir in onion. Cook 2 to 3 minutes, stirring occasionally, until onion is tender.

2 Stir in broth, water and carrots. Heat to boiling. Cook 5 minutes over medium heat.

3 Stir in broccoli, noodles, basil and garlic-pepper blend. Heat to boiling. Reduce heat; simmer uncovered 8 to 10 minutes, stirring occasionally, until vegetables and noodles are tender. Top each serving with cheese.

1 Serving: Calories 170; Total Fat 6g (Saturated Fat 2g, Trans Fat 0g); Cholesterol 35mg; Sodium 730mg; Total Carbohydrate 14g (Dietary Fiber 2g) **Exchanges:** ½ Other Carbohydrate, 1 Vegetable, 2 Very Lean Meat, 1 Fat **Carbohydrate Choices:** 1

budget smart

"The vegetables in this Italian take on comforting chicken noodle soup give it a nice, fresh flavor. For more recipe using boneless skinless chicken breasts, see the handy list on pages 314–15."

$1.22
per serving

Turkey–Wild Rice Soup

Prep Time: **10 Minutes** || Start to Finish: **30 Minutes** || **6 Servings (1½ cups each)**

2 tablespoons butter or margarine

½ cup all-purpose flour

2 cans (14 oz each) fat-free chicken broth with 33% less sodium

1 package (8 oz) 98% fat-free oven-roasted turkey breast, cubed (about 2 cups)

2 cups water

2 tablespoons dried chopped onion

1 package (6 oz) original-flavor long-grain and wild rice mix

2 cups original-flavored soymilk or fat-free (skim) milk

1 In 5-quart Dutch oven, melt butter over medium heat. Stir in flour with wire whisk until well blended. Slowly stir in broth with wire whisk.

2 Stir in turkey, water, onion, rice and contents of seasoning packet. Heat to boiling over high heat, stirring occasionally. Reduce heat to medium-low; cover and simmer about 25 minutes or until rice is tender.

3 Stir in soymilk; heat just to boiling.

1 Serving: Calories 260; Total Fat 6g (Saturated Fat 3g, Trans Fat 0g); Cholesterol 45mg; Sodium 720mg; Total Carbohydrate 33g (Dietary Fiber 0g) **Exchanges:** 1½ Starch, ½ Other Carbohydrate, 2 Very Lean Meat, 1 Fat **Carbohydrate Choices:** 2

budget smart

" Wild rice is not really rice at all, but the seed of an aquatic grass. Here, the wild rice adds a delicious nutty flavor and slightly chewy texture to this quick and tasty soup. Wild rice can be expensive, but a little goes a long way, so look for it mixed with other rices, as in the long-grain and wild rice mix called for here. "

$1.10
per serving

Southwestern Pork Soup

Prep Time: **25 Minutes** || Start to Finish: **35 Minutes** || **5 Servings (1¼ cups each)**

2 teaspoons vegetable oil

1 lb pork boneless loin, trimmed of fat, cut into ½-inch cubes

4 medium green onions, sliced (¼ cup)

1 small jalapeño chile, seeded, finely chopped

1 clove garlic, finely chopped

★ 2 cans (14 oz each) 33%-less-sodium chicken broth

★ 2 cans (15 to 16 oz each) great northern beans, rinsed, drained

½ cup loosely packed chopped fresh cilantro

¼ cup loosely packed chopped fresh parsley

1 In 3-quart nonstick saucepan, heat oil over medium-high heat. Add pork; cook 3 to 5 minutes, stirring occasionally, until browned. Add onions, chile and garlic; cook and stir 1 minute.

2 Add broth and beans. Heat to boiling; reduce heat. Cover and simmer about 10 minutes or until pork is no longer pink in center. Stir in cilantro and parsley; cook until heated through.

1 Serving: Calories 400; Total Fat 11g (Saturated Fat 3g, Trans Fat 0g); Cholesterol 60mg; Sodium 380mg; Total Carbohydrate 45g (Dietary Fiber 11g) **Exchanges:** 3 Starch, 4½ Very Lean Meat, ½ Fat **Carbohydrate Choices:** 2

Simple Swap: One pound of pork boneless loin chops, cut into cubes, would also work well for this recipe.

budget smart

❝ A blend of Southwestern flavors paired with pork loin and beans makes for a substantial soup with a fun kick. There's plenty of meat, but the beans add even more body to the soup while keeping the costs low. This soup would be absolutely delicious—and serve even more people—ladled over white rice (a great idea if you've got any leftovers). ❞

★ **Best Budget Picks** (for more uses, see pages 314–15)

$2.03
per serving

Chunky Vegetable Chowder

Prep Time: **10 Minutes** || Start to Finish: **20 Minutes** || **6 Servings**

1 tablespoon butter

1 medium green bell pepper, coarsely chopped (1 cup)

1 medium red bell pepper, coarsely chopped (1 cup)

8 medium green onions, sliced (1/2 cup)

3 cups water

3/4 lb small red potatoes, cut into 1-inch pieces (2 1/2 cups)

1 tablespoon chopped fresh or 1 teaspoon dried thyme leaves

1/2 teaspoon salt

1 cup fat-free half-and-half

1/8 teaspoon pepper

2 cans (14.75 oz each) cream-style corn

1 In 4-quart Dutch oven, melt butter over medium heat. Add bell peppers and onions; cook 3 minutes, stirring occasionally.

2 Stir in water, potatoes, thyme and salt. Heat to boiling. Reduce heat to low; cover and simmer about 10 minutes or until potatoes are tender.

3 Stir in remaining ingredients; cook about 1 minute or until hot (do not boil).

1 Serving: Calories 240; Total Fat 4g (Saturated Fat 2g, Trans Fat 0g); Cholesterol 5mg; Sodium 570mg; Total Carbohydrate 43g (Dietary Fiber 5g) **Exchanges:** 2 Starch, 1/2 Other Carbohydrate, 1 Vegetable, 1/2 Fat **Carbohydrate Choices:** 3

budget smart

" You can cut the cost of this soup even more by using 2 green bell peppers instead of 1 green and 1 red. The soup won't be as colorful, but it will taste just as good. "

$1.96 per serving

★ **Best Budget Picks** (for more uses, see pages 314–15)

Italian Tomato Soup with Pesto-Cheese Toasts

Prep Time: **15 Minutes** || Start to Finish: **15 Minutes** || **4 Servings**

1 cup water

★ 2 cans (14 oz each) diced tomatoes with Italian herbs, undrained

1 can (11.5 oz) tomato juice

4 slices rosemary, Italian or French bread, ½ inch thick

2 tablespoons basil pesto

2 tablespoons shredded Parmesan cheese

1 In 3-quart saucepan, heat water, tomatoes and tomato juice to boiling.

2 Set oven control to broil. Place bread on ungreased cookie sheet. Spread with pesto; sprinkle with cheese. With tops 4 to 6 inches from heat, broil 1 to 2 minutes or until edges of bread are golden brown.

3 Into 4 soup bowls, ladle soup. Top each serving with bread slice.

1 Serving: Calories 260; Total Fat 7g (Saturated Fat 2g, Trans Fat 0g); Cholesterol 0mg; Sodium 910mg; Total Carbohydrate 39g (Dietary Fiber 4g) **Exchanges:** 1½ Starch, ½ Other Carbohydrate, 2 Vegetable, 1½ Fat **Carbohydrate Choices:** 2½

budget smart

$1.01 per serving

"This super-fast soup gets a boost of flavor from the quick pesto-cheese toasts. Basil pesto is often available in small containers in the supermarket's refrigerator section. Better yet, make pesto and freeze it in small portions (see the tip on page 136); then just pull some out to use in this recipe. If you don't have rosemary, Italian or French bread, use bread you have on hand, such as whole wheat."

Fire-Roasted Tomato Basil Soup

Prep Time: **30 Minutes** || Start to Finish: **30 Minutes** || **5 Servings (1½ cups each)**

1 tablespoon olive or vegetable oil

1 large onion, chopped (1 cup)

2 medium carrots, chopped (1 cup)

★ 2 cans (14.5 oz each) fire-roasted diced tomatoes, undrained

2 cans (14 oz each) chicken broth

1 cup water

1 teaspoon red pepper sauce

½ cup uncooked orzo pasta

1 teaspoon dried basil leaves

1 In 4-quart saucepan, heat oil over medium heat. Add onion and carrots. Cook 2 to 3 minutes, stirring occasionally, until softened.

2 Stir in tomatoes, broth, water and pepper sauce. Heat to boiling. Stir in pasta. Heat to boiling; reduce heat to medium. Cook uncovered 10 to 15 minutes, stirring occasionally, until pasta and carrots are tender.

3 Stir in basil. Cook about 1 minute, stirring constantly.

1 Serving: Calories 160; Total Fat 4g (Saturated Fat 0.5g, Trans Fat 0g); Cholesterol 0mg; Sodium 990mg; Total Carbohydrate 23g (Dietary Fiber 4g) **Exchanges:** 1½ Starch, 1 Vegetable, ½ Fat **Carbohydrate Choices:** 1½

budget smart

"Starting with fire-roasted diced tomatoes is an easy and inexpensive way to add extra flavor to this 30-minute soup. They have a lightly smoky flavor and cost only a few cents per serving more than plain diced tomatoes.

If you have any leftover cooked short- or small-type pasta, add it at the end to make this dish yield even more servings. Add leftover cooked chicken and top with grated Parmesan."

$1.01
per serving

★ **Best Budget Picks** (for more uses, see pages 314–15)

Cheddar Cheese and Broccoli Soup

Prep Time: **30 Minutes** || Start to Finish: **30 Minutes** || **6 Servings (1⅓ cups each)**

★ **2 cans (10¾ oz each) condensed Cheddar cheese soup**

2 cups water

5 cups frozen broccoli florets

2 cups milk

½ teaspoon ground mustard

¼ teaspoon salt

¼ teaspoon garlic powder

⅛ teaspoon pepper

2 cups shredded Cheddar cheese (8 oz)

1 In 4-quart saucepan, mix soup and water. Heat over high heat, stirring constantly, until boiling and smooth.

2 Add broccoli. Heat to boiling; reduce heat to medium. Cover; cook 8 to 10 minutes, stirring occasionally, until broccoli is tender.

3 Stir in milk, mustard, salt, garlic powder and pepper. Cook uncovered 3 to 5 minutes, stirring occasionally, until thoroughly heated. Stir in cheese until melted.

1 Serving: Calories 340; Total Fat 22g (Saturated Fat 13g, Trans Fat 1.5g); Cholesterol 60mg; Sodium 1300mg; Total Carbohydrate 16g (Dietary Fiber 2g) **Exchanges:** ½ Starch, ½ Other Carbohydrate, 2½ High-Fat Meat, ½ Fat **Carbohydrate Choices:** 1

budget smart

❝Broccoli and cheddar cheese are such a great flavor combination, not to mention a great way to get picky eaters to eat their green vegetables! If you love this combo, look for the 24-pack of soup to save money on the case price. Try another recipe featuring this soup: Chicken-Veggie Casserole (page 288).❞

$1.21 per serving

Tortellini Soup

Prep Time: **40 Minutes** || Start to Finish: **40 Minutes** || **5 Servings**

2 tablespoons butter or margarine

1 medium stalk celery, chopped (1/2 cup)

1 medium carrot, chopped (1/2 cup)

1 small onion, chopped (1/4 cup)

1 clove garlic, finely chopped

6 cups water

2 extra-large vegetarian vegetable bouillon cubes

2 1/2 cups dried cheese-filled tortellini (10 oz)

1 tablespoon chopped fresh parsley

1/2 teaspoon ground nutmeg

1/4 teaspoon pepper

Freshly grated Parmesan cheese, if desired

1 In 4-quart Dutch oven, melt butter over medium heat. Add celery, carrot, onion and garlic; cook, stirring frequently, until crisp-tender.

2 Stir in water and bouillon cubes. Heat to boiling. Reduce heat to low; stir in tortellini. Cover; simmer about 20 minutes, stirring occasionally, until tortellini are tender.

3 Stir in parsley, nutmeg and pepper. Sprinkle individual servings with cheese.

1 Serving: Calories 280; Total Fat 10g (Saturated Fat 5g, Trans Fat 0g); Cholesterol 55mg; Sodium 1420mg; Total Carbohydrate 38g (Dietary Fiber 2g) **Exchanges:** 2 1/2 Starch, 1/2 High-Fat Meat, 1 Fat **Carbohydrate Choices:** 2 1/2

budget smart

" Dried tortellini is less expensive than frozen fresh tortellini, and it works very well in this toothsome soup. The celery, carrot, onion and garlic will enhance the flavor of the vegetable bouillon cubes; you can also use chicken bouillon if you like. "

93¢
per serving

CHAPTER 6

Slow Cooker
Main Dishes

Jazzed-Up Sandwiches

Part of the magic of using a slow cooker is being able to make enough food to enjoy dinner a second time—without cooking twice! Let your leftover meats inspire you to make sandwiches of greatness with these tips.

- **Think outside the bread box.** Try bagels, croissants, biscuits, dinner rolls or tortillas for great beginnings.

- **Hot or cold?** It doesn't matter! If you want a hot, hearty sandwich, reheat your meat (and possibly sauce); otherwise for ease, just pile on cold leftovers.

- **Fresh is best.** Adding items such as fresh vegetables, cheese slices or chopped nuts gives your leftovers a lift by adding texture and taste.

- **Go with the flow.** There is no right or wrong in sandwich making. Use your own tastes and creativity to make your own "new" sandwich.

- **One more time.** If you have lots of leftovers, freeze sandwich-size portions of meat in resealable freezer plastic bags or small containers. Future sandwiches can be made, individually, in minutes with the help of a microwave.

Garlic Chicken with Italian Beans

Prep Time: **20 Minutes** || Start to Finish: **7 Hours 35 Minutes** || **4 Servings**

8 large chicken thighs and drumsticks (about 2 lbs)

½ teaspoon salt

¼ teaspoon pepper

1 tablespoon olive or vegetable oil

1 medium bulb garlic, separated into cloves and peeled (about 15 cloves)

★ 1 can (14.5 oz) diced tomatoes with balsamic vinegar, basil and olive oil, undrained

½ cup chicken broth

★ 2 cans (15 to 16 oz each) great northern beans, rinsed, drained

Basil pesto, if desired (page 136)

1 Sprinkle chicken with salt and pepper. In 12-inch skillet, heat oil over medium-high heat. Cook chicken in oil over medium-high heat until brown on all sides; drain.

2 Place chicken and garlic in 3½- to 4-quart slow cooker. Pour tomatoes and broth over chicken.

3 Cover and cook on Low heat setting 7 to 8 hours or until chicken is no longer pink when centers of thickest pieces are cut.

4 Remove chicken from cooker; keep warm. Skim fat from surface of juices in cooker. Stir in beans; cover and cook on Low heat setting about 15 minutes or until heated through. Serve chicken with pesto.

1 Serving: Calories 590; Total Fat 19g (Saturated Fat 5g, Trans Fat 0); Cholesterol 115mg; Sodium 680mg; Total Carbohydrate 49g (Dietary Fiber 11g) **Exchanges:** 3 Starch, 1 Vegetable, 6 Lean Meat **Carbohydrate Choices:** 4

budget smart

"Don't be alarmed by the amount of garlic in this recipe. When garlic cooks in a slow cooker for hours, it sweetens and mellows, and loses much of the sharp taste associated with raw garlic. Chicken thighs and drumsticks are both great budget buys and are perfect for this Italian-style dish."

★ **Best Budget Picks** (for more uses, see pages 314–15)

$2.16
per serving

Teriyaki Barbecued Chicken Sandwiches

Prep Time: **10 Minutes** || Start to Finish: **6 Hours 10 Minutes** || **10 sandwiches**

2 packages (20 oz each) boneless, skinless chicken thighs (about 24 thighs)

1 envelope (1 oz) stir-fry seasoning mix

¹⁄₂ cup ketchup

¹⁄₄ cup stir-fry sauce

2¹⁄₂ cups coleslaw mix

10 kaiser rolls

1 Place chicken in 3½- to 4-quart slow cooker. In small bowl, mix seasoning mix (dry), ketchup and stir-fry sauce; pour over chicken.

2 Cover and cook on Low heat setting 6 to 7 hours or until juice of chicken is no longer pink when centers of thickest pieces are cut and chicken is tender.

3 Pull chicken into shreds, using 2 forks. Stir well to mix chicken with sauce. To serve, place ¼ cup coleslaw mix on roll and top with chicken. Chicken mixture will hold on Low heat setting up to 2 hours.

1 Sandwich: Calories 350; Total Fat 11g (Saturated Fat 3g, Trans Fat 0.5); Cholesterol 70mg; Sodium 900mg; Total Carbohydrate 34g (Dietary Fiber 1g) **Exchanges:** 2 Starch, 1 Vegetable, 3 Lean Meat **Carbohydrate Choices:** 2

budget smart

"Try these teriyaki sandwiches at your next outdoor potluck! If you want to transport the meat in the slow cooker, wrap the slow cooker in a towel or newspaper to keep it warm and place in a box that will stay flat in your car. Serve within an hour, or plug in the slow cooker at the new destination and set on Low to keep the food warm for hours."

99¢
per serving

Mediterranean Chicken Stew

Prep Time: **10 Minutes** || Start to Finish: **5 Hours 20 Minutes** || **5 Servings (1½ cups each)**

2 teaspoons olive or vegetable oil

2 lb boneless skinless chicken thighs

1 teaspoon garlic salt

¼ teaspoon pepper

2 teaspoons dried oregano leaves

★ 2 cans (14.5 oz each) diced tomatoes with garlic and onion, undrained

1 can (14 oz) quartered artichoke hearts, drained

1 package (10 oz) couscous (1½ cups)

1 can (6 oz) pitted medium ripe olives, drained

1 In 12-inch skillet, heat oil over medium-high heat. Sprinkle chicken with garlic salt, pepper and oregano. Cook chicken in oil 8 minutes, turning once, until brown on both sides; drain. In 4- to 4½-quart slow cooker, place chicken, tomatoes and artichokes.

2 Cover and cook on Low heat setting 5 to 6 hours.

3 Cook couscous as directed on package. Stir olives into stew. To serve, spoon stew over couscous.

1 Serving: Calories 620; Total Fat 21g (Saturated Fat 5g, Trans Fat 0); Cholesterol 110mg; Sodium 980mg; Total Carbohydrate 60g (Dietary Fiber 10g) **Exchanges:** 3 Starch, ½ Other Carbohydrate, 1 Vegetable, 5 Lean Meat, 1 Fat **Carbohydrate Choices:** 4

Simple Swap: Not an onion lover? Diced tomatoes with roasted garlic can be substituted for the diced tomatoes with garlic and onion.

budget smart

" This savory stew is underway in just 10 minutes and all ready by the time you're home for dinner. The addition of couscous makes this stew a meal in itself. "

$2.64 per serving

★ **Best Budget Picks** (for more uses, see pages 314–15)

Creamy Herbed Chicken Stew

Prep Time: **20 Minutes** || Start to Finish: **7 Hours 30 Minutes** || **12 Servings (1½ cups each)**

4 cups ready-to-eat baby-cut carrots

4 medium Yukon gold potatoes, cut into 1½-inch pieces

1 large onion, chopped (1 cup)

2 medium stalks celery, sliced (1 cup)

1 teaspoon dried thyme leaves

½ teaspoon salt

½ teaspoon pepper

2 lb boneless skinless chicken thighs

3 cups chicken broth

2 cups fresh sugar snap peas

1 cup whipping cream

½ cup all-purpose flour

1 teaspoon dried thyme leaves

1 In 5- to 6-quart slow cooker, place carrots, potatoes, onion and celery. Sprinkle with 1 teaspoon thyme, the salt and pepper. Top with chicken. Pour in broth.

2 Cover; cook on Low heat setting 7 to 8 hours, adding peas for last 5 to 10 minutes of cooking.

3 Remove chicken and vegetables from cooker to serving bowl, using slotted spoon; cover to keep warm. Increase heat setting to High. In small bowl, mix whipping cream, flour and 1 teaspoon thyme; stir into liquid in cooker. Cover; cook about 10 minutes or until thickened. Pour sauce over chicken and vegetables.

1 Serving: Calories 270; Total Fat 13g (Saturated Fat 6g, Trans Fat 0g); Cholesterol 70mg; Sodium 430mg; Total Carbohydrate 19g (Dietary Fiber 3g) **Exchanges:** 1 Starch, 1 Vegetable, 2 Medium-Fat Meat, ½ Fat **Carbohydrate Choices:** 1

budget smart

Perfect for a wintry weeknight dinner for a crowd, this can be quickly assembled before you go off to work, and it'll be piping hot when you get home. Yukon gold potatoes are somewhere between starchy baking potatoes and waxy boiling potatoes; they're perfect at absorbing the chicken stew flavors while holding their shape.

$1.13 per serving

Herbed Turkey Breast

Prep Time: **5 Minutes** || Start to Finish: **7 Hours 5 Minutes** || **8 Servings**

4- to 5-lb bone-in turkey breast, thawed if frozen

2 tablespoons honey mustard

1/2 teaspoon dried rosemary leaves, crumbled

1/2 teaspoon dried thyme leaves

1/2 teaspoon dried basil leaves

1/2 teaspoon garlic pepper

1/4 teaspoon salt

1/2 cup chicken broth

1 Spray 5- to 6-quart slow cooker with cooking spray. Place turkey in cooker. Brush with honey mustard. Sprinkle with rosemary, thyme, basil, garlic pepper and salt. Pour broth around turkey.

2 Cover and cook on Low heat setting 7 to 8 hours.

1 Serving: Calories 280; Total Fat 12g (Saturated Fat 3.5g, Trans Fat 0g); Cholesterol 115mg; Sodium 270mg; Total Carbohydrate 0g (Dietary Fiber 0g) **Exchanges:** 6 Very Lean Meat, 1½ Fat **Carbohydrate Choices:** 0

Simple Swap: If you don't have honey mustard, stir 2 teaspoons of honey into 1½ tablespoons of plain mustard.

budget smart

“ As we learn every year at Thanksgiving, turkey is the bird that keeps right on giving. It yields plenty, and costs less per pound than most meats.

Use leftover herbed turkey in casseroles, soups and salads. Or slice it for turkey sandwiches. Wrap the breast tightly and store in the fridge for up to 3 days. ”

$1.61 per serving

★ **Best Budget Picks** (for more uses, see pages 314–15)

Turkey–Butternut Squash Ragout

Prep Time: **15 Minutes** || Start to Finish: **7 Hours 15 Minutes** || **4 Servings**

1½ lb turkey thighs (about 2 medium), skin removed

1 small butternut squash (about 2 lb), peeled, seeded and cut into 1½-inch pieces (3 cups)

1 medium onion, cut in half and sliced

★ 1 can (16 oz) baked beans, undrained

★ 1 can (14.5 oz) diced tomatoes with Italian seasonings, undrained

2 tablespoons chopped fresh parsley, if desired

1 Spray 3- to 4-quart slow cooker with cooking spray. In cooker, mix all ingredients except parsley.

2 Cover and cook on Low heat setting 7 to 8 hours.

3 Place turkey on cutting board. Remove meat from bones; discard bones. Return turkey to cooker. Just before serving, sprinkle with parsley.

1 Serving: Calories 380; Total Fat 6g (Saturated Fat 2g, Trans Fat 0g); Cholesterol 115mg; Sodium 730mg; Total Carbohydrate 46g (Dietary Fiber 10g) **Exchanges:** 3 Starch, 1 Vegetable, 3 Very Lean Meat **Carbohydrate Choices:** 3

budget smart

" Turkey thighs—and most other turkey parts—are often on sale right after Thanksgiving, but turkey is a fairly economical meat year-round. After 7 to 8 hours in a slow cooker, the meat will practically fall right off the bone. "

$2.85 per serving

Turkey–Wild Rice Casserole

Prep Time: **25 Minutes** || Start to Finish: **5 Hours 25 Minutes** || **5 Servings**

4 slices bacon, cut into $\frac{1}{2}$-inch pieces

1 lb turkey breast tenderloins, cut into $\frac{1}{2}$- to 1-inch pieces

2 medium carrots, coarsely chopped (1 cup)

1 medium onion, coarsely chopped ($\frac{1}{2}$ cup)

1 medium stalk celery, sliced ($\frac{1}{2}$ cup)

1 cup uncooked wild rice

★ 1 can (10$\frac{3}{4}$ oz) condensed cream of chicken soup

2$\frac{1}{2}$ cups water

2 tablespoons reduced-sodium soy sauce

$\frac{1}{4}$ to $\frac{1}{2}$ teaspoon dried marjoram leaves

$\frac{1}{8}$ teaspoon pepper

1 In 12-inch skillet, cook bacon over medium heat, stirring occasionally, until almost crisp. Stir in turkey, carrots, onion and celery. Cook about 2 minutes, stirring frequently, until turkey is brown.

2 Spoon turkey mixture into 3- to 4-quart slow cooker. Stir in remaining ingredients.

3 Cover; cook on Low heat setting 5 to 6 hours.

1 Serving: Calories 340; Total Fat 8g (Saturated Fat 2.5g, Trans Fat 0g); Cholesterol 70mg; Sodium 870mg; Total Carbohydrate 38g (Dietary Fiber 4g) **Exchanges:** 2$\frac{1}{2}$ Starch, 3 Very Lean Meat, 1 Fat **Carbohydrate Choices:** 2$\frac{1}{2}$

budget smart

"Turkey makes such wonderful soups, stews and casseroles—and it's so inexpensive—that it's a shame not to have it more often through the year instead of just at Thanksgiving. This lightly creamy casserole gets a lot of flavor from the bacon that gets sautéed at the start."

★ **Best Budget Picks** (for more uses, see pages 314–15)

$1.99
per serving

Herbed Beef Roast

Prep Time: **15 Minutes** || Start to Finish: **6 Hours 15 Minutes** || **12 Servings**

3-lb beef boneless tip roast

1 teaspoon mixed dried herb leaves (such as marjoram, basil and oregano)

1 teaspoon salt

½ teaspoon pepper

2 cloves garlic, finely chopped

1 cup balsamic or red wine vinegar

1 If beef roast comes in netting or is tied, do not remove. Spray 12-inch skillet with cooking spray; heat over medium-high heat. Cook beef in skillet about 5 minutes, turning occasionally, until brown on all sides. Sprinkle with herbs, salt and pepper.

2 In 4- to 5-quart slow cooker, place garlic. Place beef on garlic. Pour vinegar over beef.

3 Cover and cook on Low heat setting 6 to 8 hours. Remove netting or strings from beef.

1 Serving: Calories 170; Total Fat 8g (Saturated Fat 3g, Trans Fat 0g); Cholesterol 60mg; Sodium 250mg; Total Carbohydrate 1g (Dietary Fiber 0g) **Exchanges:** 3 Lean Meat **Carbohydrate Choices:** 0

budget smart

" Tip roast is an inexpensive cut of beef and it works perfectly in this slow-cooked roast. If it's not tied, see if the butcher at the market will tie it for you, for more even browning and cooking. A cup of vinegar may seem like a lot, but you'll find the beef comes out perfectly tender and delicious. "

$1.42 per serving

★ **Best Budget Picks** (for more uses, see pages 314-15)

Italian Shredded Beef Hoagies

Prep Time: **15 Minutes** ‖ Start to Finish: **8 Hours 15 Minutes** ‖ **8 sandwiches**

2-lb beef boneless arm roast, trimmed of fat

2 medium onions, sliced

★ **1 can (14.5 oz) Italian-seasoned diced tomatoes, undrained**

¼ cup tomato paste

8 hoagie buns, toasted if desired

2 cups shredded mozzarella cheese (8 oz)

1 If beef roast comes in netting or is tied, remove netting or strings. In 4- to 5-quart slow cooker, place onions. Place beef on onions. In small bowl, mix diced tomatoes and tomato paste; pour over beef.

2 Cover; cook on Low heat setting 8 to 10 hours.

3 Remove beef from cooker; place on cutting board. Use 2 forks to pull beef into shreds. Return beef to cooker. Spoon about ½ cup beef mixture onto each bun. Top each with ¼ cup cheese.

1 Sandwich: Calories 280; Total Fat 14g (Saturated Fat 7g, Trans Fat 0g); Cholesterol 80mg; Sodium 350mg; Total Carbohydrate 7g (Dietary Fiber 1g); **Exchanges:** 1 Vegetable, 4½ Lean Meat **Carbohydrate Choices:** ½

$1.87 per serving

budget smart

" The warm shredded beef will melt the mozzarella right in the hoagie buns. One of the great things about slow cookers is that the most inexpensive cuts of meat are often the best, as they require long, slow cooking to become tender and juicy. "

Beef and Potato Stew

Prep Time: **20 Minutes** || Start to Finish: **8 Hours 35 Minutes** || **6 Servings**

1 cup sun-dried tomatoes (not in oil)

1½ lb beef stew meat

12 small new potatoes (1½ lb), cut in half

1 medium onion, cut into 8 wedges

1½ cups ready-to-eat baby-cut carrots

1 can (14 oz) beef broth

1½ teaspoons seasoned salt

1 dried bay leaf

½ cup water

¼ cup all-purpose flour

1 Cover dried tomatoes with boiling water. Let stand 10 minutes; drain. Coarsely chop tomatoes.

2 In 3½- to 4-quart slow cooker, mix tomatoes and remaining ingredients except water and flour.

3 Cover and cook on Low heat setting 8 to 9 hours.

4 Mix water and flour; gradually stir into stew. Increase heat setting to High. Cover and cook 10 to 15 minutes or until slightly thickened. Remove bay leaf.

1 Serving: Calories 350; Total Fat 14g (Saturated Fat 5g, Trans Fat 0.5g); Cholesterol 70mg; Sodium 900mg; Total Carbohydrate 34g (Dietary Fiber 4g) **Exchanges:** 2 Starch, 1 Vegetable, 3 Lean Meat **Carbohydrate Choices:** 2

budget smart

" When picking out stew meat, do some comparison shopping. Chuck is often the cut of meat used in beef stew, so if the beef chuck costs less per pound than the precut stew meat, buy that instead. To use, just cut it into ¾-inch pieces. "

Beef and Bean Chili

Prep Time: **25 Minutes** || Start to Finish: **8 Hours 25 Minutes** || **5 Servings**

1 tablespoon olive or
  vegetable oil

2 medium onions, coarsely
  chopped (1 cup)

2 teaspoons finely chopped
  garlic

2 tablespoons chili powder

1 tablespoon ground cumin

1 teaspoon salt

$\frac{1}{8}$ teaspoon pepper

2 lb beef stew meat

★ 2 cans (14.5 oz each) diced
  tomatoes with green chiles,
  undrained

★ 2 cans (15 oz each) black beans,
  rinsed, drained

$\frac{1}{2}$ cup water

1 In 12-inch skillet, heat oil over medium-high heat. Cook onions and garlic in oil 4 to 5 minutes, stirring frequently, until onions are softened.

2 Stir in chili powder, cumin, salt, pepper and beef. Cook 6 to 8 minutes, stirring occasionally, until beef is lightly browned.

3 Place beef mixture in 3- to 4-quart slow cooker. Stir in tomatoes, beans and water. Cover and cook on Low heat setting 8 to 10 hours. Stir well before serving.

Parmesan Bread Bowls

1 package regular or quick active dry yeast

$\frac{1}{4}$ cup warm water (105°F to 115°F)

2 tablespoons sugar

3 cups all-purpose flour

3 teaspoons baking powder

$\frac{3}{4}$ teaspoon salt

$\frac{1}{3}$ cup grated Parmesan cheese

$\frac{1}{4}$ cup shortening

1 cup buttermilk

1 In small bowl, dissolve yeast in warm water. Stir in sugar; set aside.

2 In large bowl, mix flour, baking powder, salt and cheese. Cut in shortening, using pastry blender or crisscrossing 2 knives, until mixture looks like fine crumbs. Stir in yeast mixture and just enough buttermilk so dough leaves side of bowl and forms a ball. Place dough on lightly floured surface. Knead about 1 minute or until smooth. Cover and let rise in warm place 10 minutes.

3 Heat oven to 375°F. Grease outsides of six 10-ounce custard cups. In ungreased 15×10-inch pan, place cups upside down. Divide dough into 6 equal parts. Pat or roll each part into 7-inch circle. Shape dough circles over outsides of custard cups. (Do not allow to curl under edges of cups.)

4 Bake 18 to 22 minutes or until golden brown. Carefully lift bread bowls from custard cups—custard cups and bread will be hot. Cool bread bowls upright on cooling rack.

budget smart

❝ Foods like canned tomatoes with chiles give you two ingredients for the price of one! Make this chili serve even more people by serving it over bowls of white rice or try making the Parmesan Bread Bowls pictured on the facing page. ❞

★ **Best Budget Picks** (for more uses, see pages 314-15)

$2.70
per serving

Beef and Barley Soup

Prep Time: **20 Minutes** || Start to Finish: **9 Hours 50 Minutes** || **8 Servings**

1½ lb beef stew meat

3 medium carrots, sliced (1½ cups)

1 large onion, chopped (1 cup)

2 cloves garlic, finely chopped

⅔ cup frozen whole kernel corn, thawed (from 12-oz bag)

⅔ cup uncooked pearl barley

½ teaspoon salt

½ teaspoon pepper

★ 1 can (14.5 oz) diced tomatoes, undrained

3 cans (14 oz each) beef broth

1 cup frozen sweet peas, thawed (from 12-oz bag)

1 Spray 5- to 6-quart slow cooker with cooking spray. In cooker, mix all ingredients except peas.

2 Cover; cook on Low heat setting 9 to 10 hours.

3 Stir in peas. Increase heat setting to High. Cover; cook 20 to 30 minutes longer or until peas are tender.

1 Serving: Calories 280; Total Fat 11g (Saturated Fat 4g, Trans Fat 0g); Cholesterol 50mg; Sodium 930mg; Total Carbohydrate 25g (Dietary Fiber 5g) **Exchanges:** 1 Starch, ½ Other Carbohydrate, 1 Vegetable, 2 Medium-Fat Meat **Carbohydrate Choices:** 1½

budget smart

" If you have the time, brown the stew meat in a large skillet over medium heat before putting it into the slow cooker and proceeding with the recipe. This will increase the beefy flavors in almost the same time that it will take you to chop the onion and slice the carrots. "

$1.64
per serving

Italian Meatballs with Marinara Sauce

Prep Time: **15 Minutes** || Start to Finish: **6 Hours 50 Minutes** || **6 Servings (4 meatballs each)**

★ ¾ lb ground beef

¾ lb ground pork

1 small onion, chopped (¼ cup)

2 cloves garlic, finely chopped

2 teaspoons Italian seasoning

¼ cup Italian-style dry bread crumbs

1 egg, slightly beaten

1 jar (28 oz) marinara sauce

1 Heat oven to 375°. Line jelly roll pan, 15×10×1 inch, with foil; spray with cooking spray. In large bowl, mix all ingredients except marinara sauce. Shape mixture into twenty-four 1½-inch balls. Place in pan. Bake 30 to 35 minutes or until no longer pink in center.

2 Place meatballs in 3½- to 4-quart slow cooker. Pour marinara sauce over meatballs.

3 Cover and cook on Low heat setting 6 to 7 hours to blend and develop flavors.

1 Serving: Calories 390; Total Fat 20g (Saturated Fat 6g, Trans Fat 0); Cholesterol 105mg; Sodium 780mg; Total Carbohydrate 29g (Dietary Fiber 2g) **Exchanges:** ½ Starch, 1 Other Carbohydrate, 1 Vegetable, 3 Medium-Fat Meat, 1 Fat **Carbohydrate Choices:** 2

budget smart

"The juiciness of the ground pork makes these meatballs especially tender. Serve the meatballs and sauce (or any reheated leftovers) over a bowl of hot cooked pasta."

★ **Best Budget Picks** (for more uses, see pages 314–15)

$1.21
per serving

Large-Crowd Sloppy Joes

Prep Time: **20 Minutes** || Start to Finish: **7 Hours 20 Minutes** || **24 sandwiches**

★ **3 lb lean (at least 80%) ground beef**

1 large onion, coarsely chopped (1 cup)

1½ medium stalks celery, chopped (¾ cup)

1 cup barbecue sauce

1 can (26.5 oz) sloppy joe sauce

24 sandwich buns, split

1 In 4-quart Dutch oven, cook beef and onion over medium-high heat 5 to 7 minutes, stirring occasionally, until beef is thoroughly cooked; drain.

2 Mix beef mixture and remaining ingredients except buns in 3½- to 4-quart slow cooker.

3 Cover and cook on Low heat setting 7 to 9 hours.

4 Stir well before serving. To serve, fill each bun with about ⅓ cup beef mixture. Beef mixture will hold on Low heat setting up to 2 hours; stir occasionally.

1 Sandwich: Calories 250; Total Fat 8g (Saturated Fat 3g, Trans Fat 0.5); Cholesterol 35mg; Sodium 540mg; Total Carbohydrate 29g (Dietary Fiber 1g) **Exchanges:** 1½ Starch, ½ Other Carbohydrate, 1 Vegetable, 1½ Medium-Fat Meat **Carbohydrate Choices:** 2

budget smart

" Maybe your babysitter made Sloppy Joes for you in a time gone by. They're one of the ultimate comfort foods, and this version uses only 3 lb beef for 24 servings. Try them instead of pizza delivery for a kid's birthday, or whenever you need to feed a hungry crowd. "

79¢ per serving

★ **Best Budget Picks** (for more uses, see pages 314–15)

Jerk Pork Sandwiches

Prep Time: **20 Minutes** || Start to Finish: **9 Hours 20 Minutes** || **8 sandwiches**

1 boneless pork shoulder roast (2¹⁄₂- to 3-lb)

1 medium onion, chopped (¹⁄₂ cup)

3 tablespoons Caribbean jerk seasoning

¹⁄₂ cup chili sauce

¹⁄₂ cup purchased corn relish

2 tablespoons chopped fresh cilantro

1 cup shredded lettuce

8 pita fold breads or split potato rolls

1 Spray 3- to 4-quart slow cooker with cooking spray. Remove netting or strings from pork roast; cut pork into 2-inch pieces. Place pork and onion in cooker. Sprinkle with jerk seasoning; toss to coat. Pour chili sauce over top.

2 Cover and cook on Low heat setting 9 to 11 hours.

3 Place pork on cutting board; use 2 forks to pull pork into shreds. Return pork to cooker. In small bowl, mix corn relish and cilantro. To serve, layer lettuce, pork mixture and corn relish in pita fold breads.

1 Sandwich: Calories 450; Total Fat 18g (Saturated Fat 6g, Trans Fat 0g); Cholesterol 90mg; Sodium 760mg; Total Carbohydrate 36g (Dietary Fiber 3g) **Exchanges:** 2¹⁄₂ Starch, 4 Lean Meat, ¹⁄₂ Fat **Carbohydrate Choices:** 2¹⁄₂

budget smart

"Look for Caribbean jerk seasoning in the spice section of the supermarket. Pork shoulder is one of the least expensive cuts of pork, and one of the most flavorful."

$3.35 per serving

Hearty Pork Stew

Prep Time: **35 Minutes** || Start to Finish: **7 Hours 20 Minutes** || **6 Servings (1½ cups each)**

1 tablespoon vegetable oil

1½ lb boneless pork loin roast, cut into 1-inch cubes

3 medium carrots, cut into ¼-inch slices (1½ cups)

1 medium onion, chopped (½ cup)

2 cups ½-inch cubes peeled parsnips

1½ cups 1-inch cubes peeled butternut squash

4 cups chicken broth

1 tablespoon chopped fresh or 1 teaspoon dried sage leaves

2 teaspoons chopped fresh or ¾ teaspoon dried thyme leaves

½ teaspoon salt

½ teaspoon pepper

3 tablespoons all-purpose flour

3 tablespoons butter or margarine, softened

1 In 10-inch skillet, heat oil over medium-high heat. Cook pork in oil 6 to 8 minutes, stirring occasionally, until browned on all sides.

2 In 3-quart slow cooker, mix pork and remaining ingredients except flour and butter.

3 Cover; cook on Low heat setting 6 to 7 hours.

4 In small bowl, mix flour and butter; gradually stir into stew until blended. Increase heat setting to High. Cover; cook 30 to 45 minutes, stirring occasionally, until thickened.

1 Serving: Calories 340; Total Fat 16g (Saturated Fat 6g, Trans Fat 0g); Cholesterol 90mg; Sodium 980mg; Total Carbohydrate 20g (Dietary Fiber 4g) **Exchanges:** 1 Starch, ½ Other Carbohydrate, 4 Lean Meat, ½ Fat **Carbohydrate Choices:** 1

budget smart

" The aromas created by this stew will have your mouth watering the moment you enter your home for dinner. If you have additional carrots on hand, use those instead of parsnips. "

$2.37
per serving

Saucy Barbecued Ribs

Prep Time: **10 Minutes** || Start to Finish: **7 Hours 10 Minutes** || **6 Servings**

3½ lb pork loin back ribs
  or pork spareribs

½ teaspoon salt

¼ teaspoon pepper

½ cup water

1⅓ cups barbecue sauce

Chopped green onions,
  if desired

1 Spray inside of 5- to 6-quart slow cooker with cooking spray. Cut ribs into 2- or 3-rib portions. Place ribs in cooker. Sprinkle with salt and pepper. Pour water into cooker.

2 Cover and cook on Low heat setting 6 to 7 hours. Remove ribs from cooker; place in shallow baking pan. Drain and discard liquid from cooker.

3 Brush both sides of ribs with barbecue sauce. Return ribs to cooker. Pour any remaining sauce over ribs. Cover and cook on Low heat setting about 1 hour or until ribs are glazed and sauce is desired consistency. Sprinkle with green onions.

1 Serving: Calories 580; Total Fat 39g (Saturated Fat 14g, Trans Fat 0g); Cholesterol 155mg; Sodium 870mg; Total Carbohydrate 20g (Dietary Fiber 0g) **Exchanges:** 1 Starch, 1 Vegetable, 4 High-Fat Meat, 1½ Fat **Carbohydrate Choices:** 1

budget smart

"These ribs get a double-cooking for twice the flavor. Loin back ribs are a good deal less expensive than baby back ribs or country-style ribs, and they benefit from long, slow cooking. Serve these with potato salad and a green vegetable."

$2.53
per serving

Asian Hoisin Ribs

Prep Time: **10 Minutes** || Start to Finish: **8 Hours 10 Minutes** || **4 Servings**

3 lbs pork bone-in country-style ribs

1 medium onion, sliced

½ cup hoisin sauce

⅓ cup seasoned rice vinegar

¼ cup soy sauce

1 tablespoon grated gingerroot or 1 teaspoon ground ginger

2 teaspoons sesame oil, if desired

Fresh cilantro leaves, if desired

1 Place ribs in 3½- to 4-quart slow cooker. Cover with onion slices. In small bowl, mix remaining ingredients except cilantro; pour over ribs and onion.

2 Cover and cook on Low heat setting 8 to 10 hours or until ribs are tender.

3 Remove ribs to serving platter; keep warm. Skim fat from surface of juices in cooker. Serve ribs with sauce; sprinkle with cilantro.

1 Serving: Calories 450; Total Fat 23g (Saturated Fat 8g, Trans Fat 0); Cholesterol 120mg; Sodium 1490mg; Total Carbohydrate 18g (Dietary Fiber 1g) **Exchanges:** 1 Other Carbohydrate, 6 Lean Meat, 1 Fat **Carbohydrate Choices:** 1

Simple Swaps: The sesame oil adds a nice subtle sesame flavor to the ribs. However, if you don't have sesame oil, sprinkle the ribs with toasted sesame seed (page 34) before serving.

budget smart

"Hoisin sauce is available bottled in the Asian aisle of most supermarkets, as is sesame oil. Country-style ribs are the meatiest ribs of all, and they are often on sale."

$3.74
per serving

Ham and Wild Rice Soup

Prep Time: **10 Minutes** || Start to Finish: **8 Hours 25 Minutes** || **8 Servings (1 cup each)**

2 cups diced cooked ham

³/₄ cup uncooked wild rice

1 medium onion, chopped
(¹/₂ cup)

1 bag (12 oz) frozen mixed
vegetables, thawed, drained

1 can (14 oz) chicken broth

★ 1 can (10³/₄ oz) cream of celery
soup

¹/₄ teaspoon pepper

3 cups water

¹/₂ cup half-and-half

1 In 3- to 4-quart slow cooker, mix all ingredients except half-and-half.

2 Cover; cook on Low heat setting 8 to 9 hours.

3 Stir in half-and-half. Increase heat setting to High. Cover; cook 10 to 15 minutes longer or until hot.

1 Serving: Calories 210; Total Fat 6g (Saturated Fat 2.5g, Trans Fat 0g); Cholesterol 25mg; Sodium 920mg; Total Carbohydrate 25g (Dietary Fiber 4g) **Exchanges:** 1¹/₂ Starch, 1 Vegetable, 1 Lean Meat, ¹/₂ Fat **Carbohydrate Choices:** 1¹/₂

budget smart

"Rich and creamy, with the nutty flavor of wild rice, this soup would make the perfect dinner appetizer or weekend lunch."

★ **Best Budget Picks** (for more uses, see pages 314–15)

$1.33
per serving

Barbecued Beans and Polish Sausage

Prep Time: **10 Minutes** || Start to Finish: **5 Hours 10 Minutes** || **6 Servings**

★ **2 cans (15 to 16 oz each) great northern beans, rinsed, drained**

★ **2 cans (15 oz each) black beans, rinsed, drained**

1 large onion, chopped (1 cup)

1 cup barbecue sauce

¼ cup packed brown sugar

1 tablespoon ground mustard

1 tablespoon Worcestershire sauce

2 teaspoons chili powder

1 ring (1 to 1¼ lbs) fully cooked smoked Polish sausage

1 Spray 3- to 4-quart slow cooker with cooking spray. Mix all ingredients except sausage in cooker. Place sausage ring on bean mixture.

2 Cover and cook on Low heat setting 5 to 6 hours.

1 Serving: Calories 750; Total Fat 23g (Saturated Fat 8g, Trans Fat 0.5g); Cholesterol 45mg; Sodium 1740mg; Total Carbohydrate 102g (Dietary Fiber 19g) **Exchanges:** 7 Starch, 1½ Medium-Fat Meat **Carbohydrate Choices:** 7

budget smart

" This bean-and-sausage pot can be prepped in the time it takes the kids to get ready for school. The hearty flavors of the smoked Polish sausage, also called kielbasa, infuse the beans in this low-cost dish. "

$1.06 per serving

★ **Best Budget Picks** (for more uses, see pages 314–15)

Mixed-Bean and Sausage Minestrone

Prep Time: **25 Minutes** || Start to Finish: **9 Hours 55 Minutes** || **8 Servings (1¾ cups each)**

1 package (20 oz) 15-dried-bean soup mix, sorted, rinsed

8 cups water

12 oz bulk Italian sausage

1 medium onion, chopped (½ cup)

2 medium carrots, chopped (1 cup)

2 cans (14 oz each) beef broth

2 cups water

★ 2 cans (14.5 oz each) Italian-style stewed tomatoes, undrained, large pieces cut up

½ cup uncooked small pasta shells

¼ cup shredded Parmesan cheese

2 tablespoons chopped fresh parsley

1 If bean soup mix comes with seasoning mix, save for another use. In 4-quart saucepan, heat beans and 8 cups water to boiling; reduce heat to low. Simmer uncovered 10 minutes; remove from heat. Cover and let stand 1 hour.

2 In 10-inch nonstick skillet, cook sausage and onion over medium heat, stirring occasionally, until sausage is no longer pink; drain if necessary.

3 Drain beans and discard water. In 5- to 6-quart slow cooker, mix beans, sausage mixture, carrots, broth and 2 cups water.

4 Cover and cook on Low heat setting 8 to 9 hours.

5 Stir in tomatoes and pasta. Increase heat setting to High. Cover and cook about 30 minutes longer or until pasta is tender. Sprinkle individual servings with cheese and parsley.

1 Serving: Calories 440; Total Fat 10g (Saturated Fat 3.5g, Trans Fat 0g); Cholesterol 25mg; Sodium 1400mg; Total Carbohydrate 64g (Dietary Fiber 9g) **Exchanges:** 4 Starch, 1 Vegetable, 1 Lean Meat **Carbohydrate Choices:** 4

budget smart

"If you see bulk sausage on sale, pick up more than you need and freeze some in small portions for future recipes."

$1.26 per serving

Creole Jambalaya

Prep Time: **10 Minutes** || Start to Finish: **7 Hours 40 Minutes** || **4 Servings (about 1 cup each)**

2 medium stalks celery, chopped (1 cup)

4 cloves garlic, finely chopped

★ 2 cans (14.5 oz each) diced tomatoes with green pepper and onion, undrained

½ cup chopped fully cooked smoked sausage

½ teaspoon dried thyme leaves

¼ teaspoon pepper

¼ teaspoon red pepper sauce

12 oz uncooked deveined peeled medium (26 to 30 count) shrimp, thawed if frozen, tail shells removed

⅔ cup uncooked long-grain white rice

1⅓ cups water

1 In 3- to 3½-quart slow cooker, mix all ingredients except shrimp, rice and water.

2 Cover; cook on Low heat setting 7 to 8 hours or until vegetables are tender.

3 Stir in shrimp. Cover; cook on Low heat setting about 30 minutes longer or until shrimp are pink. Meanwhile, cook rice in water as directed on package, omitting butter and salt. Serve jambalaya with rice.

1 Serving: Calories 300; Total Fat 6g (Saturated Fat 2g, Trans Fat 0g); Cholesterol 130mg; Sodium 910mg; Total Carbohydrate 43g (Dietary Fiber 3g)**Exchanges:** 1½ Starch, 1 Other Carbohydrate, 1 Vegetable, 2 Lean Meat **Carbohydrate Choices:** 3

budget smart

" You don't have to wait till Fat Tuesday (Mardi Gras) to cook this fabulous jambalaya. For the most authentic stew, try to find cooked Cajun andouille sausage, generally available in large supermarkets. Any extra sausage will keep very well, refrigerated, for snacking purposes, or chop and mix it with scrambled eggs. "

★ **Best Budget Picks** (for more uses, see pages 314–15)

$3.26
per serving

Mediterranean Bulgur and Lentils

Prep Time: **15 Minutes** || Start to Finish: **3 Hours 30 Minutes** || **8 Servings**

1 cup uncooked bulgur wheat or cracked wheat

1/2 cup dried lentils, sorted, rinsed

1 teaspoon ground cumin

1/4 teaspoon salt

3 cloves garlic, finely chopped

1 can (15.25 oz) whole kernel corn, drained

2 cans (14 oz each) vegetable or chicken broth

2 medium tomatoes, chopped (1 1/2 cups)

1/2 cup drained pitted kalamata olives

1 cup crumbled reduced-fat Feta cheese (4 oz)

1 In 3- to 4-quart slow cooker, mix all ingredients except tomatoes, olives and cheese.

2 Cover; cook on Low heat setting 3 to 4 hours or until lentils are tender.

3 Stir in tomatoes and olives. Increase heat setting to High. Cover; cook 15 minutes longer. Top with cheese.

1 Serving: Calories 210; Total Fat 4g (Saturated Fat 1.5g, Trans Fat 0g); Cholesterol 0mg; Sodium 880mg; Total Carbohydrate 33g (Dietary Fiber 7g) **Exchanges:** 2 Starch, 1/2 Very Lean Meat, 1/2 Fat **Carbohydrate Choices:** 2

budget smart

" Bulgur—wheat kernels that have been boiled, dried, and crushed—and lentils are an integral and beloved part of the Mediterranean and Middle Eastern cooking. Both are fairly inexpensive, but yield a vegetarian stew that's toothsome and hearty. "

$1.68
per serving

Zesty Black Bean Soup

Prep Time: **25 Minutes** || Start to Finish: **11 Hours 25 Minutes** || **9 Servings**

★ **2 cups dried black beans (1 lb), sorted, rinsed**

10 cups water

8 cups vegetable broth

★ **2 cans (14.5 oz each) diced tomatoes with green chiles, undrained**

2 medium carrots, coarsely chopped (1 cup)

2 medium onions, coarsely chopped (1 cup)

¼ cup chopped fresh cilantro

2 teaspoons finely chopped garlic

1 teaspoon salt

¼ teaspoon pepper

⅛ teaspoon ground red pepper (cayenne)

Sour cream, if desired

Chopped fresh cilantro, if desired

1 In 4-quart Dutch oven, heat beans and water to boiling; reduce heat. Simmer uncovered 10 minutes; remove from heat. Cover and let stand 1 hour.

2 Drain beans. In 6-quart slow cooker, place beans and remaining ingredients except sour cream and cilantro.

3 Cover and cook on Low heat setting 10 to 12 hours.

4 Serve soup topped with sour cream and cilantro.

1 Serving: Calories 175; Total Fat 1g (Saturated Fat 0g, Trans Fat 0g); Cholesterol 0mg; Sodium 1410mg; Total Carbohydrate 40g (Dietary Fiber 8g) **Exchanges:** 2 Starch, 1 Vegetable **Carbohydrate Choices:** 2½

budget smart

" Dried beans are often much less expensive than canned, but they need to cook a long time. This makes them perfect for the slow cooker since you don't have to be around while they cook. "

★ **Best Budget Picks** (for more uses, see pages 314–15)

$1.22
per serving

Three-Bean Beer Pot

Prep Time: **20 Minutes** || Start to Finish: **4 Hours 20 Minutes** || **16 Servings** (¹/₂ cup each)

8 slices uncooked bacon, cut into small pieces

1 large onion, chopped (1 cup)

1 cup barbecue sauce

³/₄ cup regular or nonalcoholic dark beer

¹/₄ cup packed brown sugar

★ 2 cans (15 oz each) black beans, drained, rinsed

★ 2 cans (15 oz each) pinto beans, drained

★ 1 can (19 oz) cannellini beans, drained

1 In 10-inch skillet, cook bacon and onion over medium heat 7 to 10 minutes, stirring occasionally, until bacon is crisp; drain.

2 Spray 3- to 4-quart slow cooker with cooking spray. In cooker, place bacon mixture and remaining ingredients; mix well.

3 Cover; cook on Low heat setting 4 to 6 hours.

1 Serving: Calories 270; Total Fat 2.5g (Saturated Fat 0.5g, Trans Fat 0g); Cholesterol 0mg; Sodium 650mg; Total Carbohydrate 47g (Dietary Fiber 13g) **Exchanges:** 2 Starch, 1 Other Carbohydrate, 1 Lean Meat **Carbohydrate Choices:** 3

budget smart

"Sometimes it only takes a little meat to flavor a huge pot of beans, which helps keep the cost per serving small but the flavor big. The dark beer and sugar give the beans a wonderful caramel flavor that will make these the hit of your next outdoor potluck."

45¢ per serving

★ **Best Budget Picks** (for more uses, see pages 314–15)

Lentil Soup

Prep Time: **15 Minutes** || Start to Finish: **8 Hours 15 Minutes** || **8 Servings**

1 lb smoked ham shanks

8 cups chicken broth

1 package (16 oz) dried lentils (2¼ cups), sorted, rinsed

4 medium stalks celery, chopped (2 cups)

4 medium carrots, chopped (2 cups)

3 tablespoons chopped fresh parsley

3 cloves garlic, finely chopped

2 cups shredded fresh spinach

1 In 5- to 6-quart slow cooker, mix all ingredients except spinach.

2 Cover and cook on Low heat setting 8 to 9 hours or until lentils are tender.

3 Remove ham from cooker; place on cutting board. Pull meat from bones, using 2 forks; discard bones and skin. Stir ham and spinach into soup. Stir well before serving.

1 Serving: Calories 205; Total Fat 3g (Saturated Fat 1g, Trans Fat 0g); Cholesterol 5mg; Sodium 810mg; Total Carbohydrate 37g (Dietary Fiber 14g) **Exchanges:** 2 Starch, 1 Vegetable, 1 Very Lean Meat **Carbohydrate Choices:** 2½

budget smart

" This classic, rustic soup is easy on the wallet and healthy to boot. If you don't have the spinach, it's fine to omit. "

$2.12 per serving

CHAPTER 7

Budget
Bisquick Recipes

A Quick Crispy Coating

Bisquick mix is the perfect pantry staple to turn to whenever you need a crispy coating for chicken, fish and pork chops. This basic coating is ready in less than 5 minutes.

MIX

$2/3$ **cup Original Bisquick mix**

1$^1/_2$ **teaspoons paprika**

1 teaspoon salt

$^1/_4$ **teaspoon pepper**

COAT

2$^1/_2$ **to 3$^1/_2$ lb cut-up chicken or**

1 lb fish fillets or

1$^1/_4$ **to 1$^1/_2$ lb pork chops,**
    $^1/_2$ **to $^1/_4$ inch thick**

Melt 1 tablespoon butter or margarine in 13×9-inch (3-quart) glass baking dish.

Chicken: Bake 50 minutes, skin sides down, turning chicken after 35 minutes, until juice of chicken is clear when thickest piece is cut to bone (170°F for breasts; 180°F for thighs and drumsticks).

Fish: Bake 25 to 30 minutes or until fish flakes easily with a fork.

Pork: Bake 50 minutes, turning pork chops after 25 minutes, until no longer pink in center. (For pork chops that are $^3/_4$ inch thick, bake until pork is no longer pink and meat thermometer inserted in center reads 160°F.)

Very Veggie Pizza Pie

Prep Time: **15 Minutes** || Start to Finish: **40 Minutes** || **8 Servings**

1 package (8 oz) sliced
    mushrooms (3 cups)

1 small zucchini, sliced (1 cup)

1 medium bell pepper, sliced

1 clove garlic, finely chopped

2 cups Bisquick Heart Smart®
    mix

$1/4$ cup process cheese sauce or
    spread (room temperature)

$1/4$ cup very hot water

$1/2$ cup pizza sauce

$3/4$ cup shredded reduced-fat
    mozzarella cheese (3 oz)

1 Heat oven to 375°F. Spray cookie sheet with cooking spray. Spray 10-inch skillet with cooking spray; heat over medium-high heat. In skillet, cook mushrooms, zucchini, bell pepper and garlic about 5 minutes, stirring occasionally, until vegetables are crisp-tender.

2 In medium bowl, stir Bisquick mix, cheese sauce and hot water until soft dough forms. Place dough on surface sprinkled with Bisquick mix; roll in Bisquick mix to coat. Shape into a ball; knead about 5 times or until smooth. Roll or pat dough into 14-inch circle on cookie sheet. Spread pizza sauce over dough to within 3 inches of edge. Top with vegetable mixture. Sprinkle with cheese. Fold edge of dough over mixture.

3 Bake 23 to 25 minutes or until crust is golden brown and cheese is bubbly.

1 Serving: Calories 180; Total Fat 6g (Saturated Fat 2.5g, Trans Fat 0); Cholesterol 10mg; Sodium 470mg; Total Carbohydrate 25g (Dietary Fiber 1g) **Exchanges:** $1/2$ Starch, 1 Vegetable, 1 Fat **Carbohydrate Choices:** $1/2$

budget smart

" If you're having a party, this recipe is very easy to double, and it costs a lot less than sending out for pizza! It's almost as fast, too, thanks to dough that comes together in just a few minutes. This veggie version also helps keeps the cost down, but feel free to throw on some pepperoni or leftover cooked meat if you like. "

$1.09
per serving

Pizza Biscuit Bake

Prep Time: **15 Minutes** || Start to Finish: **40 Minutes** || **8 Servings**

3⅓ cups Original Bisquick® mix

1 cup milk

2 cans (8 oz each) pizza sauce

1 package (8 oz) sliced pepperoni

2 cups shredded mozzarella cheese (8 oz)

1 Heat oven to 375°F. Spray 13×9-inch (3-quart) glass baking dish with cooking spray. In medium bowl, stir Bisquick mix and milk until soft dough forms.

2 Drop half of dough by spoonfuls evenly over bottom of baking dish (dough will not completely cover bottom of dish). Drizzle 1 can pizza sauce over dough. Scatter half of the pepperoni over sauce. Top with 1 cup of the cheese. Repeat layers with remaining dough, pizza sauce, pepperoni and cheese.

3 Bake 20 to 25 minutes or until golden brown.

1 Serving: Calories 450; Total Fat 24g (Saturated Fat 10g, Trans Fat 2g); Cholesterol 50mg; Sodium 1530mg; Total Carbohydrate 41g (Dietary Fiber 2g) **Exchanges:** 2 Starch, ½ Other Carbohydrate, 2 High-Fat Meat, 1½ Fat **Carbohydrate Choices:** 3

budget smart

An unusual and economical spin on pizza, you can't beat this five-ingredient deep-dish crowd pleaser for its convenience (no rolling needed!). Feel free to add your favorite pizza toppings to the filling: Try crumbled cooked sausage, sliced green bell pepper, onion or olives.

$1.26
per serving

Oven-Baked Chicken

Prep Time: **10 Minutes** ‖ Start to Finish: **1 Hour** ‖ **5 Servings**

1 tablespoon butter or margarine

²/₃ cup **Original Bisquick mix**

1½ teaspoons paprika

1 teaspoon salt or garlic salt

1 teaspoon Italian seasoning, if desired

¼ teaspoon pepper

1 cut-up whole chicken (3 to 3½ lb)

1 Heat oven to 425°F. In 13×9-inch (3-quart) glass baking dish, melt butter in oven.

2 In medium bowl, stir together Bisquick mix, paprika, salt, Italian seasoning and pepper. Coat chicken with Bisquick mixture. Place skin side down in heated dish.

3 Bake 35 minutes. Turn chicken; bake about 15 minutes longer or until juice of chicken is clear when thickest piece is cut to bone (170°F for breasts; 180°F for thighs and drumsticks).

1 Serving: Calories 360; Total Fat 20g (Saturated Fat 7g, Trans Fat 1g); Cholesterol 110mg; Sodium 780mg; Total Carbohydrate 11g (Dietary Fiber 0g) **Exchanges:** ½ Starch, 4½ Lean Meat, 1½ Fat **Carbohydrate Choices:** 1

budget smart

"Just like fried chicken but lighter and less messy, this is sure to become a household favorite. If you love dark meat and see chicken drumsticks or thighs on sale, snap them up and use them instead of a whole cut-up chicken. The baked chicken can be served hot, room temperature or cold, and it's a very welcome leftover!"

$1.17 per serving

★ **Best Budget Picks** (for more uses, see pages 314–15)

Mustardy Chicken and Dumplings

Prep Time: **15 Minutes** ‖ Start to Finish: **35 Minutes** ‖ **6 Servings**

1 tablespoon vegetable oil

★ 4 boneless skinless chicken breasts (about 1¼ lb), cut into bite-size pieces

1 medium onion, chopped (½ cup)

2 cups milk

2 cups frozen mixed vegetables

★ 1 can (10¾ oz) condensed cream of chicken soup

1 tablespoon yellow mustard

1½ cups Original Bisquick mix

1 In 4-quart Dutch oven, heat oil over medium-high heat. Cook chicken and onion in oil 6 to 8 minutes, stirring occasionally, until chicken is no longer pink in center and onion is tender.

2 Stir in 1½ cups of the milk, the mixed vegetables, soup and mustard. Heat to boiling.

3 In small bowl, stir Bisquick mix and remaining ½ cup milk until soft dough forms. Drop dough by 6 spoonfuls onto chicken mixture; reduce heat to low. Cover; cook 20 minutes.

1 Serving: Calories 390; Total Fat 15g (Saturated Fat 4g, Trans Fat 1g); Cholesterol 65mg; Sodium 930mg; Total Carbohydrate 36g (Dietary Fiber 3g) **Exchanges:** 2 Starch, ½ Other Carbohydrate, 3 Very Lean Meat, 2½ Fat **Carbohydrate Choices:** 2½

budget smart

❝ To make this zesty one-dish meal zestier, add another teaspoon of mustard. ❞

$1.62 per serving

Sweet-and-Sour Chicken Stir-Fry

Prep Time: **30 Minutes** || Start to Finish: **30 Minutes** || **6 Servings (1¼ cups each)**

1 cup Original Bisquick mix

½ teaspoon pepper

2 eggs

★ **1 lb boneless skinless chicken breasts, cut into 1-inch cubes**

¼ cup vegetable oil

3 medium carrots, cut diagonally into ¼-inch slices (1½ cups)

1 medium green bell pepper, cut into strips (1 cup)

1 small onion, thinly sliced, separated into rings (⅓ cup)

1 can (20 oz) pineapple chunks, drained

½ cup sweet-and-sour sauce

1 In large resealable food-storage plastic bag, mix Bisquick mix and pepper.

2 In medium bowl, beat eggs slightly. Stir in chicken until combined. Using slotted spoon, remove chicken from eggs; place in bag with Bisquick mix. Seal bag; shake until chicken is coated.

3 In 12-inch skillet, heat 1 tablespoon of the oil over medium-high heat. Add carrots; cook 2 minutes, stirring frequently. Add bell pepper and onion; cook 2 minutes longer, stirring frequently. Remove from skillet.

4 In same skillet, heat remaining oil. Add chicken; cook, stirring frequently, until golden brown on outside and no longer pink in center. Add vegetables; cook about 2 minutes, stirring frequently, until thoroughly heated. Stir in pineapple and sweet-and-sour sauce; cook until thoroughly heated.

1 Serving: Calories 370; Total Fat 16g (Saturated Fat 3.5g, Trans Fat 1g); Cholesterol 115mg; Sodium 410mg; Total Carbohydrate 34g (Dietary Fiber 3g) **Exchanges:** ½ Starch, 1½ Other Carbohydrate, 1 Vegetable, 2½ Very Lean Meat, 3 Fat **Carbohydrate Choices:** 2

budget smart

" This is like making your own Chinese takeout, but it's a lot less expensive (and tastier too!). Serve it over steamed white rice. You'll find sweet-and-sour sauce in the Asian aisle of most supermarkets. "

$1.77
per serving

Chicken Cutlets with Creamy Mushroom Gravy

Prep Time: **30 Minutes** || Start to Finish: **30 Minutes** || **4 Servings**

★ **4 boneless skinless chicken breasts (about 4 oz each)**

¹/₂ cup Original Bisquick mix

¹/₂ teaspoon garlic powder

1 egg

3 tablespoons vegetable oil

1¹/₂ cups sliced fresh mushrooms

3 tablespoons Original Bisquick mix

2 medium green onions, sliced (2 tablespoons)

1 cup milk

1¹/₂ teaspoons soy sauce

1 Between pieces of plastic wrap or waxed paper, place each chicken breast smooth side down; gently pound with flat side of meat mallet or rolling pin until about ¼ inch thick.

2 In shallow dish, stir ½ cup Bisquick mix and the garlic powder. In another shallow dish, beat egg. Dip chicken in egg, then coat with Bisquick mixture.

3 In 12-inch nonstick skillet, heat 2 tablespoons of the oil over medium heat. Add chicken. Cook about 3 minutes or until golden brown. Turn chicken; cover and cook 4 to 6 minutes longer or until chicken is no longer pink in center. Remove to serving platter; cover to keep warm.

4 In same skillet, heat remaining 1 tablespoon oil over medium heat. Add mushrooms; cook 3 to 4 minutes, stirring frequently, until browned. Add 3 tablespoons Bisquick mix and the onions; cook and stir until mixed. Stir in milk and soy sauce. Cook until mixture is thick and bubbly. Serve over chicken.

1 Serving: Calories 370; Total Fat 19g (Saturated Fat 4.5g, Trans Fat 1g); Cholesterol 125mg; Sodium 470mg; Total Carbohydrate 18g (Dietary Fiber 0g) **Exchanges:** ¹/₂ Starch, ¹/₂ Other Carbohydrate, 4 Very Lean Meat, 3¹/₂ Fat **Carbohydrate Choices:** 1

budget smart

❝ With this easy weeknight entrée, all you need for a complete dinner is a simple salad for four. If you don't have a meat mallet or rolling pin, pound down the chicken with the bottom of a saucepan or skillet. ❞

$1.75 per serving

★ **Best Budget Picks** (for more uses, see pages 314–15)

Italian Chicken Fingers

Prep Time: **20 Minutes** || Start to Finish: **40 Minutes** || **4 Servings**

1 egg

1 package (14 oz) uncooked chicken breast tenders (not breaded)

1¼ cups Original Bisquick mix

1 teaspoon Italian seasoning

3 tablespoons butter or margarine, melted

1 cup tomato pasta sauce, heated

1 Heat oven to 450°F. Spray 15×10×1-inch pan with cooking spray. In medium bowl, beat egg slightly. Add chicken; toss to coat.

2 In resealable food-storage plastic bag, place Bisquick mix and Italian seasoning; seal bag and shake to mix. Add chicken; seal bag and shake to coat chicken with Bisquick mixture. Place chicken in single layer in pan. Drizzle with butter.

3 Bake 14 to 16 minutes, turning chicken after 6 minutes, until chicken is brown and crisp on the outside and no longer pink in center. Serve with pasta sauce for dipping.

1 Serving: Calories 410; Total Fat 17g (Saturated Fat 8g, Trans Fat 2g); Cholesterol 120mg; Sodium 950mg; Total Carbohydrate 36g (Dietary Fiber 2g) **Exchanges:** 1½ Starch, 1 Other Carbohydrate, 3 Lean Meat, 1½ Fat **Carbohydrate Choices:** 2½

budget smart

"Dine out at home with Italian-style oven-baked chicken fingers, served with warm tomato dipping sauce! Trim costs further by preparing your own chicken breast tenders from uncooked boneless skinless chicken breasts; just slice them lengthwise into strips about 1¼ inches wide and proceed with the recipe."

91¢
per serving

Easy Chicken Pot Pie

Prep Time: **10 Minutes** || Start to Finish: **40 Minutes** || **6 Servings**

1 bag (12 oz) frozen mixed
   vegetables, thawed, drained

1 cup diced cooked chicken

★ 1 can (10¾ oz) condensed
   cream of chicken soup

1 cup Original Bisquick mix

½ cup milk

1 egg

1 Heat oven to 400°F. In ungreased 2-quart casserole, mix vegetables, chicken and soup until blended.

2 In medium bowl, stir all remaining ingredients with wire whisk or fork until blended. Pour over chicken mixture.

3 Bake uncovered about 30 minutes or until crust is golden brown.

1 Serving: Calories 240; Total Fat 9g (Saturated Fat 3g, Trans Fat 1g); Cholesterol 60mg; Sodium 670mg; Total Carbohydrate 28g (Dietary Fiber 4g) **Exchanges:** 1½ Starch, 1 Vegetable, 1 Lean Meat, 1 Fat **Carbohydrate Choices:** 2

budget smart

" Use what you've got in this incredibly easy chicken pot pie casserole. Condensed cream of mushroom soup is a fine substitute if that's what's in your pantry. Need to use up leftover vegetables? Swap them for the frozen vegetables. And if you don't have leftover cooked chicken, you can make some up in a jiffy and freeze the extras—see page 9. "

★ **Best Budget Picks** (for more uses, see pages 314–15)

86¢
per serving

Chicken-Veggie Casserole

Prep Time: **20 Minutes** || Start to Finish: **45 Minutes** || **6 Servings**

★ **1 can (10³/₄ oz) condensed Cheddar cheese soup**

1 cup milk

2 tablespoons dried minced onion

2 cups frozen mixed vegetables, thawed, drained

1¹/₂ cups cut-up cooked chicken

2 cups Original Bisquick mix

¹/₄ cup sliced green onions

2 tablespoons mayonnaise or salad dressing

1 egg

1 Heat oven to 400°F. In 3-quart saucepan, heat soup, milk and dried minced onion to boiling, stirring constantly. Stir in vegetables and chicken. Pour into ungreased 11×7-inch (2-quart) glass baking dish.

2 In medium bowl, mix all remaining ingredients with fork until crumbly. Sprinkle over chicken mixture.

3 Bake uncovered about 25 minutes or until topping is golden brown and soup is bubbly.

1 Serving: Calories 400; Total Fat 17g (Saturated Fat 5g, Trans Fat 2g); Cholesterol 80mg; Sodium 1050mg; Total Carbohydrate 42g (Dietary Fiber 4g) **Exchanges:** 2¹/₂ Starch, ¹/₂ Other Carbohydrate, 1¹/₂ Lean Meat, 2 Fat **Carbohydrate Choices:** 3

budget smart

"Green onions give a nice edge to the flavors in this delightful cheesy casserole. This is a great "use up your leftovers dish": Whether you've got leftover cooked chicken or vegetables (or both) in your fridge, use them in this recipe. Save even more by purchasing the condensed Cheddar cheese soup in large quantity; then try another recipe that calls for it, Cheddar Cheese and Broccoli Soup (page 229)."

★ **Best Budget Picks** (for more uses, see pages 314–15)

$1.23
per serving

Easy Turkey Club Bake

Prep Time: **10 Minutes** || Start to Finish: **30 Minutes** || **6 Servings**

2 cups Original Bisquick mix

¹⁄₃ cup mayonnaise or salad dressing

¹⁄₃ cup milk

2 cups cubed cooked turkey

2 medium green onions, sliced (2 tablespooons)

6 slices bacon, crisply cooked, crumbled

¹⁄₄ cup mayonnaise or salad dressing

1 large tomato, chopped (1 cup)

1 cup shredded Colby–Monterey Jack cheese (4 oz)

1 Heat oven to 450°F. Spray cookie sheet with cooking spray. In medium bowl, stir Bisquick mix, ⅓ cup mayonnaise and the milk until soft dough forms. On cookie sheet, press dough into 12×8-inch rectangle.

2 Bake 8 to 10 minutes or until crust is golden brown.

3 In medium bowl, mix turkey, onions, bacon and ¼ cup mayonnaise. Spoon over crust to within ¼ inch of edges. Sprinkle with tomato and cheese.

4 Bake about 5 minutes or until mixture is hot and cheese is melted.

1 Serving: Calories 530; Total Fat 35g (Saturated Fat 10g, Trans Fat 2g); Cholesterol 75mg; Sodium 950mg; Total Carbohydrate 29g (Dietary Fiber 1g) **Exchanges:** 1 Starch, 1 Other Carbohydrate, 3 Lean Meat, 5 Fat **Carbohydrate Choices:** 2

budget smart

"Your freezer can save you a lot of money! Take bacon, for example. It's great to have on hand, but you don't always need to use a whole package. So freeze any remaining strips on a cookie sheet till frozen, then store in a plastic freezer storage bag. That way, you can take out and defrost the exact number of strips you need, whenever you need them."

Impossibly Easy Taco Pie

Prep Time: **15 Minutes** || Start to Finish: **50 Minutes** || **6 Servings**

1 lb ground turkey breast

1 medium onion, chopped
(½ cup)

1 package (1 oz) taco seasoning
mix

1 can (4.5 oz) chopped green
chiles, undrained

½ cup Original Bisquick mix

1 cup milk

2 eggs

½ cup shredded Colby-
Monterey Jack cheese blend
(2 oz)

1 medium tomato, chopped
(¾ cup)

1½ cups shredded lettuce

2 medium green onions, sliced
(2 tablespoons), if desired

1 Heat oven to 400°F. Spray 9-inch glass pie plate with cooking spray.

2 In 10-inch skillet, cook turkey and onion over medium-high heat 5 to 7 minutes, stirring occasionally, until turkey is no longer pink. Stir in taco seasoning mix. Spread in pie plate. Top evenly with chiles.

3 In medium bowl, stir Bisquick mix, milk and eggs with wire whisk or fork until blended. Pour into pie plate.

4 Bake 25 minutes. Top with cheese and tomato. Bake 2 to 3 minutes longer or until cheese is melted. Let stand 5 minutes before serving. Sprinkle with lettuce and green onions.

1 Serving: Calories 250; Total Fat 11g (Saturated Fat 4.5g, Trans Fat 0.5g); Cholesterol 135mg; Sodium 880mg; Total Carbohydrate 15g (Dietary Fiber 1g); **Exchanges:** ½ Starch, ½ Other Carbohydrate, 3 Lean Meat, ½ Fat **Carbohydrate Choices:** 1

Impossibly Easy Beef Taco Pie: Substitute 1 lb lean (at least 80%) ground beef for the turkey, cooking until beef is thoroughly cooked. Drain before stirring in taco seasoning mix.

budget smart

" This easy pie gives you all those wonderful Tex-Mex flavors with half the work of regular tacos—and no pricey taco shells to pay for! The pie is also much easier to eat. If your crowd likes spicy food, pass a small bowl of chopped, stemmed and seeded jalapeño chiles at the table. And a bowl of baked tortilla chips would surely be welcome. "

$1.49
per serving

★ **Best Budget Picks** (for more uses, see pages 314-15)

Impossibly Easy Cheeseburger Pie

Prep Time: **15 Minutes** || Start to Finish: **40 Minutes** || **6 Servings**

★ **1 lb lean (at least 80%) ground beef**

1 large onion, chopped (1 cup)

¹⁄₂ teaspoon salt

1 cup shredded Cheddar cheese (4 oz)

¹⁄₂ cup Original Bisquick mix

1 cup milk

2 eggs

1 Heat oven to 400°F. Spray 9-inch glass pie plate with cooking spray.

2 In 10-inch skillet, cook beef and onion over medium-high heat 5 to 7 minutes, stirring occasionally, until beef is thoroughly cooked; drain. Stir in salt. Spread in pie plate. Sprinkle with cheese.

3 In medium bowl, stir remaining ingredients with wire whisk or fork until blended. Pour into pie plate.

4 Bake about 25 minutes or until knife inserted in center comes out clean.

1 Serving: Calories 300; Total Fat 19g (Saturated Fat 9g, Trans Fat 1g); Cholesterol 140mg; Sodium 510mg; Total Carbohydrate 11g (Dietary Fiber 0g) **Exchanges:** ¹⁄₂ Starch, 3 Medium-Fat Meat, 1 Fat **Carbohydrate Choices:** 1

budget smart

"This is one of the most-requested Bisquick recipes of all time! It's a big hit with kids and a very tasty way to stretch a pound of ground beef to serve six. Serve with a salad or oven fries—and don't forget the ketchup!"

88¢ per serving

Beef and Peppers with Cheese Biscuits

Prep Time: **20 Minutes** || Start to Finish: **30 Minutes** || **6 Servings**

1³⁄₄ cups Original Bisquick mix

¹⁄₂ cup milk

¹⁄₂ cup shredded Swiss or provolone cheese (2 oz)

★ 1 can (10.75 oz) condensed French onion soup

2 packages (5 oz each) deli-style sliced cooked beef, cut into thin strips

2 small bell peppers, sliced

¹⁄₂ teaspoon garlic-pepper blend

1¹⁄₃ cups water

¹⁄₃ cup all-purpose flour

1 Heat oven to 450°F. In medium bowl, stir Bisquick mix, milk and cheese until soft dough forms; beat 20 strokes. Place dough on surface generously sprinkled with Bisquick mix; gently roll in Bisquick mix to coat. Shape into a ball; knead 10 times.

2 Press or roll dough until ¼ inch thick. With 3-inch round cutter, cut into 6 biscuits. On ungreased cookie sheet, place biscuits.

3 Bake 6 to 8 minutes or until golden brown.

4 Meanwhile, in 2-quart saucepan, mix soup, beef, bell peppers, garlic-pepper blend and 1 cup of the water. Heat to boiling over medium-high heat. Reduce heat to medium-low. In small bowl, stir remaining ¹⁄₃ cup water and the flour until mixed; stir into beef mixture. Heat to boiling, stirring frequently, until thickened.

5 Split biscuits. Serve beef mixture over biscuits.

1 Serving: Calories 300; Total Fat 10g (Saturated Fat 4g, Trans Fat 1.5g); Cholesterol 35mg; Sodium 1340mg; Total Carbohydrate 36g (Dietary Fiber 2g) **Exchanges:** 1¹⁄₂ Starch, 1 Other Carbohydrate, 2 Lean Meat, ¹⁄₂ Fat **Carbohydrate Choices:** 2¹⁄₂

budget smart

❝ If you're more of a sliced turkey person than a beef person, you can substitute deli-style sliced cooked turkey for the beef. Making your own biscuits really saves money here, and the recipe is still ready in 30 minutes! ❞

★ **Best Budget Picks** (for more uses, see pages 314–15)

$1.62
per serving

Heart Smart Deluxe Cheeseburger Melt

Prep Time: **15 Minutes** || Start to Finish: **45 Minutes** || **8 Servings**

1⅓ cups Bisquick Heart Smart mix

¼ cup water

½ cup fat-free egg product or 4 egg whites

1½ cups shredded reduced-fat Cheddar cheese (6 oz)

★ 1 lb extra-lean (at least 90%) ground beef

1 can (10.75 oz) condensed 98% fat-free cream of mushroom soup

1 cup frozen mixed vegetables

1 Heat oven to 400°F. Spray 13×9-inch pan with cooking spray. In medium bowl, stir Bisquick mix, water, egg product and 1 cup of the cheese. Spread mixture in pan.

2 In 10-inch skillet, cook beef over medium-high heat 5 to 7 minutes, stirring frequently, until thoroughly cooked; drain. Stir in soup and vegetables; heat until hot. Spread over batter in pan.

3 Bake 23 to 25 minutes or until edges are light golden brown. Sprinkle with remaining ½ cup cheese. Bake 1 to 3 minutes longer or until cheese is melted.

1 Serving: Calories 240; Total Fat 8g (Saturated Fat 3g, Trans Fat 0g); Cholesterol 40mg; Sodium 770mg; Total Carbohydrate 20g (Dietary Fiber 1g) **Exchanges:** 1½ Starch, 2 Lean Meat **Carbohydrate Choices:** 1

Simple Swaps: Substitute ground turkey breast for the extra-lean ground beef.

budget smart

"You don't have to give up delicious dishes to eat heart smart and cheaply, as this recipe proves. It's the perfect dinner solution when you've got staples on hand like condensed cream of mushroom soup and frozen vegetables. Serve the cheeseburger melt with baked potato chips and spinach salad with low-fat dressing."

★ **Best Budget Picks** (for more uses, see pages 314–15)

$1.05
per serving

Creamy Beef Fold-Over Pie

Prep Time: **15 Minutes** || Start to Finish: **55 Minutes** || 6 Servings

★ 1 lb lean (at least 80%) ground beef

1 small onion, chopped (¼ cup)

★ 1 can (10¾ oz) condensed cream of mushroom soup

1½ cups frozen mixed vegetables, thawed

1 tablespoon ketchup

2 cups Original Bisquick mix

½ cup boiling water

¼ cup shredded Cheddar cheese (1 oz)

1 Move oven rack to lowest position. Heat oven to 375°F. Spray 12-inch pizza pan with cooking spray.

2 In 10-inch skillet, cook beef and onion over medium-high heat 5 to 7 minutes, stirring occasionally, until beef is thoroughly cooked; drain. Stir in soup, vegetables and ketchup. Cook 3 to 4 minutes, stirring occasionally, until thoroughly heated.

3 In medium bowl, stir Bisquick mix and boiling water until soft dough forms. Place dough on surface sprinkled with Bisquick mix; gently roll in Bisquick mix to coat. Shape dough into a ball; knead about 5 times or until smooth. Roll dough into 14-inch circle; place on pizza pan.

4 Spoon beef mixture over dough to within 2 inches of edge. Fold edge of dough up over beef mixture. Bake 24 to 27 minutes or until crust is golden brown. Top with cheese. Bake 3 to 4 minutes longer or until cheese is melted. Let stand 5 minutes before cutting.

1 Serving: Calories 390; Total Fat 19g (Saturated Fat 6g, Trans Fat 1.5g); Cholesterol 55mg; Sodium 1030mg; Total Carbohydrate 35g (Dietary Fiber 3g) **Exchanges:** 2 Starch, ½ Other Carbohydrate, 2 Medium-Fat Meat, 1½ Fat **Carbohydrate Choices:** 2

budget smart

"Some may see this fold-over pie as a big-size variation on the Midwestern "pastie," an 800-year-old Cornish pastry that is a full meal baked in a crust. Pasties arrived in Michigan's Upper Peninsula 150 years ago when immigrants came to the area to work the copper and iron mines. Miners needed a portable and substantial lunch, and these pocket-sized pastries filled the bill. This fold-over pie is every bit as economical as those pasties once were, not to mention just as hearty and delicious!"

$1.10 per serving

★ **Best Budget Picks** (for more uses, see pages 314–15)

Italian Beef Bake

Prep Time: **15 Minutes** || Start to Finish: **40 Minutes** || **6 Servings**

★ **1 lb lean (at least 80%) ground beef**

1¼ cups tomato pasta sauce

1 cup shredded mozzarella cheese (4 oz)

2 cups Original Bisquick mix

¾ cup milk

¼ cup grated Parmesan cheese

Additional tomato pasta sauce, warmed, if desired

1 Heat oven to 400°F. Spray 8-inch square (2-quart) glass baking dish with cooking spray.

2 In 10-inch skillet, cook beef over medium-high heat 5 to 7 minutes, stirring occasionally, until thoroughly cooked; drain. Stir in 1¼ cups pasta sauce. Heat to boiling; spoon into baking dish. Top with mozzarella cheese.

3 Meanwhile, in medium bowl, stir Bisquick mix, milk and Parmesan cheese until soft dough forms. Drop dough by 12 tablespoonfuls onto beef mixture.

4 Bake 20 to 24 minutes or until topping is golden brown and toothpick inserted in topping comes out clean. Serve topped with additional warmed pasta sauce.

1 Serving: Calories 440; Total Fat 21g (Saturated Fat 8g, Trans Fat 2g); Cholesterol 65mg; Sodium 960mg; Total Carbohydrate 38g (Dietary Fiber 2g) **Exchanges:** 2 Starch, ½ Other Carbohydrate, 2½ Medium-Fat Meat, 1½ Fat **Carbohydrate Choices:** 2½

$1.13 per serving

budget smart

" This budget-friendly Italian-style casserole is simple, good and easy—a real pantry pleaser. Use whatever tomato pasta sauce you have on hand: And if you've got cooked ground beef stored in the freezer, just thaw it in the microwave and dinner's ready even faster! "

Cowboy Casserole

Prep Time: **15 Minutes** || Start to Finish: **45 Minutes** || **6 Servings**

★ **1 lb lean (at least 80%) ground beef**

★ **1 can (16 oz) baked beans**

$\frac{1}{2}$ **cup barbecue sauce**

2 cups Original Bisquick mix

$\frac{2}{3}$ **cup milk**

1 tablespoon butter or margarine, softened

$\frac{1}{2}$ **cup shredded Cheddar cheese (2 oz)**

1 Heat oven to 425°F. In 10-inch skillet, cook beef over medium-high heat 5 to 7 minutes, stirring frequently, until thoroughly cooked; drain. Stir in baked beans and barbecue sauce. Heat to boiling, stirring occasionally. Pour into ungreased 2-quart casserole.

2 Meanwhile, in medium bowl, stir Bisquick mix, milk and butter until soft dough forms. Drop dough by 12 spoonfuls onto beef mixture.

3 Bake uncovered 18 to 22 minutes or until topping is golden brown. Sprinkle with cheese. Bake about 3 minutes longer or until cheese is melted.

1 Serving: Calories 470; Total Fat 20g (Saturated Fat 8g, Trans Fat 2.5g); Cholesterol 70mg; Sodium 1160mg; Total Carbohydrate 50g (Dietary Fiber 5g) **Exchanges:** 2 Starch, 1$\frac{1}{2}$ Other Carbohydrate, 2$\frac{1}{2}$ Lean Meat, 2 Fat **Carbohydrate Choices:** 3

budget smart

" Are there hungry kids (and picky eaters) who need to be fed in less than an hour? Round 'em up for this sure-to-please chuck wagon casserole! (It's also a great way to use those canned beans that have been lurking in the back of your cupboard.) Vary the topping with any melting type cheese you have on hand, like Monterey Jack, mozzarella or Muenster. Pass additional warmed barbecue sauce around at the table. "

★ **Best Budget Picks** (for more uses, see pages 314-15)

Beef Pot Pie with Potato Crust

Prep Time: **20 Minutes** || Start to Finish: **55 Minutes** || **6 Servings**

1 slice (½ lb) deli roast beef, cubed (1½ cups)

2 cups frozen mixed vegetables

1 medium onion, chopped (½ cup)

1 jar (12 oz) beef gravy

⅔ cup plain mashed potato mix (dry)

⅔ cup hot water

1½ cups Original Bisquick mix

3 tablespoons milk

1 tablespoon freeze-dried chopped chives

1 Heat oven to 375°F. In 2-quart saucepan, heat beef, frozen vegetables, onion and gravy to boiling over medium heat, stirring frequently. Boil and stir 1 minute. Keep warm.

2 In medium bowl, stir potato mix and hot water until well mixed; let stand until water is absorbed. Stir in Bisquick mix, milk and chives until dough forms.

3 Place dough on surface sprinkled with Bisquick mix; gently roll in Bisquick mix to coat. Shape into a ball; knead 10 times. Press into 11×7-inch rectangle. Fold dough crosswise into thirds.

4 Pour beef mixture into ungreased 11×7-inch (2-quart) glass baking dish. Carefully unfold dough onto beef mixture.

5 Bake uncovered 30 to 35 minutes or until crust is golden brown.

1 Serving: Calories 260; Total Fat 6g (Saturated Fat 2.5g, Trans Fat 1g); Cholesterol 20mg; Sodium 1100mg; Total Carbohydrate 37g (Dietary Fiber 4g) **Exchanges:** 2 Starch, 1 Vegetable, 1 Lean Meat, ½ Fat **Carbohydrate Choices:** 2½

Simple Swaps: Substitute 1½ cups cooked cubed chicken for the beef and chicken gravy for the beef gravy.

budget smart

" Feel free to leave out the chives if you don't have any, or substitute a tablespoon of chopped green onion. "

$2.14 per serving

Impossibly Easy Ham and Swiss Pie

Prep Time: **10 Minutes** || Start to Finish: **55 Minutes** || **6 Servings**

1½ **cups cut-up cooked ham**

1 **cup shredded Swiss cheese (4 oz)**

4 **medium green onions, sliced (¼ cup)**

½ **cup Original Bisquick mix**

1 **cup milk**

¼ **teaspoon salt**

⅛ **teaspoon pepper**

2 **eggs**

1 **medium tomato, sliced, if desired**

1 **medium red, yellow or green bell pepper, cut into rings, if desired**

1 Heat oven to 400°F. Spray 9-inch glass pie plate with cooking spray. Sprinkle ham, cheese and onions in pie plate.

2 In medium bowl, stir remaining ingredients except tomato and bell pepper until blended. Pour into pie plate.

3 Bake 35 to 40 minutes or until knife inserted in center comes out clean. Let stand 5 minutes before serving. Garnish with tomato and bell pepper.

1 Serving: Calories 220; Total Fat 12g (Saturated Fat 6g, Trans Fat 0g); Cholesterol 110mg; Sodium 820mg; Total Carbohydrate 10g (Dietary Fiber 0g) **Exchanges:** ½ Starch, ½ Other Carbohydrate, 2 Lean Meat, 1 Fat **Carbohydrate Choices:** ½

budget smart

Ham and Swiss cheese are classic companions, so why not bake them into a pie? This is a foolproof and wallet-friendly dish. Since mustard goes so well with a ham and Swiss cheese sandwich, why not pass some around at the table?

$1.04 per serving

Chili with Cornbread Dumplings

Prep Time: **15 Minutes** || Start to Finish: **55 Minutes** || **6 Servings**

★ 1½ lb ground beef

1 large onion, chopped (¾ cup)

1 can (15.25 oz) whole kernel corn, undrained

★ 1 can (14.5 oz) stewed tomatoes, undrained

1 can (16 oz) tomato sauce

2 tablespoons chili powder

1 teaspoon red pepper sauce

1⅓ cups Original Bisquick mix

⅔ cup cornmeal

⅔ cup milk

3 tablespoons chopped fresh cilantro or parsley, if desired

1 In 4-quart Dutch oven, cook beef and onion over medium heat, stirring occasionally, until beef is brown; drain. Reserve ½ cup of the corn. Stir remaining corn with liquid, tomatoes, tomato sauce, chili powder and pepper sauce into beef mixture. Heat to boiling; reduce heat. Cover and simmer 15 minutes.

2 In medium bowl, mix Bisquick mix and cornmeal. Stir in milk, cilantro and reserved ½ cup corn just until moistened.

3 Heat chili to boiling. Drop dough by rounded tablespoonfuls onto chili; reduce heat to low. Cook uncovered 10 minutes. Cover and cook about 10 minutes longer or until dumplings are dry.

1 Serving: Calories 500; Total Fat 18g (Saturated Fat 6g, Trans Fat 2); Cholesterol 75mg; Sodium 1200mg; Total Carbohydrate 57g (Dietary Fiber 5g) **Exchanges:** 3 Starch, ½ Other Carbohydrate, 1 Vegetable, 2 Medium-Fat Meat, 1½ Fat **Carbohydrate Choices:** 4

budget smart

❝ This fun twist on chili and cornbread combines them into a one-dish meal. What could be better to serve up on a cold winter night? ❞

$1.40
per serving

Barbecue Pork Chops

Prep Time: **10 Minutes** || Start to Finish: **30 Minutes** || **6 Servings**

1 cup barbecue-flavored potato
  chips (about 1 oz)

¹/₂ cup Original Bisquick mix

1 egg, beaten

2 tablespoons barbecue sauce

6 boneless pork loin chops,
  ¹/₂ inch thick (about 1¹/₂ lb)

1 tablespoon vegetable oil

³/₄ cup barbecue sauce

1 Place potato chips in 1-gallon resealable food-storage plastic bag; crush with rolling pin. Add Bisquick mix to chips; mix well.

2 In small shallow dish, mix egg and 2 tablespoons barbecue sauce. Dip pork chops into egg mixture, then shake in bag to coat with Bisquick mixture.

3 In 12-inch nonstick skillet, heat oil over medium-low heat. Add pork chops; cook 15 to 18 minutes, turning once, until golden brown and pork is no longer pink in center. Serve with ¾ cup barbecue sauce.

1 Serving: Calories 330; Total Fat 15g (Saturated Fat 4g, Trans Fat 0g); Cholesterol 105mg; Sodium 590mg; Total Carbohydrate 24g (Dietary Fiber 0g) **Exchanges:** ¹/₂ Starch, 1 Other Carbohydrate, 3¹/₂ Lean Meat, 1 Fat **Carbohydrate Choices:** 1¹/₂

budget smart

" If there's an almost-finished bag of barbecue potato chips in your pantry, you can use the broken chips at the bottom of the bag for the 1 cup crushed chips in this recipe. "

$2.00 per serving

Coconut Shrimp

Prep Time: **30 Minutes** || Start to Finish: **30 Minutes** || **6 Servings**

1 lb uncooked deveined peeled medium shrimp (31 to 35), thawed if frozen, tail shells removed

1 cup Original Bisquick mix

³⁄₄ cup milk

1 egg

1 cup vegetable oil

2¹⁄₂ cups flaked coconut

¹⁄₂ cup chili sauce

¹⁄₂ cup apricot preserves

1 Pat shrimp dry with paper towels. In medium bowl, stir Bisquick mix, milk and egg with wire whisk or fork until blended. Add shrimp; gently stir to coat well.

2 In 10-inch skillet, heat oil over medium heat to 375°F. In shallow dish, place half of the coconut (add remaining coconut after coating half of the shrimp). Cooking in batches, remove shrimp one at a time from batter and coat with coconut; place in oil in single layer.

3 Cook 3 to 4 minutes, turning once, until coating is crispy and golden brown and shrimp are pink (cut 1 shrimp open to check doneness). Drain on paper towels.

4 In small bowl, mix chili sauce and apricot preserves. Serve shrimp with sauce for dipping.

1 Serving: Calories 440; Total Fat 21g (Saturated Fat 11g, Trans Fat 0g); Cholesterol 110mg; Sodium 520mg; Total Carbohydrate 50g (Dietary Fiber 3g) **Exchanges:** 1 Starch, 2 Other Carbohydrate, 1¹⁄₂ Very Lean Meat, 4 Fat **Carbohydrate Choices:** 3

budget smart

"Shrimp can be pricey, but medium shrimp are a good deal less expensive than large or jumbo, and that means more shrimp for all! To ensure the shrimp come out just right, make sure to cook them in batches; if you overcrowd the skillet, the shrimp won't crust up properly. Serve with lightly buttered fluffy white rice."

$2.45
per serving

Herbed Fish

Prep Time: **15 Minutes** || Start to Finish: **15 Minutes** || **2 Servings**

½ lb cod or other mild-flavored fish fillets, about ½ inch thick

¼ cup Bisquick Heart Smart mix

2 tablespoons garlic herb dry bread crumbs

1½ teaspoons chopped fresh or ½ teaspoon dried basil leaves

⅛ teaspoon salt

2 tablespoons fat-free egg product or 1 egg white

1 tablespoon olive or vegetable oil

1 Cut fish into 2 serving pieces. In small shallow dish, stir Bisquick mix, bread crumbs, basil and salt. In another shallow dish, beat egg white.

2 In 8-inch skillet, heat oil over medium heat. Dip fish into egg white, then coat with Bisquick mixture.

3 Reduce heat to medium-low. Cook fish in oil 8 to 10 minutes, turning once, until fish flakes easily with fork and is brown on both sides.

1 Serving: Calories 250; Total Fat 9g (Saturated Fat 1.5g, Trans Fat 0g); Cholesterol 60mg; Sodium 560mg; Total Carbohydrate 15g (Dietary Fiber 0g) **Exchanges:** 1 Starch, 3 Lean Meat **Carbohydrate Choices:** 1

budget smart

" When there are just two of you, turn to this easy fish recipe. Serve with baked French fries and pass around a bottle of malt vinegar, and you've got a terrific low-budget version of British-style fish and chips! "

$3.09
per serving

Easy Garden Bake

Prep Time: **15 Minutes** || Start to Finish: **55 Minutes** || **4 Servings**

1 cup chopped zucchini

1 large tomato, chopped (1 cup)

1 medium onion, chopped (1 cup)

1/3 cup grated Parmesan cheese

1/2 cup Bisquick Heart Smart mix

1 cup fat-free (skim) milk

1/2 cup fat-free egg product or 2 eggs

1/2 teaspoon salt

1/8 teaspoon pepper

1 Heat oven to 400°F. Lightly grease 8-inch square baking dish or 9-inch pie plate. Sprinkle zucchini, tomato, onion and cheese in baking dish.

2 In small bowl, stir remaining ingredients until blended. Pour over vegetables and cheese.

3 Bake uncovered about 35 minutes or until knife inserted in center comes out clean. Cool 5 minutes.

1 Serving: Calories 210; Total Fat 6g (Saturated Fat 3g, Trans Fat 0g); Cholesterol 15mg; Sodium 830mg; Total Carbohydrate 21g (Dietary Fiber 2g) **Exchanges:** 1/2 Starch, 1/2 Other Carbohydrate, 1 Vegetable, 2 Lean Meat **Carbohydrate Choices:** 1 1/2

budget smart

"Zucchini and onions are some of the least expensive vegetables in the whole supermarket. Learn to like zucchini—it has nice delicate flavors and is a highly versatile vegetable."

$2.66 per serving

Impossibly Easy Vegetable Pie

Prep Time: **15 Minutes** || Start to Finish: **55 Minutes** || **6 Servings**

- 2 cups chopped fresh broccoli or sliced fresh cauliflower florets
- 1/3 cup chopped onion
- 1/3 cup chopped green bell pepper
- 1 cup shredded Cheddar cheese (4 oz)
- 1/2 cup Original Bisquick mix
- 1 cup milk
- 1/2 teaspoon salt
- 1/4 teaspoon pepper
- 2 eggs

1 Heat oven to 400°F. Spray bottom and side of 9-inch glass pie plate with cooking spray. In 2-quart saucepan, heat 1 inch water (salted if desired) to boiling. Add broccoli; cover and return to boiling. Cook about 5 minutes or until broccoli is almost tender; drain thoroughly.

2 In pie plate, mix broccoli, onion, bell pepper and cheese. In small bowl, stir remaining ingredients until blended. Pour into pie plate.

3 Bake 30 to 35 minutes or until golden brown and knife inserted in center comes out clean. Let stand 5 minutes before cutting.

1 Serving: Calories 160; Total Fat 10g (Saturated Fat 5g, Trans Fat 0g); Cholesterol 95mg; Sodium 420mg; Total Carbohydrate 9g (Dietary Fiber 1g) **Exchanges:** 2 Vegetable, 1/2 Medium-Fat Meat, 1 1/2 Fat **Carbohydrate Choices:** 1/2

Impossibly Easy Spinach Pie: Use a 9-oz package of frozen spinach, thawed and squeezed to drain, in place of the broccoli; do not cook. Omit bell pepper. Substitute Swiss cheese for the Cheddar cheese. Add 1/4 teaspoon ground nutmeg with the pepper. Bake about 30 minutes.

66¢ per serving

budget smart

“No need to buy or make a crust in this easy vegetable pie—it makes it's own crust! If there are meat lovers in your family, you could stir in some chopped cooked ham.”

★ BEST BUDGET PICKS

bottled dressing

Caesar Chicken Paninis, 210
Fajita Salad, 84
Feta-Topped Chicken, 28
Flank Steak with Smoky Honey
   Mustard Sauce, 77
Grilled Mushroom-Pepper
   Whole Wheat Sandwiches, 218
Grilled Steak and Potato Salad, 82
Italian Chopped Salad, 44
Italian Frittata with Vinaigrette
   Tomatoes, 182
Summer Harvest Chicken-Potato
   Salad, 45
Turkey Pasta Primavera, 114
Veggie Focaccia Sandwiches, 216

canned beans

Barbecued Beans and Polish
   Sausage, 264
Beef and Bean Chili, 248
Beef and Bean Tortilla Bake, 62
Chili, 70
Chile-Sausage Pasta, 121
Chipotle and Black Bean
   Burritos, 178
Cowboy Casserole, 300
Easy Chili Mole, 68
Fiesta Taco Casserole, 60
Garlic Chicken with Italian
   Beans, 234
Grilled Barbecued Beef and Bean
   Burgers, 201
Ham Steak with Barbecued
   Beans, 97
Italian Chopped Salad, 44
Mexi Shells, 120
Peppers Stuffed with Broccoli,
   Beans and Rice, 184
Quinoa with Black Beans, 168
Red Bean and Rice Cakes, 187
Rice and Bean Bake, 162
Skillet Nacho Chili, 72
Southwestern Bean Skillet, 170
Southwestern Pork Soup, 224
Taco Supper Skillet, 67
Three-Bean Beer Pot, 272
Turkey–Butternut Squash
   Ragout, 241
Vegetarian Chili, 188
Veggie and Bean Burgers, 186
Zesty Black Bean Soup, 270

canned soup

Beef and Peppers with Cheese
   Biscuits, 294
Cheddar Cheese and Broccoli
   Soup, 229
Chicken and Noodles Skillet, 40
Chicken Tortilla Casserole, 18
Chicken-Veggie Casserole, 288
Creamy Beef Fold-Over Pie,
   298
Curried Turkey Stir-Fry, 50
Easy Chicken Pot Pie, 286
Florentine Tuna Tetrazzini,
   126
Ham and Wild Rice Soup, 262
Italian Chicken Noodle Soup,
   220
Mustardy Chicken and
   Dumplings, 281
Onion-Topped Turkey Divan, 49
Skillet Nacho Chili, 72
Southwestern Pork Soup, 224
Spanish Rice Bake, 160
Spicy Parmesan Meatballs with
   Angel Hair Pasta, 118
Turkey–Wild Rice Casserole,
   242

canned tomatoes

Beef and Barley Soup, 250
Beef and Bean Chili, 248
Beef and Bean Tortilla Bake, 62
Beef and Kasha Mexicana, 64
Cacciatore-Style Chicken, 37
Chili, 70

Chili with Cornbread
Dumplings, 304
Chile-Sausage Pasta, 121
Creole Jambalaya, 266
Easy Chili Mole, 68
Fire-Roasted Tomato Basil Soup,
228
Garlic Chicken with Italian
Beans, 234
Italian Shredded Beef Hoagies,
245
Italian Tomato Soup with
Pesto-Cheese Toasts, 227
Mediterranean Chicken Stew,
238
Mexi Shells, 120
Mexican Chicken Pizza with
Cornmeal Crust, 147
Mixed-Bean and Sausage
Minestrone, 265
Overnight Rotini Bake, 116
Penne with Spicy Sauce, 134
Sage and Garlic Vegetable Bake,
154
Spicy Parmesan Meatballs with
Angel Hair Pasta, 118
Turkey–Butternut Squash
Ragout, 241
Vegetarian Chili, 188
Zesty Black Bean Soup, 270

chicken breasts

Bow Ties with Chicken and
Asparagus, 112
Cacciatore-Style Chicken, 37

Caesar Chicken Paninis, 210
Chicken Cutlets with Creamy
Mushroom Gravy, 284
Chicken Marsala, 23
Chicken Milano, 30
Chicken and Noodles Skillet,
40
Chicken with Oregano-Peach
Sauce, 26
Chicken-Rice Skillet, 38
Chicken Tortilla Casserole, 18
Crunchy Garlic Chicken, 19
Feta-Topped Chicken, 28
Grilled Sesame-Ginger Chicken,
34
Grilled Taco-Barbecue Chicken,
36
Italian Chicken Noodle Soup,
220
Lemon Chicken with Olives, 22
Lime- and Chili-Rubbed
Chicken Breasts, 24
Mediterranean Chicken Packets,
32
Mexican Chicken Pizza with
Cornmeal Crust, 147
Mustardy Chicken and
Dumplings, 281
Parmesan-Dijon Chicken, 20
Southwestern Chicken
Scaloppine, 25
Summer Harvest Chicken-Potato
Salad, 45
Sweet-and-Sour Chicken
Stir-Fry, 282
Zesty Roasted Chicken and
Potatoes, 17

ground beef

Beef and Bean Tortilla Bake, 62
Beef and Kasha Mexicana, 64
Beefy Rice Skillet, 66
Broiled Dijon Burgers, 202
Chili, 70
Chili with Cornbread
Dumplings, 304
Cowboy Casserole, 300
Creamy Beef Fold-Over Pie,
298
Easy Chili Mole, 68
Fiesta Taco Casserole, 60
Grilled Barbecued Beef and Bean
Burgers, 201
Grilled Hamburger Steaks with
Roasted Onions, 73
Heart Smart Deluxe
Cheeseburger Melt, 296
Impossibly Easy Cheeseburger
Pie, 293
Italian Beef Bake, 299
Italian Meatballs with Marinara
Sauce, 252
Italian Sausage Burgers, 204
Large-Crowd Sloppy Joes, 254
Meat Loaf, 58
Mexi Shells, 120
Overnight Rotini Bake, 116
Skillet Nacho Chili, 72
Spicy Parmesan Meatballs with
Angel Hair Pasta, 118
Spinach and Beef Enchiladas, 63
Taco Supper Skillet, 67

|| METRIC CONVERSION GUIDE ||

VOLUME

U.S. Units	Canadian Metric	Australian Metric
¼ teaspoon	1 mL	1 ml
½ teaspoon	2 mL	2 ml
1 teaspoon	5 mL	5 ml
1 tablespoon	15 mL	20 ml
¼ cup	50 mL	60 ml
⅓ cup	75 mL	80 ml
½ cup	125 mL	125 ml
⅔ cup	150 mL	170 ml
¾ cup	175 mL	190 ml
1 cup	250 mL	250 ml
1 quart	1 liter	1 liter
1½ quarts	1.5 liters	1.5 liters
2 quarts	2 liters	2 liters
2½ quarts	2.5 liters	2.5 liters
3 quarts	3 liters	3 liters
4 quarts	4 liters	4 liters

WEIGHT

U.S. Units	Canadian Metric	Australian Metric
1 ounce	30 grams	30 grams
2 ounces	55 grams	60 grams
3 ounces	85 grams	90 grams
4 ounces (¼ pound)	115 grams	125 grams
8 ounces (½ pound)	225 grams	225 grams
16 ounces (1 pound)	455 grams	500 grams
1 pound	455 grams	½ kilogram

MEASUREMENTS

Inches	Centimeters
1	2.5
2	5.0
3	7.5
4	10.0
5	12.5
6	15.0
7	17.5
8	20.5
9	23.0
10	25.5
11	28.0
12	30.5
13	33.0

TEMPERATURES

Fahrenheit	Celsius
32°	0°
212°	100°
250°	120°
275°	140°
300°	150°
325°	160°
350°	180°
375°	190°
400°	200°
425°	220°
450°	230°
475°	240°
500°	260°

NOTE: The recipes in this cookbook have not been developed or tested using metric measures. When converting recipes to metric, some variations in quality may be noted.

INDEX

Page numbers in *italics* indicate illustrations.

Recommended intake for a daily diet of 2,000 calories as set by the Food and Drug Administration

Total Fat	Less than 65g
Saturated Fat	Less than 20g
Cholesterol	Less than 300mg
Sodium	Less than 2,400mg
Total Carbohydrate	300g
Dietary Fiber	25g

Complete your cookbook library with these *Betty Crocker* titles

Betty Crocker Baking Basics

Betty Crocker Baking for Today

Betty Crocker's Best Bread Machine Cookbook

Betty Crocker's Best Chicken Cookbook

Betty Crocker's Best of Baking

Betty Crocker's Best of Healthy and Hearty Cooking

Betty Crocker's Best-Loved Recipes

Betty Crocker's Bisquick® Cookbook

Betty Crocker Bisquick® II Cookbook

Betty Crocker Bisquick® Impossibly Easy Pies

Betty Crocker Celebrate!

Betty Crocker Christmas Cookbook

Betty Crocker's Complete Thanksgiving Cookbook

Betty Crocker's Cook Book for Boys and Girls

Betty Crocker's Cook It Quick

Betty Crocker Cookbook, 10th Edition— *The* **BIG RED** *Cookbook*®

Betty Crocker Cookbook, Bridal Edition

Betty Crocker Cookbook, Heart Health Edition

Betty Crocker Cookie Book

Betty Crocker Cooking Basics

Betty Crocker's Cooky Book, Facsimile Edition

Betty Crocker Country Cooking

Betty Crocker Decorating Cakes and Cupcakes

Betty Crocker's Diabetes Cookbook

Betty Crocker Dinner Made Easy with Rotisserie Chicken

Betty Crocker Easy Everyday Vegetarian

Betty Crocker Easy Family Dinners

Betty Crocker's Easy Slow Cooker Dinners

Betty Crocker's Eat and Lose Weight

Betty Crocker's Entertaining Basics

Betty Crocker's Flavors of Home

Betty Crocker 4-Ingredient Dinners

Betty Crocker Grilling Made Easy

Betty Crocker Healthy Heart Cookbook

Betty Crocker's Healthy New Choices

Betty Crocker's Indian Home Cooking

Betty Crocker's Italian Cooking

Betty Crocker Just the Two of Us Cookbook

Betty Crocker Kids Cook!

Betty Crocker's Kitchen Library

Betty Crocker's Living with Cancer Cookbook

Betty Crocker Low-Carb Lifestyle Cookbook

Betty Crocker's Low-Fat, Low-Cholesterol Cooking Today

Betty Crocker More Slow Cooker Recipes

Betty Crocker's New Chinese Cookbook

Betty Crocker One-Dish Meals

Betty Crocker's A Passion for Pasta

Betty Crocker's Picture Cook Book, Facsimile Edition

Betty Crocker Quick & Easy Cookbook

Betty Crocker's Slow Cooker Cookbook

Betty Crocker 30-Minute Meals for Diabetes

Betty Crocker Ultimate Bisquick® Cookbook

Betty Crocker's Ultimate Cake Mix Cookbook

Betty Crocker Whole Grains Cookbook

Betty Crocker Why It Works

Betty Crocker Win at Weight Loss Cookbook